OBJECT
LESSONS

ADVANCES IN OBJECT TECHNOLOGY

Dr. Richard S. Wiener
Series Editor
Editor: *Journal of Object-Oriented Programming*
SIGS Publications, Inc.
New York, New York

and

Department of Computer Science
University of Colorado
Colorado Springs, Colorado

1. Object Lessons: Lessons Learned in Object-Oriented
Development Projects, *Tom Love*

Additional Volumes in Preparation

OBJECT LESSONS

Lessons Learned in Object-Oriented Development Projects

Tom Love

**OrgWare, Inc.
Roxbury, Connecticut**

New York

Tom Love is the owner of the service mark OBJECT*Lessons*^{SM} and offers various professional seminars and training courses related to object-oriented programming. For more information contact the author at OrgWare, Inc., 30 East Woods Road, Roxbury, CT 06783 or call (203) 350-4331.

PUBLISHED BY
SIGS Books, Inc.
588 Broadway, Suite 604
New York, New York, 10012

Library of Congress Catalog Card Number: 93-84410
ISBN 0-9627477-3-4

This book is printed on acid-free paper.

Printed in United States of America
10 9 8 7 6 5 4 3 2 1

Preface

As a consultant I am often asked to review projects that are perceived by someone as being "in trouble." Often by the time I arrive, I feel like a doctor at the scene of a major disaster site. More damage has been done than can ever be repaired, more people are injured than can be helped, and basic systems are not available to help anyone. Reviewing such software projects is a tough job for a consultant. Like the doctor in the field, one must quickly assess each situation, decide who can be helped and does not require immediate assistance and who cannot be saved. Software company triage is what I call this work. Careers are likely to be damaged, a company's reputation may be at stake, and the business itself may be in danger of collapse. *Object Lessons* can't teach one how to perform software project triage but it can help to avoid such a disaster.

This book was designed to answer questions that arise at the inception of a major project. If you are already working on such a project, read quickly and make changes to the project immediately! Time is your worst enemy. If you are not working on such a project, read quickly anyway to equip you for future projects.

One major problem is that communicating via print media, a very slow communication line, is difficult as information in this industry changes very rapidly. Therefore, described in the book are fundamental issues and trends rather than specific products or services; so, I will not provide you with a set of prescriptions for specific products or services because the information will be hopelessly out of date by the time it is read. However, described are fundamental characteristics of products that one should be aware of as selections are made. You may find more questions than answers in these chapters but not to worry, you will find plenty of specific advice and recommendations about software intensive businesses. These recommendations will be very specific and practical—most of which have never been printed before.

This book will aid technical leaders and managers responsible for building commercial software. It has two objectives: to encourage project leaders to build innovative but successful software products with higher quality and lesser risk and; to help these project leaders make interesting new mistakes on projects rather than uninteresting old mistakes that have been made many times before. The book explains how these two objectives can be accomplished as pragmatically as I know how. References to more extensive sources are provided where possible.

While I think you should read the first chapter first and the last chapter last, the others can be read in the order that pleases you. Each chapter of the book is designed to be read independently; on a short airplane ride or on a lunch break.

The craft of system programming still has its tar pits,* yet the joys and challenges of this profession continue to attract the best and brightest the world has to offer. This book was written for these hard working professionals with the hope that concrete assistance could be provided to increase the chances of creating a software product superstar.

Tom Love

---

*Fred Brooks, *The Mythical Man-Month*, Addison-Wesley, 1975.

Acknowledgements

During the process of developing and publishing this manuscript, the efforts of some people have been exceptional. Frederick Trapnell, formerly of Amdahl Corporation, provided me with detailed comments on an earlier draft of the manuscript along with several "in person" lessons on how to improve my technical writing. What you read is surely better due to his efforts but not yet up to his high standards.

Kurt Schmucker of Apple Computer, Mel Conway, formerly of Wang Labs, and Leo Nabben of Philips Components also provided important technical critiques and elaboration of the chapters. Many people developed raw material for Chapter Four, which provides a detailed object programming example. Their capable efforts allowed that chapter to be written.

I also want to provide special thanks to the employees and the private and professional investors in the Stepstone Corporation. Without their support, many of the experiences described here would never have happened. Together we have learned that being first does not always provide the largest rewards.

The person who has read and re-read this manuscript tirelessly for at least four years is my wife, Mary Hughes. She has found and removed enough "very's" from this manuscript to fill a small book. Thank you very, very, very much!

Our children and office staff, Emily, Claire, and Gayle have made numerous copies of this manuscript, collated photographs and even proofread parts of the manuscript. You know how special I think you are.

Tom Love

Introduction

It is a pleasure to introduce *Object Lessons* by Tom Love. This is the first of many books in the series *Advances in Object Technology* that will deal with object technology. It will be of great value to software managers, analysts, designers, and implementors who wish to learn about the challenges, opportunities, successes and failures associated with large-scale commercial software development in general and object-oriented software engineering in particular.

The author shares with us his depth of experience and wisdom concerning every aspect of modern software development and the opportunities that exist in changing to object technology. Only by learning from our past failures and errors do we have any chance of repairing them. Dr. Love provides many examples and stories of such failures. He also describes useful and important techniques and strategies for avoiding these problems in the future.

I believe the readership will obtain many important insights from *Object Lessons* and some inspiration as well.

Dr. Richard S. Wiener
Series Editor

Contents

Preface   iii

Acknowledgments   v

Introduction   vii

1.   Object Lessons from 1628   1

2.   Assessing Our Craft   9

3.   Hope with Objects   25

4.   Greed: An Example Program   49

5.   Experiences with Objects   79

6.   Where Do the Objects Come From?   99

7.   Pickled Objects   125

8.   Providing an Environment   143

9.   Educating Your People   157

10. Software Construction Management   169

11. Building in Quality   183

12. A Road Map for Change   199

13. Lessons Learned   215

14. Software Component Foundries   235

15. Software Development—2002   249

Index   257

Permissions   265

OBJECT LESSONS

BJÖRN LANDSTRÖM 1974

1

Object Lessons from 1628

*Experience has shown that someone's proven ability
to do an excellent job on a given scale is by no means
a guarantee that, when faced with a much larger job,
he will not make a mess of it.*

E. W. Dijkstra
"Notes on Structured Programming"
Structured Programming
O. J. Dahl, E. W. Dijkstra, and A. Hoare, Eds., Academic Press, New York, 1972, p. 39.

In 1625, the Swedish Navy was victorious in the Baltic waters. It was so successful that King Gustav commissioned the construction of a new flagship for his
fleet — to be the grandest flagship in all of Europe.

To build this ship, the *Vasa*, he selected Hendrick Hybertszoon, a master shipwright from Holland. After a brief meeting to discuss the "requirements" for this
ship, the master shipwright returned to his small workshop and built a scale model
of the proposed flagship. The king was delighted by the model and appropriated a
small oak forest to provide the timbers for his new ship.

There were no written specifications. Lumber was cut under the assumption
that the ship would be approximately 108 feet in length. At the first review meeting, the king requested that the ship be made larger by 135 feet. The master shipwright complied by patching the keel, adding a new length of timber, and extending the ship to 120 feet. As leveling of the forest began, the king departed for a
summer vacation in the south of Sweden.

*Figure 1.1.
Cutting timbers
for a new ship
was rather
specialized in
1625. Trees
of the proper
shape and size
were selected
for each major
timber required.*

While on vacation, the king discovered that the Danish king also had recently
commissioned the construction of a flagship, but the Danish ship was to have three
gun decks — one more than the Swedish vessel. Therefore, upon his return to
Stockholm, King Gustav demanded a project review. He was impressed with the
ship's architecture and proposed decorations, and so approved the design with one
modification — the addition of a third enclosed gundeck with 50 brass, 24-lb can-
nons.* He also commanded the shipwrights to complete the ship several months
ahead of schedule — no matter the cost.

The shipwright was stunned; How could he request such a major structural

---

*This would be the weight of the cannonball, not the cannon itself. Each cannon was different,
but most weighed 1 ton or more.*

change after the keel had been laid and the planking nearly completed? But because the customer was king, the shipwright reluctantly complied.*

Mathematics and physics were not well developed in 1625. It was more than a decade before analytic geometry was discovered by Descartes and five decades before Newton's first publication of the calculus. So in 1625 a shipwright would guess, model, build, and learn.

It was also the tradition among shipwrights of that era to keep the specifications for successful ships a closely guarded secret. None of the calculations accounted for 50 tons of added weaponry, nor for a heavy multistory brick oven for cooking. The builder surmised that adding a new gun deck would require the addition of some planking along the sides and some additional ballast (130 tons added to the 122 tons already planned). However, there was not enough room for another 130 tons of rock under the existing deck, so it was left out for the time being. Using the best tools available, master builder Hybertszoon calculated the changes required to the planking and communicated those changes to the shipwright. The shipwright, without asking, added about 5 inches to the width of the ship just to be sure.

When the flagship's modification was complete, a navy admiral conducted a stability test by instructing 30 sailors to run from side to side on the deck. The test was considered "successful enough" even though the ship nearly tipped over the third time the sailors ran from side to side. Approval was given because nobody could figure out how to solve the problem, and the king demanded that the ship be completed on schedule.

After vespers one Sunday in August 1628, the *Vasa* set sail from Stockholm harbor. Amid glorious celebration, the ship sailed out into the Stockholm archipelago. About one mile from the harbor, a modest gust of wind caught the mainsail and the ship "turned turtle," sinking immediately.

OBJECT LESSONS

The state of software building today bears striking parallels to the state of shipbuilding in the early 1600s:

- Shipbuilding was a craft with an inadequate underlying science and "engineering practice."
- Specification was accomplished in an *ad hoc* manner — typically verbally.
- Design methods were inadequate — just make a sketch or two, build a model, and extrapolate to the real thing.

---

* *Due in part to the stress, Mr. Hybertszoon became seriously ill and died a year before the* Vasa *was completed. His brother and business partner, Arent Hybertszoon de Groote, became the new master shipwright despite the fact that he had considerably less experience than his brother.*

Figure 1.2. The Vasa's ornate carvings included about 1,000 sculptures. "[The sterncastle] is crowned with an ornamental flower bud decked with acanthus leaves; immediately below appears the decorously draped torso of a turbaned herm, then a large grotesque mask, and below that a king wearing Roman armour and holding a sword in one hand; at his feet is a convoluted shield displaying griphons [sic]."[1] Expensive gold and indigo paints adorned the carvings. Golden lions' heads protected each gun port hatch.

- The full implications of a change were not understood — the addition of a gun deck could not be accommodated by simply adding more ballast as more weight might cause the waterline to rise above the first gun deck!
- Indications of trouble from empirical testing were often ignored.
- Far too much time and effort were wasted carving lions' heads and other statuary prior to determining if the ship would sail.
- "Success breeds failure." It is not enough to continue doing what has worked in the past.
- In 1626, shipwrights had not learned how to tell their clients "no," even if the client *was* king.

Other lessons emerge from the *Vasa* tragedy. After 333 years of sitting peacefully on the not very salty bottom of Stockholm harbor, Anzer Franzén discovered the remains of the *Vasa* and convinced the government to finance its recovery and reconstruction (see Figure 1.3).

After two decades of work and thousands of gallons of polyethylene glycol (a preservative of green or wet wood), the *Vasa* once again is moored in Stockholm harbor. From this experience, software developers should remember:

1. The systems we build may last far longer than we ever imagine (333 years).
2. Maintenance costs often exceed the original development costs — even for unsuccessful products!
3. Tiny pieces of what we build today may be carefully examined and scrutinized decades or even centuries from now.

During the next major war in which Sweden became engaged nearly 50 years later, King Karl XI commissioned a new flagship for his fleet, the *Kronan*.[2] The *Kronan* was built using a design similar to the *Vasa*, but it was almost twice as long and carried nearly three times the weight of cannon.

The *Kronan* sailed successfully for nearly four years. But on June 1, 1676 it was engaged by the Danish and Dutch fleet near the Swedish island of Öland. In response to the attack, the *Kronan* turned too tightly, its third gun deck flooded, and the ship sank, killing some 800 men. Forty-nine years and 10 months after the sinking of the *Vasa*, the consequences of an initial design error resulted in an even greater loss of life.

Ship design, construction, and maintenance in the 1600s bear a striking resemblance to the experiences many of us have had while building software systems in the 1980s. The goal of this book is to motivate a change process that has the possibility of fundamentally altering the way in which software systems are built. We'll begin with a look at some successful software products to understand their com-

Figure 1.3.
The Vasa as it was
raised from Stockholm
harbor 333 years
after it capsized.

mon properties. Then, an important new software technology will be described and an explanation of how this technology can be put into commercial practice today with a minimum of risk will be provided. The book concludes with a look ahead at where the software industry is taking us and how soon it will get us there.

NOTES

1. Björn Landström, *The Royal Warship Vasa*, Interpublishing, Stockholm, Sweden, 1980 [available at the Vasa museum in Stockholm].
2. *National Geographic*, April 1989.

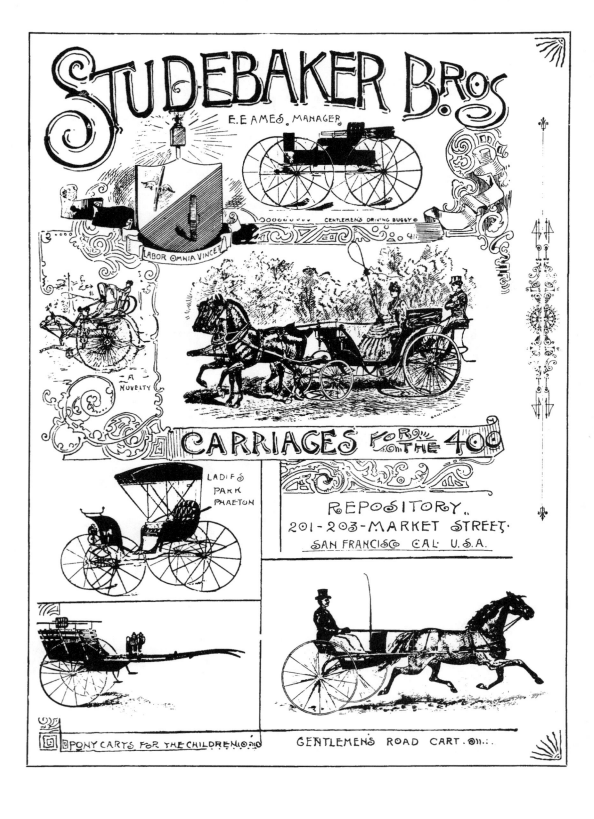

2

Assessing Our Craft

The tyranny of large systems sets up a numbers barrier to future advances if we must rely on individual discrete components for producing larger systems.

J. A. Morton
International Science and Technology
July 1966, p. 38.

The software industry is young but not new. It began growing during the 50s, the years of Studebakers, bobbie socks, and Sputnik. Today, billions of lines of software are used daily and most companies have a critical dependency upon computer software. Few people realize the extent of this dependency and how much is being spent on software annually.

For instance, one large electronics company recently estimated that their annual output of new software, if printed, would yield a stack of paper 28 stories high. They also found that the median age of software running on their mainframe computers was more than 10 years. An equal amount of externally developed software operates within the company. So the paper equivalent of 500 stories of computer software supports that $20 billion business. That's a stack of paper more than four times the height of the Sears Tower in Chicago, Illinois, the world's tallest building.

How many programmers do you suppose it takes to debug 500 stories of software? How many errors remain in that amount of code? Operating at half the current industry average of 10 errors per 1,000 lines of code, we can assume there are as many as 5,000,000 errors remaining in that corporation's software.

Yet, if one reads any publication regarding software, one finds there is an urgent demand for more software in increasingly complicated electronic systems and applications. This chapter assesses the ability of the industry to service this demand and concludes with the observation that it is time for us to rethink the fundamentals of our industry. It is also a fair guess that we don't need more software but rather, less software with more function and flexibility.

DEMAND FOR THE CRAFT

Contemporary corporations, governments, institutions, and individuals require, or at least use massive quantities of software. Yet few feel satisfied with the systems they have, and most are working furiously to improve what they are currently using. As a result, the annual budget for software within corporations is growing substantially from year to year. Although large and growing steadily, software costs rarely appear as a separate line item in the budget. Instead, these costs radiate outward to negatively impact expenses in most other areas.[1]

Billion dollar corporations and other large institutions have been ruined or are endangered by their inability to build software in a reliable and cost-effective manner. Examples of software criticality include:

- The U.S. Department of Defense requires the construction of tens of millions of lines of computer software annually. Building such software is extremely expensive, dangerously error prone, and a critical path item for deployment of most weapons systems.

- ITT, once the world's second-largest telecommunications company with sales exceeding $25 billion, was forced to divest its telecommunications business because of the failure of a software project. The company failed to modify the System 1240 software for the North American market, despite efforts that cost the company more than $1 billion in direct expenses.

- General Motors (GM) management decided to build a new car company called Saturn. While building the manufacturing facilities for Saturn, GM also decided to construct a contemporary information-sharing infrastructure within Saturn. The buzzwords are computer-integrated manufacturing (CIM), computer-aided design (CAD), and computer-aided manufacturing (CAM). An internal analysis showed that the Saturn plant would require 10 million lines of new software. Software became the critical path item for Saturn.

- Success in politics and with public interest groups is partially attributed to the quality of the software that controls mailing campaigns, opinion survey analysis, and fund-raising.

- Scientific breakthroughs in nuclear physics, biomedicine, genetics, material sciences, electronics, and chemistry require innovative computer software as well as high-performance computers.

Software has become a critical technology for most enterprises large and small. Just as the semiconductor industry faced a "tyranny of numbers" prior to the introduction of the electronics industry, so the software industry faces a "tyranny of source lines of code" (SLOC).

Successful microcomputer software products

Let's begin our assessment of the software industry with a closer look at successful software products (see Table 2.1). Success will be measured in terms of installed base, durability of the product, and estimated revenue generated.[2] What distinguishes these products from thousands of competing products that have had mediocre to poor sales? Were these products better engineered? Did their authors have a common experience? Were the development tools or methods different from those used on other products? After investigating the facts concerning these successful software products, we will attempt to answer these questions.

CP/M was really the first operating system used widely on microcomputers. It was designed by Gary Kildall with the support of John Torode, who did important low-level optimizations of the system. Both were computer scientists from the University of Washington teaching in California. They worked without development tools on a new microprocessor.

Table 2.1. Successful microcomputer software products.

Product	CP/M[3,4]	Microsoft Basic[5]	Microsoft MS/DOS	Lotus 1-2-3[6]
Authors	Kildall/Torode	Gates/Allen	Tim Patterson[7]	Kapor/Sachs
Background	Computer science/Physics	Physics	Physics	Business/ Psychology
Age at creation	20s	20s	20s	20s
Motivation	Entrepreneurial	Entrepreneurial	Entrepreneurial	Entrepreneurial
Work environment	Basement	Dorm room	Tiny company	Home
Previous software experience	Academic mainframes	High school	Micros	n/a
Development machine	Intel 8080	Altair 8800	8086 IBM PC	
Development language	PL/M	Assembler	Assembler	Assembler
Development time (yr)	1	1	1	1.5
Use of software engineering methods (1 = low; 10 = high)	5	1	2	2
Initial sales price	$75	$200	$500	$200
Number of copies sold before 1990	10,000,000+	500,000+	20,000,000+	5,000,000+

Microsoft Basic was developed by Bill Gates and Paul Allen as an entrepre-neurial endeavor. Gates believed these new and inexpensive microcomputers could support the Basic programming language and accepted the challenge from Allen that it could be done. Gates modestly describes the secret of their success as his ability to write bug-free compilers—slick, tight code. They were also young, aggressive, and willing to take substantial risks—including claiming to Altair that they had Basic running before they even got delivery of the computer. Nevertheless, they managed to accomplish the impossible and have built the world's largest microcomputer software company.

Microsoft MS/DOS was a similar success, but due more to marketing and sales prowess than to technical innovation. Microsoft was originally asked to design an operating system for the new IBM PC. When this effort seemed mired with technical obstacles, Gates decided to acquire 86-QDOS from Tim Patterson and improve upon it for delivery to IBM. The rest is history. 86-QDOS was a reimplementation of CP/M.

Lotus 1-2-3, like MS/DOS, was a second-generation product. It was an attempt by a highly skilled programmer, Jonathan Sachs, and a marketer, Mitch Kapor, to dominate a developing market for spreadsheets. The development process was iterative and had the particular characteristic that 1-2-3 began as a simple working program and continued to be a working program throughout its development. The development period was 10 months of "nothing but eating, sleeping, and working." Sachs had more than the usual distrust of other people's code; he says he doesn't use any tools or programs that he didn't either write or have some control over. Lotus 1-2-3 was a one-man development project with regular support from Kapor.

First, note that these products were not built with established software engineering techniques or tools. In fact, all were built by a pair of hackers in start-up mode. Some of these hackers were extremely well trained in the software profession; others had little relevant academic training. Most were from the Seattle area; none from Silicon Valley.

These products had no formal specifications, designs, or even management reviews. High-quality technical reviews occurred on a regular basis as each product evolved. Keep in mind that each of these "superproducts" was built by one or two people in a short period of time. The initial operational version of MS/DOS was called 86-QDOS and developed by a single programmer. Some consider this to have been a reengineering effort and as such it is surely different from the other products.[8]

The initial version of each of these products was built using a spiral development process. Albeit informal at times, each product was specified, designed, built, and tested. This process was repeated several times. With their success, each of these products now has hundreds, if not thousands, of person-years of effort invested in their continued extension and support.

All these developers were aggressive advocates of small, tight code that provided the maximum benefit for a modest consumption of machine resources. All were young, gifted, and hard working. The "gifted" attribute may be an important discriminator. John Torode is certainly one of the smartest computer scientists I have ever worked with. Bill Gates scored a perfect 800 on the math section of his SAT exam.

It was remarkably difficult to select only four successful software products built for large computers. Clearly each product shown in Table 2.2 has been a major success.

Four large computer software success stories

UNIX was created by Dennis Ritchie and Kenneth Thompson to increase their own productivity. They had just completed work on a mammoth operating system being developed by a three-party consortium. It contained wonderful new concepts but was always a major resource hog. UNIX was created on a surplus PDP-7 beginning in 1969. It achieved increasing notoriety because of its power, simplicity, modularity, and portability. It also created an easy "buy vs. build" decision for corporate managers needing a new operating system (O/S). How could you justify an expensive new O/S development project, replete with risks, when UNIX could be delivered complete from AT&T with all of its source code for $43,000?

In 1982 I wrote a business plan that projected there would be 24,000 UNIX licenses by 1986. Everyone who saw that projection thought I was a madman. In fact, it was an underestimate by more than an order of magnitude!

Just before this section was written, the developers of Customer Information Control System (CICS) held a week-long celebration to recognize their success. CICS was IBM's first program product. Its purpose was to provide interactive access to data held within a batch-oriented system. Described in today's terms, it added transaction management features to OS/360. CICS was developed at IBM regional headquarters in Chicago for customers in the public utility industry. Utility customers needed online access to their data.

Two people working in Detroit, Ben Riggins and Jerry Anderson, were the originators of the CICS concept. Riggins was the technical guy; Anderson was the project leader and product definition man. Riggins regards the key to CICS's success as providing an efficient solution to an important customer problem. The product was small in the beginning (19,000 card images, 300 of which were blank to provide room for growth!). But, like all other successful software products, it has steadily grown. Today, it is about 20 times larger than the original, although its architecture has remained remarkably intact.

Riggins says that one reason the development project was so short and the program so small was that the computer was 12 blocks away from their offices. Every day, each of the programmers would make one or two walks to the computer room. Everyone realized the importance of completing the project before the onset of winter in the Windy City.

Oracle has become a $1 billion software company. The company was bootstrapped by Larry Ellison, Bob Miner, and Bruce Scott. The first version of the Oracle database management system (DBMS) was built by Bob Miner and Bruce Scott. In his 30s, Miner had been involved in several commercial software projects; Scott was a newcomer with important compiler development skills from the university. They worked on a PDP-11 using RSX-11 with few development tools. Ellison assisted with product definition, but (more importantly) he also did consulting to help pay for product development. As Miner described it to me, they have always had an aggressive approach to product development: build and deliver

Table 2.2. Successful large computer software companies

Product	AT&T UNIX[9]	IBM's CICS	Oracle	SAS's stat pack
Authors	Ritchie/ Thompson	Riggins/ Anderson	Miner/Scott	Barr/Goodnight
Background	Mathematics/ Electrical engineering	Physics/ Business	Computer science	Physics/Statistics
Age at creation	20s	30s	30s/20s	20s
Motivation	Research	Customer service	Entrepreneurial	Research
Work environment	Corporate laboratory	Corporate	Tiny company	University
Previous software experience	Multics	Application development	DBMCs;O/S	Government software[10]
Development machine	PDP-7/GE	IBM360/30	PDP-11	IBM360
Development language	Assembler, then C	Assembler	Assembler	Assembler/ FORTRAN
Development time (yr)	2	1	1	2
Use of software engineering methods (1 = low; 10 = high)	4	2	2	5
Initial sales price	$100[11]	$600/mo	$50,000	$35
Number of copies sold before 1990	1,000,000+	30,000+	100,000+	40,000+MF 100,000+PC

needed functionality to the users as quickly as possible. It was never clear to them that software engineering techniques would help expedite product development or delivery. Money was never spent on tools either. More machine resources always seemed to help, but better tools were often questionable.

The SAS Institute is an out-of-the-way, quarter of a billion dollar software company that has been highly successful financially and remains remarkably secure. The company builds the leading statistics package for mainframe and, arguably, for personal computers. One key to their success has been that they license their software on an annual basis. The first version of Statistical Analysis System (SAS) was designed at North Carolina State University by Jim Goodnight and implemented largely by Tony Barr. Initially, the SAS product was supported by a variety of government agencies and was essentially in the public domain. Later, the SAS Institute was created and "took the product private." SAS proliferated quickly because it was available for only $35 in the beginning. As users began to appreciate its power and quality, its use quickly spread out of universities and into corporations and government. It has now been completely recoded three times, from IBM Assembler to PL/1 and again to C. It comprises over 2.5 million lines of code and requires hundreds of developers to support, port, and extend.

COMMON PROPERTIES OF SUCCESSFUL SOFTWARE PRODUCTS

As I was doing research on these products, I was surprised to discover that two of them were priced so low that they were basically given away in the beginning. But "giving away" the product resulted in the rapid creation of a strong and substantial user group. Each of these products had the important characteristic of giving the user "a little more than they expected."[12]

I was amazed to discover that the initial versions of six of these software products were developed by just two people. Only the product developed by IBM involved more than two people. (There were four, but there were two original champions for the project.) In general, one person understood the need for a product while the other provided the technical wizardry to make it happen quickly. In no sense does one get the impression that these products were built using accepted software engineering methods. Craftsmen built these products with a keen feel for good design and an intense desire to build a quality product. Like other old world craftsmen, they were all concerned with efficiency and resource constraints. Several of the products were conceived to make their creator's own work more efficient and pleasant.

None of the products was built using the software engineering methods and process being advocated by academics and technologists at the time. "Designs" were more likely to be written on the back of a placemat than in an engineering notebook. Assembler was the language of choice. Written requirements, formal technical reviews, testing plans, and independent quality assurance groups were not the norm! Development "teams" were always small. Support teams become small armies.

"NO SILVER BULLETS"

The December 1973 issue of *Datamation* declared that a software revolution would be fomented by structured programming. That issue contained several articles written by practicing IBM Federal Systems Division programmers and managers who had previously completed a major project for the *New York Times* using this "revolutionary" new technology. IBM was prepared to recommend the widespread adoption of structured programming. However, revolutions in the software industry are more often proclaimed than delivered.

Professor E. W. Dijkstra originally defined structured programming as the development of programs using three control flow constructs—concatenation, selection, and repetition.[13] Later, the term grew to include design methodologies, testing schemes, project teams, organizational guidelines, and documentation styles.

Most of today's professional programmers have never read Dijkstra's *Notes on Structured Programming;* many don't even know his name. Yet, most agree that structured programming has helped the software industry by improving programming languages and programming style. But the effect of structured programming has hardly been revolutionary.[14]

The state of the "software craft" was recently summarized by Professor Fred Brooks[15] as follows:

1. COBOL, FORTRAN, Assembler language, and Basic are still the four most popular programming languages.

2. "None of the truly innovative software products developed during the past decade have been developed using the accepted software engineering life cycle and methodologies." He cited examples such as UNIX, VisiCalc, Pascal, and CP/M.

3. Experimental comparisons of the use of structured programming techniques have demonstrated only marginal productivity and quality effects.[16]

4. Software development is more a craft than an engineering discipline. Increasing numbers of professional programmers are creating "craft shops" to develop and sell their particular "wares." The personal computer software market is the most visible example of this trend.

5. While the artificial intelligence (AI) community has developed a substantial technology for solving classes of problems within a defined context,[17] and stimulated some significant innovations in programming environments,[18] AI technology has not yet had a noticeable effect on the "craft of programming."[19]

My assessment of successful software projects does not differ significantly from the conclusions of Professor Brooks. Software development is a craft; there is no magic to cause our problems to go away; and "time and space always matter." We can thank a few brilliant craftsmen for the software products we depend upon today.

But what about the failures? What can we learn from them? How were they different?

UNSUCCESSFUL SOFTWARE PROJECTS

We rarely read about failed software projects and products. Corporate executives and lawyers hardly ever approve papers describing failure. What if news of failed automobiles was never made public? Or nuclear power plants? Or telephone exchanges?

Our profession must become mature enough to publicly admit its weaknesses and even its failures. Analyzing these failures will help us as an industry much more than basking in our occasional successes.[20]

Personal experiences

In my nearly two decades of commercial experience in the software industry, I have held positions as a software engineer, first-line manager, second-line manager, corporate staffer, president of a start-up company, and management consultant. As I began to think about formulating this chapter, I went back to my journals to analyze the projects with which I have had significant association. I selected only those projects where I personally spent at least one month working with or on the project, and only projects involving more than 50 person-years of effort.

Analyzing these 16 major system development projects (7 countries and 6 very different companies)[21] reveals the following:

- Nine of the projects involved significant assembly language programming and several key members of each project were specialists in "hexadecimal dump analysis."
- Large, commercial operating systems such as MVS and VMS were used in conjunction with a microprocessor development "environment" on eight projects. Six used home-grown development environments.
- Most of the software line managers had never heard of software management gurus such as Barry Boehm, Fred Brooks, Jerry Weinberg, or Capers Jones.
- Only one of the managers had previously managed a project of comparable size and complexity.
- Only three of the project managers could sit down at a terminal and write a simple program in the language used on their project.

- Little ongoing training was available to the software developers, their managers, or the support staff.
- Some of the more spectacular failures were projects that had made the most aggressive use of structured analysis or design techniques.
- Only 1 of the 16 systems was delivered without a major restructuring (usually to dramatically reduce the ambition level of the project).
- Software reusability was an unrealized dream in every one of these projects. Across the 16 projects, no significant code was reused from previous efforts. (All were build-it-from-scratch projects.)
- Only five projects were actually completed and delivered to customers.

As a consultant or corporate staff person, one is not called upon to work on projects unless they are in trouble. Most commonly, one arrives after the patient has had open heart surgery for the fifth time and is now in a coma on life-support systems. Software project triage has been my business.

Looking across this particular collection of projects, I was struck by how inexperienced and poorly trained the managers were. The one project that delivered the product *on time* was also the project being led by the most experienced manager.

Another key observation is that high-level programming languages and programming environments are not being used as widely as many assume. Many commercial systems are still being built in Assembler with primitive development tools.

More often than not, projects got derailed during the specification or design phases, not the coding phase. I would characterize the derailing as loss of contact with reality or excessive ambition. It was easy to write wish lists that could never be fulfilled. Few projects adopted the important adage, "never attempt a project that is more than 20% different from one your organization and management has successfully completed before."

Until you have lived through one of these major development efforts, you cannot imagine how hard it is to accomplish what you set out to do. Project managers, architects, designers, and even developers must in turn ask themselves "the 20% question." If you are not satisfied that they understand the key issues involved in the development effort and have accomplished something similar, begin to reduce the ambition level of the project immediately. Remember, you can always add functionality in version 2.0, or version 6.0, if you succeed in getting version 1.0 delivered.

In stark contrast, every software development project involving five or fewer developers has been completed and often considered very successful.

Troubled projects

Let's examine some other software projects that either failed or were troubled (too little, too late, at too high a price). Publicly discussed failures include IBM's Future

System (FS), AT&T's Advanced Communication System (ACS and several other names as it began to fail), ITT's 1240 North America, and Standard Electric Lorenz's Bildschrimtext. Major reliability problems have been reported for AT&T switching systems, McDonnell Douglas's F-16 navigation software (the plane could have inverted itself upon crossing the equator), IBM's space shuttle software, Ericsson's MD-110 PABX, and AT&T's billing system for international calls (billions of dollars in lost revenue). Less publicly described failures include:

- a worldwide computer timesharing and communications system (after investing approximately 200 person-years of effort)
- a testing environment for distributed processing systems (more than 100 person-years of effort)
- many integrated services digital network (ISDN) projects and innovative PABX projects that have either failed or been scaled down radically in functionality
- most software reusability projects
- one or more programming environment projects within most large technology companies

Tom DeMarco provides a similar summary of his experiences: "One of the major reasons that the user community distrusts and dislikes software developers is based on performance: users are accustomed to achieving goals in their own fields with a consistency that is unheard of in the software world."[22] A remarkable observation from my admittedly limited experience is that the more aggressively you attempt to "engineer software," the more likely the project is to fail. The successes come from craftsmen, the failures from engineers!

Successes also seem to come from the "bottom," failures from the "top." When a corporation says, "we're behind and have to spend whatever it takes to regain our leadership position," a spectacular failure looms large on the horizon—not unlike the one in Stockholm harbor in 1628 (Chapter One). When a couple of competent and experienced programmers are given the freedom to solve a known problem, they might just create a spectacular success. The first version of the UNIX operating system was developed by two craftsmen, and it was not even a formal project.

Large, complex systems fail today for reasons remarkably similar to the reasons the Vasa failed in 1628:

- We don't know how to design large, complex software.
- We can't reliably manage large development teams.
- Specifications do change and systems quickly become inflexible.
- We have not learned how to say "no" often or effectively enough.

The only difference is that software failures are not as dramatic as 300 tons of hand-carved oak, painted with gold, capsizing into Stockholm harbor. Software failures can be detected only through a detailed inspection of the corporate balance sheet—look for a few hundred million dollars of additional engineering expense.

TIME TO RETHINK THE FUNDAMENTALS

How can it be that a multibillion dollar industry of critical importance finds itself in such disarray? As commercial systems builders, we must find a better way to develop large, innovative systems in the 1990s. Or we need to stop trying to build such large and technically risky projects.

In an article celebrating the tenth anniversary of the invention of the computer, J. A. Morton, a Vice President of Bell Labs wrote, "For some time now, electronic man has known how 'in principle' to extend greatly his visual, tactile, and mental abilities through the digital transmission and processing of all kinds of information. However, all these functions suffer from what has been called 'the tyranny of numbers.' Such systems, because of their complex digital nature, require hundreds, thousands, and sometimes tens of thousands of electronic devices. Each element must be made, tested, packed, shipped, unpacked, retested, and interconnected one-at-a-time to produce a whole system."[23]

In the early 1990s, software engineering remains more a statement of desire than reality. The technologies most commonly available to software developers do not allow software to be engineered. Instead, it has been handcrafted by extraordinary craftsmen. Major projects start from scratch, involve substantial research and invention, and all too often simply fail.

Software projects fail because they require so much invention, so many separately designed parts, so many craftsmen, and so many connections to existing hardware and software systems. Like the hardware guys three decades ago, we software guys are suffering from a tyranny of numbers in the way we try to build software systems.

Software engineering as a discipline has failed due to inadequate technology. If we can't effectively reuse software components, we can't engineer. Until we can engineer more predictably by building systems largely composed of existing components, we must moderate our ambitions. If we don't want to moderate our ambitions, we had better learn a new technology for building software. Chapter Three provides some hope that a solution is at hand. Later chapters will convince you that this new approach to building systems will take a generation or two to fully exploit.

NOTES

1. It is an interesting exercise to see if you can find an item on any corporation's balance sheet that is not affected by computer software.

2. Unfortunately, it was not possible to obtain sufficient installed base and sales information to be sure that the products selected are the top four in each category. It is certain that all are considered highly successful software products.

3. *Byte,* February 1983, p. 433.

4. See Freiberger and Swaine's excellent book, *Fire in the Valley,* for a description of this project (McGraw-Hill, New York, 1984, pp. 136–139).

5. *Byte,* February 1983, p. 433.

6. Levering, Katz, and Moskowitz, *The Computer Entrepreneurs,* NAL Books, 1984.

7. The original version of MS/DOS was called SCP/DOS. It was developed by Patterson in his company, Seattle Computer Products. Gates and Allen acquired SCP/DOS and converted it while under contract to IBM. It thus became MS/DOS and PC/DOS.

8. Gary Kildall has publicly described SCP/DOS as being so close to CP/M that he could use it in sophisticated ways without referring to a reference manual, based upon his knowledge of CP/M.

9. Jack Scanlon, vice president, AT&T, speech at UniForum, 1986.

10. Barr also developed a furniture product (Yieldamatic) to improve yield of wood cutting, a HASP multileaving software product developed under contract, and a linking loader that was sold to UCC.

11. Initially sold only to universities under the scrap materials regulations developed for disposing of old copper wire. When sold to companies, the price went up to $43,000.

12. A motto of the Studebaker brothers in the transportation business beginning in the mid-1800s.

13. See E. W. Dijkstra, Notes on structured programming, *Structured Programming,* O. J. Dahl, E. W. Dijkstra, and A. Hoare, Eds., Academic Press, New York, 1972, p. 19.

14. Software engineering is (was) a noble effort to legitimize the "craft of programming." This effort developed symbiotically with the structured programming movement. As we will see later, a critical requirement for real engineering was missing, so today's practicing programmers rarely think of themselves as engineers.

15. Frederick Brooks, "No silver bullet: Essence and Accidents of Software Engineering," IEEE *Computer,* Apr. 1987, pp. 10-19.

16. For one of the better large studies comparing traditional approaches to structured approaches see Sheppard, S. B., Curtis, B., Millman, P. and Love, T. *Modern coding practices and programmer performance,* IEEE Computer Magazine, December 1979.

17. See Winograd and Flores' important book, *Understanding Computers and Cognition: A New Foundation for Design* (Ablex Publishing, 1986) for a comprehensive assessment of the AI field and a new set of "headware" for thinking about computers. They say, for example, "one cannot construct machines that either exhibit or successfully model intelligent behavior" and "once we move away from the blindness generated by the old questions, we can take a broader perspective on what computers can do."

18. See B. Shiel's *Power Tools for Programmers* in Datamation, November 1982 for a brief explanation of these innovations.

19. Growing interest in AI may be a bellwether indicating that a major change in software technology is about to happen.

20. I would be happy to receive written descriptions of failed projects. If the list becomes interestingly long, I will summarize and publish the information received—with proper respect for confidentiality, of course.

21. Several of which were included in the list of excellent companies described in the modernday management classic, *In Search of Excellence: lessons from America's best run companies.* T. J. Peters and R. H. Waterman, Jr., Harper and Row, 1982.

22. Tom DeMarco, *Controlling Software Projects,* Yourdon Press, Englewood Cliffs, NJ, 1982, p. 4.

23. *Proceedings of the IRE*, June 1958, p. 955.

OOPS

Xerox
tek
PPI

Apple
IBM
HP

7/17/85

Tech

D. Paterson
D. Ungar
A. Purdy {Servio}
A. W. Brock
G. Krasner
Duane Bay
T. Menow
K. Schmucker
G. Booch
L. Tesler
B. Stroustrup
J. Bidwell
J. Anderson
"NEON"
P. Smith
J. McKenna
C. Wisinski

UNIV

C. Hewitt
"Brown "
N. Meyrowitz
"Waterloo # "

T. Budd
D. Bobrow

Aug
22 · 23
29 & 30

On July 17, 1985
*Duane Bay, Glen Krasner,
Chet Wisinski, Tom Love and Larry
Tesler met for lunch in Palo Alto, CA to plan
the first conference on object-oriented programming.
This is a copy of the dinner napkin from that meeting.
About 14 months later, the first OOPSLA conference was held in
Portland, OR sponsored by the Association of Computing Machinery. Many
other people contributed to the success of this first conference and all subsequent
ones. It was considered the most successful first conference ever held by the ACM.*

3

Hope with Objects

The importance of object oriented programming is comparable to that of Whitney's interchangeable part innovation, and for many of the same reasons.

Brad Cox
Object Oriented Programming
Addison-Wesley, Reading, MA, 1986.

It is now time to learn more about a new approach for designing and developing computer software. This chapter offers an introduction to the important concepts. These new concepts will be compared to related hardware engineering concepts and contrasted with current practice in software engineering.

Just as modern corporations are structured into departments, each with its own departmental files and procedures, it makes sense to structure software in the same manner. This is the essence of an "object": the intimate linking of data with the procedures used to operate on that data.

AN OBJECT AS AN "ELECTRONIC MACHINE"

Corporate departments can be thought of as "machines" to accomplish work. Software objects can also be thought of as machines: electronic machines built from software. Let's begin by considering some of the characteristics of electronic machines. We can then use those characteristics to construct a specification for a software machine.

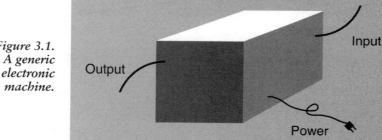

*Figure 3.1.
A generic
electronic
machine.*

Note the electronic black box (Figure 3.1) with input and output wires and a power source. Its salient characteristics are:

- It requires energy.
- It consumes space.
- It is physically isolated from other machines.
- It may contain subassemblies that are themselves electronic machines.
- It takes a finite time to accomplish predetermined tasks.

- It can allow prior requests to influence future results, i.e., it has state or the ability to remember.

In addition, it can be controlled in some manner:

- It accepts requests to perform its task by some agreed-upon communications protocol through one or more input wires.
- It indicates when its operation is completed.

An integrated circuit is an example of a well-packaged electronic machine.

A "software machine"

Objects, the primary components of object-oriented software, also have such characteristics. They:

- require energy, time, and space
- accomplish predetermined tasks
- accept requests for work from a user (a person or other object)
- notify the user when the work has been accomplished
- can allow prior requests to influence future results
- can contain subassemblies that are objects
- can interact with other objects using a standard communications protocol
- are otherwise isolated from other objects and cannot influence their operations

How is this structure different from traditional procedural programming? FORTRAN subroutines and C functions also require time, space, and energy and can perform only those tasks predetermined for them. But the resemblance ends there. In particular:

- Such subroutines or functions are not strictly coupled to specific data. A subroutine or function can be passed arguments containing arbitrary data, permitting *side effects*. The operation of one subroutine or function can alter data depended upon by another.
- Subroutines and functions cannot "remember." They do not retain state information between invocations. Therefore, prior invocations cannot influence future results.

By contrast, objects have:

- private memory to contain data that is retained between invocations of the object
- specialized routines (called *methods*) tailored to the particular type of data available in the object's private memory

In addition, objects use a predefined protocol, called message passing, to interact with other objects. An object can therefore be thought of as a "software machine" encapsulating its data with a set of predefined methods. This is the essence of object-oriented programming. Now, let's look a little closer.

WHAT IS OBJECT-ORIENTED PROGRAMMING?[1]

Object-oriented programming is accomplished by sending a message to an object requesting that object to perform some action. You can think of a message as an interdepartmental memo requesting action. (Unlike such memos, however, the current crop of object-oriented languages requires the sender of a message to wait until receiving the reply from a request before returning to work—not a practice that would be tolerated in corporations!)

What is a message?

A message contains:

- the name of the receiving object
- the name of the message
- arguments (optional) that can be objects themselves

The *message* is a request to an object to perform a routine called a method. This routine usually has the same name as the message. Objects, like machines, determine upon receipt of a message if they will respond to it and, if so, how. The sending object knows only what it wants accomplished; it does not care how. The receiver knows how to accomplish the request, including the form of the result to return. The receiver searches its list of methods for one bearing the same name as the message it has received. If one is found, control passes to it and the method executes. Only the receiver can determine which chunk of code to execute in response to a given message.

Note that methods and messages have the same name by convention. A mes-

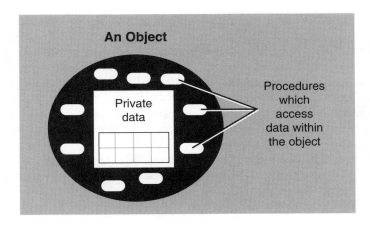

Figure 3.2.
An object.

sage, copy, is sent to an object, aParagraph. Control passes to the copy method within the object, aParagraph, which executes the code contained within the copy method. Upon completing the copy method, control is returned to the object that sent the message.

Because each object can look up a message name and find a unique chunk of code, many different kinds of objects can recognize the same message name and each object can implement that message differently, responding with its own unique method. Such multiple responses to the same message are a characteristic of the system as a whole known as *polymorphism.*

It is important to mention here that the sense in which object-oriented programming languages use the term message passing is comparable to the calling of a subroutine. It does not imply asynchronous communication of any kind. Messages are not broadcast in parallel; instead, only one thread of control exists.

Dynamic binding

Unlike the subroutine calls of traditional procedural languages, the particular method executed in response to a message is not known when the program is compiled. Instead, objects determine which method to execute at runtime; that is, as the code executes. This characteristic, called *dynamic binding,* is one of the important benefits of object-oriented languages.

For example, you might wish to display an arbitrary collection of objects on a screen. Each object is sent the message, display, but different kinds of objects will execute entirely different methods in response.[2] If an object does not have a display method defined, it returns an error saying, "I do not have this method." The system does not crash; control flows smoothly back to the sender.

Such dynamic binding has notable advantages beyond avoiding a crash. Implementors of a drawing program, for example, do not have to anticipate in version 1.0 every type of object they might ever wish to display on the screen. Instead, they can use the display message to control the general mechanism by which the drawing is displayed and implement a display method for each type of object they wish to display in the initial version. Later versions can easily add functionality by defining new kinds of objects and implementing appropriate display methods for each. The general mechanism whereby objects in the drawing are displayed is not affected.[3]

Deferring until runtime the binding of procedure names to procedure invocations allows software to be malleable in the face of changing requirements. For example, the line of code:

```
[currentLaser aimAndFire];
```

is intended to execute a procedure that will aim and fire a laser. How the laser is aimed and fired depends upon the type of laser. If you need a system with different types of lasers, it would be useful if you could send them all the same message— aimAndFire—and have them respond with distinct, appropriate aim-and-fire algorithms.

In effect, a laser distinguished as the currentLaser will choose which aimAndFire mechanism will service that request. But which laser is the currentLaser cannot be known when the program is compiled. Nor can it be "hard-wired" in any way because different objects distinguished as the currentLaser will result in different firing algorithms being invoked. If it is hard-wired, such flexibility of response is lost.

Objects bind a message to the method dynamically—when the code is running. As a result, other objects need only know that lasers know how to respond appropriately to the message aimAndFire. They can depend upon each specific laser object to know how to aim and fire itself.

Because messaging specifies only the desired response, dependencies of type cannot spread through a system. Instead, they remain within objects. Therefore, programmers can install new data types in working systems without altering, and possibly disrupting, the rest of the system.

Dynamic binding results in a significant change in the way we view a system and the pieces within it. For the first time, it makes sense to see the system behavior in terms of the *responsibilities* of the objects within it. For example, a Collection might not be responsible for knowing the types of objects it can contain. But, an OrderedCollection might make some assumptions about the ability of its component objects to respond to certain messages that allow them to be ordered.

The simplified diagram in Figure 3.3 shows the essential elements of object-oriented programming: encapsulation of data, methods of the object, and message-passing between objects.

A method within one object may not directly access data within another object. Data is bound to a particular set of procedures that access that data.

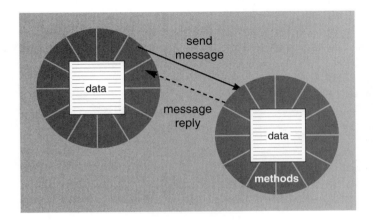

Figure 3.3. Sending a message from one object to another.

Classes and instances

So far, I have been using the phrase "kind of object" without an explanation. Indeed, the previous paragraph refers to two kinds of objects: Collection and OrderedCollection. What exactly are "kinds of objects"?

When the first object-oriented languages were used, it was quickly discovered that much work was being duplicated among similar objects. A powerful solution was to group objects into classes, just as biologists classify organisms into species.

A class is a description of similar objects. Classes describe:

- the set of data structures within objects of that class
- the set of methods that can operate on data within the objects of that class

In essence, classes provide a blueprint for the construction of new objects. They are the DNA of a newly formed object.

An *instance* is an object that is a member of a class. For example, if Children is a class, then claire, emily, and gayle could be instances of the class Children.

A *class* itself does not contain data; it merely describes the structure and function of objects of that class.[4] For example, the class List may prescribe that its instances contain a list of other objects. The class itself does not contain any particular list of objects. An instance of the class List, however, would contain a list of specific objects. Instances contain specific data; classes contain the structure and behavior shared by all instances of the class.

An implementation trick is used to make classes objects too. Let me explain. If a class is an object, then that object must be an instance of some class. It is an instance of a metaclass. Moreover, the same logic should apply to metaclasses; it does. Metaclasses are also objects. Luckily, the recursive descent stops there. Let's draw a picture or we'll never understand these connections.

If we look at one class and metaclass (Figure 3.4), we see the following relationship:

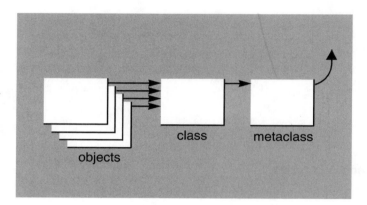

Figure 3.4.
Relationship of
objects to classes
and metaclasses.

There are several objects of a given class. There is one metaclass for each class. Objects have pointers to their class. Class objects have a pointer to their metaclass. A metaclass is an instance of the Object class's metaclass. See page 77 of Cox's *Object-Oriented Programming* or Goldberg and Robson's *Smalltalk-80* for an introduction to metaclasses. Chapter 16 of Goldberg and Robson should be consulted for all the minute details (effectively, the circuit diagrams) that most mortals are not particularly interested in knowing (see Note 6).

All this metaclass complexity exists to create simplicity. Remember the concept behind Smalltalk was that "everything is an object"—even classes and metaclasses. By adding a little complexity in the wiring diagram near the root of the inheritance tree, it was not necessary to add additional language constructs. And the less complicated the language, the more powerful the development environment that can be built for it.

It would be nice if we could say that all object-oriented languages have the same inheritance structure or use the same terminology. Nothing could be further from the truth. What has been presented here is the Smalltalk terminology, because it was the "mother of all contemporary object-oriented languages." The same concepts exist by and large within Objective-C. But, C++ is altogether different.

In Objective-C, factory methods are used to create instances. Classes are then thought of as factories. Then a class would have a factory method, new, to create a new instance of that class. In C++, constructors are called by using the class name as a function to create new objects. Destructors are used to remove objects and are called by functions indicated by ~Classname.

Encapsulation

The object-oriented approach improves reusability and avoids drawbacks by distributing information on a "need-to-know" basis—one object does not need to know how information is organized within other objects. Instead, it can only request that object to carry out some predefined activity. Objects operate autonomously, just as departments within companies; they cannot obtain information from another object without its cooperation and without using a predefined protocol for interaction ("We'll browse our own files, thank you.").

We say that an object's private data is hidden from other objects. Only the object's own methods can manipulate its data. But method names are visible to other objects. This visibility allows objects to send messages, which cause methods by the same name to be executed. But how an object responds (the implementation of a particular method) is not visible externally. This is useful because a method's implementation can now change without affecting other parts of a system. If it had a bug, fixing that bug will not introduce new bugs. The rest of the system is insulated by the messenger.

This encasing of data and methods within one object is called *encapsulation*; it ensures an object's integrity. It shields data from other parts of the system, allowing each object to operate as an independent software machine. Such a machine can be used in many different systems without affecting other working code.

How does this actually work? Suppose you sent a message size to a window. When the size message is sent, the receiving object determines if it can respond to that message. It determines this by comparing its list of available methods with the name of the incoming message. If there is a match, control is passed to the method named size and it runs until it completes. While the method is executing, it can access only the data contained within the object (including any arguments passed with the message). Upon completion, control is returned to the method from which the original message was sent.

Encapsulation releases the programmer from the heavy burden of trying to predict and account for all possible contingencies. Because data is encapsulated, programmers need only depend upon the data the object will return; the object can decide how it will construct that data.

How strong is this capsule around an object? It can be broken, one way or another, by every extant object-oriented programming language. But it need not be, and the fact that the mechanism is still imperfect should not obscure the importance of the principle.

Organizing systems of software as objects manages complexity by eliminating redundancy, encapsulating data to limit side effects, and simplifying the flow of control. It facilitates reusability by separating what the designer wants to accomplish from how it will be implemented.*The combined effect is to make genuinely reusable software possible on a scale never before achieved.*

Encapsulation is not nearly so simple a story in any hybrid language. By virtue of the fact that hybrid languages are extensions to base languages that usually have some very low-level features, it is possible to violate the encapsulation of objects through the lower-level language.

Some hybrid languages create different types of encapsulations. The diagram in Figure 3.5 shows the three different types of encapsulation available within C++. Each method and variable can have different levels of protection declared.

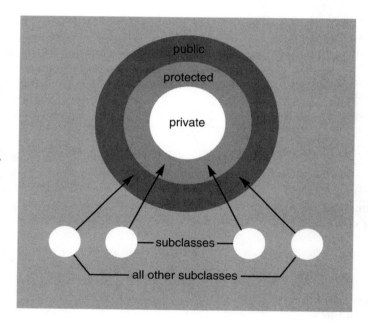

*Figure 3.5.
Inheritance
in C++.*

Inheritance

New classes are created by choosing an existing class and specifying the differences between the new class and the existing class. The new class is said to inherit the data structures and behaviors of the existing class, and it can add other data structures and behaviors as required. Behaviors added may in fact override previously defined behaviors in one or more superclasses. The intent is to make it easy to specialize generic code.

First, we begin with a hierarchy of classes (see Figure 3.6). Subclasses inherit the structures and behaviors of their superclasses. In technical terms, the new class is a said to be a *subclass;* the existing class is its *superclass.* If a Rectangle class is a subclass of a Polygon class, then all the procedures and data structures previously defined for polygons are inherited by rectangles. The designer of the Rectangle class need only describe how rectangles differ from polygons—in what way they refine the original concept.

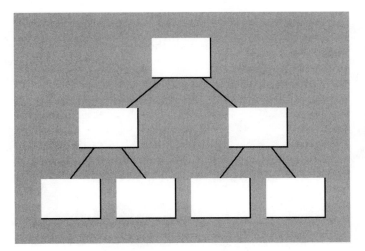

Figure 3.6.
Hierarchy of classes

Inheritance enables the software engineer to design new software components by specifying only those characteristics that differentiate the new component from an existing component. This is a particularly appropriate representation for software components because they can be designed to directly reflect existing real-world entities, such as the lasers in a manufacturing application or the business forms in a data processing application. The real world is full of entities that resemble each other. If such relationships can be represented directly, then to that extent the program faithfully models the real world. Among other benefits, inheritance makes a program easier for a maintenance programmer to understand at a later date.

For clarity, remember that a subclass is a superset of the class from which it inherits.

One class is special: the class named Object. Object is the only class without a superclass. It is at the root of the inheritance tree. All other classes within the system form a tree growing from this root. Again, for clarity we routinely draw them upside-down.

The Object class describes the structure and behavior of all objects. This root class allows all objects to share such behaviors as knowing what class they belong to, how to copy themselves, responding with their sizes or their names, writing themselves onto a disk, and so on. These can be useful and powerful behaviors, especially when you can ensure that all objects share these behaviors. By contrast, if we added additional data structures to the Object class it would be very expensive!

By convention, object names begin with a lowercase letter and class names begin with a capital letter. The name, Object, then refers to the class at the root of the inheritance tree.

Inheritance hierarchies are *generalization–specialization* trees. The more generalized classes are near the root of the tree; the leaves of the tree contain more specialized capabilities.

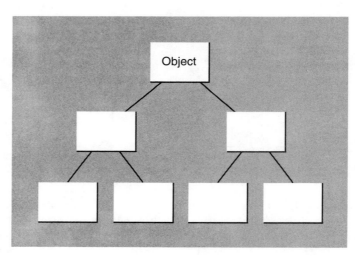

Figure 3.7.
Inheriting from the
Object class.

Class hierarchy diagrams such as the one in Figure 3.7 can be confusing at first glance because they look like other diagrams we are accustomed to seeing—those depicting the functional decomposition of a system. But the Object class does not call the two classes below it. The class hierarchy is a *static* description of the relationships between classes in a system. The diagram in Figure 3.7 implies only that the four classes on the bottom of the hierarchy inherit behavior and function from two other classes, one of which is the Object class. For each class there is a metaclass, which is shown as darker grey in Figure 3.8.

The class hierarchy can also be thought of as a hierarchically structured knowledge base for building software systems. *With each new class you define, you extend the language to create a new, application-specific, higher-level language.* Each new class raises the level of the language for application or system building. There is no fundamental constraint to this extensibility.

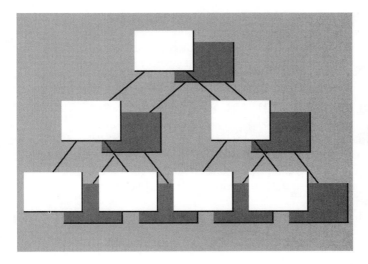

Figure 3.8.
Metaclass inheritance.

But again, languages like C++ and Eiffel allow multiple inheritance. Multiple inheritance means that a class may have more than one superclass. So inheritance trees now become inheritance lattices (see Figure 3.9). Fortunately, there is no metaclass concept in these languages.

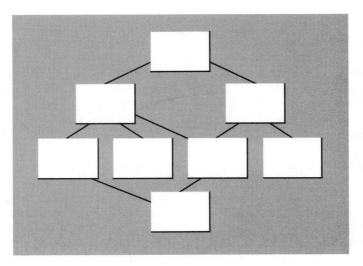

Figure 3.9.
Inheritance lattices.

Design and coding efforts are reduced by the mechanism of inheritance, which allows data or procedures to be stored without redundancy. This tree of classes effectively becomes an index to an ever-expanding catalog of reusable software components available to many applications. As we will see in a later chapter on quality, inheritance can complicate the life of a test manager. Multiple inheritance can have a brutal effect on a development project if used often.[5]

OBJECTS VS. PROCEDURAL PROGRAMMING

In traditional programming languages, data is passive. Behaviors associated with a data structure are hard-wired into the procedures by means of branching statements that examine some *ad hoc* characteristic of the data and decide how to act upon it. In effect, data and procedures are stitched together one at a time by each programmer.

These branching statements bind the input data with the blocks of code (the routines) that operate on that data. This maze of branching statements includes important assumptions about acceptable data types. But those important assumptions remain implicit. Because such assumptions are so difficult to understand, conflicting assumptions are routinely made within a modest-sized program. A large system is replete with such conflicts.

Routines in traditional programming languages depend upon the arguments or files they deal with during execution. Such things as the specific size of an array, or the types of data it contains, must all be assumed to be appropriate. However, these assumptions *are never recorded*, nor can they be enforced. So the original programmer must simply assume that the data fed to this routine throughout its life will conform to these unrecorded specifications. If this routine has a typical 10-year lifetime, most of its data will not yet even have been generated.

This places a heavy burden on programmers. The original programmer must try to code for contingencies and future changes but has no place to record these important decisions. Later, the maintenance programmer will discover that crucial information required to modify or extend the system is no longer available.

Nevertheless, this procedural or operator/operand model has allowed us to build impressive software systems. It is also the root of many fundamental problems that software developers have been grappling with for over 20 years. Software written in this procedural way tends to be bulky—many lines of code are needed to finish a job. It tends to be complex due to the intricate structure of branching statements. It tends to be rigid, inflexible, and difficult to adapt to changing requirements.

To reuse code effectively, the aspects of data that functions depend upon must be both known and enforced. Objects are a mechanism to accomplish this. Reuse also requires flexibility because it is impossible to foresee how software will change over the years.

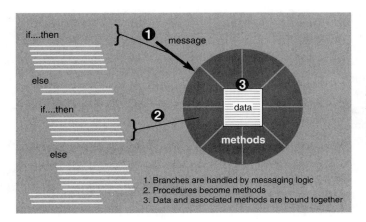

Figure 3.10. Relating traditional code to objects.

Figure 3.10 shows that:

- Branches are replaced by messaging logic.
- Procedures become methods.
- Data and associated methods are bound together to form objects.

Branching statements that bind data to procedures are replaced with a system-wide messaging routine that determines:

- the class of the object
- the name of the message
- if the receiving object can service the incoming message

Each class recognizes and responds to a finite set of messages. The methods within an object can be thought of as the blocks of code within a branching structure. Many specialized branching statements are replaced by a single heavily used branching statement: the messenger.

OBJECT-ORIENTED PROGRAMMING LANGUAGES

Hybrid vs. pure object systems

It is possible to construct remarkably capable systems with laudatory performance using only objects and messages, as shown by the fundamental successes of the Learning Research Group at Xerox PARC during the 1970s. Such purely object-oriented systems treat integers as objects and even send messages to accomplish simple addition: 2 add: 3. Yet, such purity implies inefficiency because some uncertainty must be dynamically resolved prior to determining exactly which chunk of code to execute in response to a message.

Nevertheless, powerful development tools and environments can be constructed based upon such uniform languages. For the rapid prototyping of applications, or even for systems with no inherent need for computational performance, pure object systems are ideal. As machines become more powerful and pure object systems become more efficient, the set of applications for which the technology is appropriate has begun to predominate. And, for training purposes, pure object-oriented environments are mandatory.

For systems where memory and performance impose real constraints, an attractive option is to employ a hybrid system in which objects and traditional procedural programming are freely intermixed. This allows computationally intensive operations such as fast Fourier transforms and matrix manipulation to be implemented traditionally, while components that exhibit high entropy such as user interfaces, error handling, report generation, and system administration, can be accomplished using objects.

This book directs its attention toward the construction of commercial systems. Practical experience has shown that reducing memory requirements and increasing performance always have significant commercial implications. Hybrid systems can provide most of the benefits of pure object-oriented systems while offering some significant improvements in time and space efficiency as well.

COMMERCIAL HISTORY OF OBJECT-ORIENTED TECHNOLOGY

In research institutions from Palo Alto to Cambridge to Oslo, experimental software systems have been built for two decades using objects. The most comprehensive of these systems was started in 1969 but was not fully described to the public for over 10 years—*Smalltalk-80*.[6] The first significant commercial products built using various precursors of this technology were developed by telecommunications companies. They reached the market in the late 1970s.

Until 1984, this new technology—object-oriented software engineering—was confined mostly to research labs, the intelligence community, a few universities, some governmental agencies, and the artificial intelligence community. As a result, tools were designed with little regard for the realities of the commercial software world. They were voracious consumers of machine cycles and storage, requiring programmers to work in an entirely new language (typically LISP) and operating system. A few commercial organizations however, provided training, engineering assistance, or support for these new languages and development environments. Examples included languages such as Loops (from Xerox) and KEE (from IntelliCorp).

The commercial delivery of Objective-C[7] in January 1984 by PPI (later renamed Stepstone) corrected this situation. A tiny entrepreneurial company had developed a hybrid object-oriented programming language and class library that included the entire C programming language and could run on traditional operating systems such as UNIX, VMS, Aegis, and MS-DOS. Objective-C also reduced the time and space costs of object-oriented programming to a level acceptable for many commercial system and application development projects. From Objective-C, existing programs in other languages could be accessed just as they can be from C.

Within a year of the introduction of Objective-C, a flurry of other object-oriented languages entered the market including Clascal (which became Object-Pascal), Neon (a precursor of Actor), Class C (which became C++), and Methods (later Smalltalk-V).

In retrospect, it is remarkable how many significant commercial development projects adopted these new languages prior to 1985. Even more remarkable is that most of these projects proved successful. It is no surprise that most had difficulties with the concepts and all had difficulties with the tools.

A BRIEF PROGRAMMING LESSON

In June 1983, Brad Cox and I founded PPI to build tools to provide commercial support for object-oriented software engineering. It is therefore only natural that Objective-C, a commercial product of Stepstone, is the language chosen for examples in this book.[8]

Objective-C

Objective-C adds objects, messages, and inheritance to the standard C language. C syntax remains the same.

The most basic operation in Objective-C is to send a message to an object.[9] If aLaser is an object, it can be sent the message aimAndFire:

```
[aLaser aimAndFire];
```

Square brackets designate that a message is being sent. The semicolon is the standard C line termination character.

Messages may include objects or C variables as arguments. In the following line, the argument aTarget could be either a C variable or an object:

```
[aLaser aimAt: aTarget];
```

In this case, the message is aimAt: aTarget and the method is aimAt:. The message includes the message name and all arguments.

The object aLaser determines how to respond to the message when it receives it. This is dynamic binding at work, a distinguishing feature of the object-oriented approach. When the code was written, the programmer might not even have known if the object aLaser could service the message aimAt: aTarget.

Defining a class

Objective-C includes a library of over two dozen Software-ICs.[10] Software-ICs are classes developed by Stepstone and certified to operate according to their documented specification.

Naturally, users can also define their own classes. Defining a new class requires the following information:

- identification of the superclass
- the instance methods (the behavior of instances of the class)
- the factory methods (the behavior of the class itself)
- additional data structures required for new instances of this class (called instance variables)

The example class definition below uses the Objective-C commenting convention. Comments begin with two forward slashes "//" and end at the end of the line. The name of the new class appears first, followed by a colon and the superclass from which it will inherit structure and behavior. A pointer to, and the name of, the instance variable(s) encapsulated by the class are included within the curly braces that follow. After a comment documenting the purpose of the class, the methods are declared: Factory methods begin with a plus sign "+" and instance methods begin with a minus sign "-."

```
Laser:Object { id direction }
// a comment describing the purpose and features of
// the class Laser, a subclass of the Software-IC Object.
// This class adds within each instance of a Laser
// an additional pointer (id) to the object "direction"

+ new {...}                        // a comment describing
                                   // the factory method new
- aimAndFire {...}                 // a comment describing aimAndFire
- aimAt: aDirection {...}          // a comment describing aimAt:
- test {...}                       // a method to verify that
                                   // the class performs
                                   // according to spec
```

Notice that test methods are developed for each class from the very start. These test methods are designed to test the functional behavior of the class. (See Table 2.2.)

Objects

Objects are created by sending a message to a factory object (the class itself). The factory object creates an organized data space and provides pointers to the behaviors available to that new object, thus enabling it to invoke its methods. Objects are named using standard C assignment statements. The act of creation and naming occurs this way:

```
aLaser = [Laser new];
```

This statement assumes the prior existence of the class named Laser, such as the one defined above, which recognizes the factory method new.

EXAMPLE OF THE BENEFITS OF USING OBJECTS

Let's use a specific example to see some of the benefits from this new approach to building computer software systems. Keep in mind that this is not a book introducing you to all the concepts of object technology, so we will move fast and omit much detail.

How does object-oriented software engineering represent an improvement over procedural programming? In essence, traditional programming requires that we take the conceptual model for a system (its top-level design [see Figure 3.11]) and transform it into an implementation model, the actual code. That transformation is so radical that the mapping from the conceptual model to the code and vice versa cannot be maintained as the system evolves. A semantic gap exists between the conceptual model and its implementation.

Object-oriented software engineering not only retains the conceptual model but it makes it more explicit by virtue of the language syntax. If the conceptual model of a word processing program contains sections, paragraphs, sentences, and words, then those concepts would be represented in the implementation model by classes bearing those names. As classes, those concepts would now be visible at the highest level of structure—the inheritance tree.

The importance of retaining the conceptual model, and making it visible within the implementation, cannot be overstated. We can now read the code and determine what the original designer had in mind at every step of the way (see Figure 3.12). Designed-in assumptions are now explicit. With procedural code, this is simply not possible. Basic algorithms are cluttered with information about the types of data being dealt with rather than expressing the algorithms independently of the

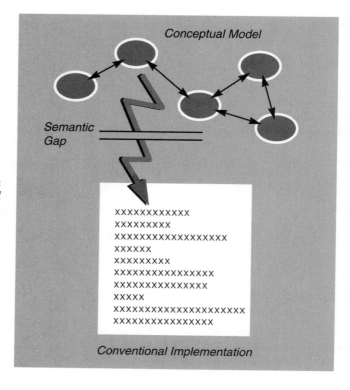

Figure 3.11.
Translating a
conceptual model
into code.

Conceptual Model

Semantic
Gap

Conventional Implementation

types of data they manipulate. This cluttering is termed static binding of procedures and data because the programming language cannot dynamically accommodate new types of data.

Let's take a simple program and compare procedural code to object-oriented
code. Consider a program that manipulates various types of space weapons, each
with a routine designed and optimized for the particular characteristics of the
weapon in question:

```
CASE weapon.tag OF
        laser:              AimAndFireLaser (weapon);
        railGun:            AimAndFireRailGun (weapon);
        directImpact:       AimAndFireDirectImpact (weapon);
        kkv:                AimAndFireKKV (weapon);
        asat:               AimAndFireASAT (weapon);
END;
```

Imagine that you had to add a new type of direct impact interceptor to this
program. To do so, you would have to scrutinize the entire program to find every

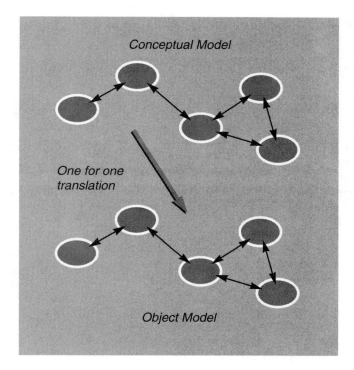

Conceptual Model

One for one translation

Object Model

Figure 3.12.
Translating a
conceptual model
into objects.

time the "tag" field was used to distinguish the various types of weapons. You would then have to differentiate the treatment of this new type from the existing direct impact interceptors and weapons by changing all these code blocks appropriately. You would then recompile, relink, and retest each function. It would be a slow, tedious, and error-prone process.

I like to apply the "trash can test"—walk to the nearest trash can, collect an unstained program, and inspect it carefully. My experience is that "if-then-else" statements or computed "go-to" statements are a lot more common than case statements. Changing a program to accept a new data structure will therefore be even more complex than the process described above. Complex changes result in discarded programs and, ultimately, the decision to start over from scratch instead of reusing what exists.

The strong link between procedures and data types makes the job of modifying a program quite difficult. The limitations of static binding can be overcome in an object-oriented language. The weapon-firing case statement becomes:

```
[aLaser aimAndFire];
```

This message-send in an object-oriented language is independent of any changes we might wish to make either to modify the simulation or improve the efficiency of any of the laser-aiming algorithms. We could add a new laser object to the simulation and reprogram an existing laser object to execute more efficient code without any changes to the way the system "hangs together."

. Theoretically, object-oriented techniques can be used in any programming language. However, this requires that the programmer construct extremely complex data structures and manipulate them consistently. While it is certainly possible to do this, my experience has shown that a simple rule applies: a single programmer working alone can create and maintain such structures and build rather large pieces of object-oriented code in a procedural language. As soon as another programmer joins the project, however, these self-enforced standards become nearly impossible to sustain.

Instead, it is far more reasonable to use a language that directly supports objects—an object-oriented language. Several such languages exist as supported products running on a wide variety of workstations and hosts: Smalltalk-80, Objective-C, Object-Pascal, C++, Smalltalk-V, LOOPS, and others. (One notable nonexample is the Ada programming language. Ada supports neither dynamic binding nor inheritance and is therefore not an object-oriented programming language.)

TERMS USED IN THIS BOOK

Object-oriented technology allows software components to be reused; it thus provides the first opportunity for software really to be engineered. The term "object-oriented software engineering" describes this application of engineering practice to the development of commercial software components and systems. The term "programming" is inappropriate. When a single word needs to be used, this book uses "modeling" instead.

SUMMARY

The software industry, while still young, has seen some significant changes since Sputnik was sent aloft. But none of the changes during the past 30 years will prove as significant as the commercial application of objects that began in the mid-1980s. Object-oriented technology is important because it finally allows us to crack the software reusability problem. Fundamental to object-oriented software engineering is never to start from scratch. This will be the single most important change we will see in the software industry in our lifetimes.

Technologists who are actively building and reusing software components have begun to create a new industry. That software components industry will become as large and as significant as the semiconductor industry. Yet, making reusability an industry-wide, day-to-day reality will require another decade or two. We are all pioneers now, making history. Many claims have yet to be staked.

NOTES

1. For a more technical description of object-oriented programming, see Brad Cox, *Object-Oriented Programming: An Evolutionary Approach,* Addison-Wesley, Reading, MA, 1986.
2. Known as polymorphic objects.
3. As it turns out, there are even more powerful ways to handle the specific case of displaying objects on the screen. I will return to this example later.
4. Classes may have data. Class variables can be used for keeping track of all objects of a given class, for example. But this concept is not fundamental to understanding what is happening, so I will gloss over some details that are not fundamental at this stage of a person's understanding of object technology.
5. To learn more about inheritance, I recommend Alan Snyder's article, Inheritance and the development of encapsulated software components, in *Research Directions in Object-Oriented Programming*, Bruce Shriver and Peter Wegner, Eds., MIT Press, Cambridge, MA, 1987. Issues raised here can provide some solid advice to newcomers regarding their use of inheritance in whatever language.
6. See the series on Smalltalk-80, especially Adele Goldberg and Kenny Robson, *Smalltalk-80: The Language and Its Implementation* (Addison-Wesley, Reading, MA, 1983) and Adele Goldberg, *Smalltalk-80: The Interactive Programming Environment* (Addison-Wesley, Reading, MA, 1984).
7. Objective-C is a registered trademark of The Stepstone Corporation.
8. For those who may have formed the premature opinion that Objective-C passed away, I offer a moment of silence. You can't always be right. Good technology is persistent, but of course it must change and improve. Companies such as NeXT are very effective in doing just that.
9. Thanks are extended to Kurt Schmucker for providing this example.
10. Software-IC is a registered trademark of The Stepstone Corporation. It is a mark that designates high-quality, commercially viable, fully tested, and documented classes.

I brought GREED to OOPSLA '89

Sponsored by Hewlett-Packard

4

Greed: An Example Program

*We need to shift our attention away from
the detailed specification of algorithms, towards
the description of the properties of
the packages and objects with which we build.*

Terry Winograd
"Beyond Programming Languages"
Interactive Programming Environments
Barstow, Shrobe, & Sandewall, Eds., McGraw-Hill, New York, 1984, p. 520.

Deciding to use a "new" technology on a critical software project requires a review of other organizations' experiences with that technology. The experienced manager searches for three examples: those small enough to be understood completely, projects of a similar size and complexity as the project at hand, and at least one example of the unsuccessful use of the new technology.

My intent here is not to teach the details of a particular object-oriented programming language but to explain the basic technology and its implications for the development process. The same example programmed in many languages will prove especially enlightening.

This chapter provides for the first time, an interesting object-oriented program that I originally specified, then was programmed by leading experts in each of the following object-oriented programming languages: C++, Object-Pascal, Smalltalk-80, Smalltalk-V, ProGraph, Complete C, HyperCard, Actor, and Eiffel. I trust you will find this example and implementation tour as interesting, enlightening, and productive as I did. I trust that managers will find this an appropriate example that is completely understandable, yet nontrivial.

GREED—THE SPECS

Good example programs are hard to find, and I spent several years looking for a suitable candidate. Such a program must satisfy some impossibly conflicting objectives:

- It must be small enough to be presented in its entirety.
- It must be large enough so that professionals believe the technology is scalable.
- It must provide good examples of the use of objects, inheritance, dynamic binding, and encapsulation.
- It must be easy to understand and preferably involve some physical modeling.
- Aspects of the example must be nonobvious from both a design and implementation perspective.
- It must demonstrate significant reuse.
- The example should not be unduly favorable to one language or development environment.

You be the judge, but I think I have found an excellent example program.

But first, let me thank the wonderful staff at Knowledge Systems Corporation

(KSC) in Cary, North Carolina, for their participation and collaboration on this project. We could not have done this without your help. I also thank Hewlett-Packard Corporation for having provided a reward to all implementors—their ownGreed T-shirt. Finally, it was the extraordinary participation by experts from many companies that made this project such a success.

It is a game program that involves physical modeling, rules, graphics, an iconic user interface, and report generation. The game was introduced to me by Capers Jones, but I have no idea of its origin. The name of the game is Greed.

To implement the game in all of the major object-oriented programming languages, we created a competition for OOPSLA '89. The rules of the Greed exercise were as follows:

1. OrgWare and Knowledge Systems Corporation (KSC) provided all participants with the same written specification by telefax several weeks before OOPSLA '89.
2. Any errors in the specification or misunderstandings arising from the specs were corrected by sending clarifications to all participants.
3. All implementors were invited to present their results at a special session one evening during the OOPSLA conference.
4. Everyone who made a presentation and submitted an implementation was provided with a copy of all other implementations and a present (an HP-provided Greed T-shirt).
5. It was assumed that all implementations were copyrighted material. Any further use of these implementations must be done with the permission of each author.
6. It was also assumed that each implementor would be experienced in the use of his or her chosen language, component library, and development environment.

In direct competition with a free bar and without public announcement, nearly 250 people attended a three-hour session on Tuesday evening of OOPSLA. Each implementor had the opportunity to describe his or her implementation, and at the end of the session most implementors did live demonstrations. I was pleased that there was not a single "my language is better than your language" comment during the three-hour session. Instead, participants sincerely wanted to understand the experiences of the many competent implementors in using their respective languages and development environments.

SPECIFICATIONS

The following specification and implementation suggestions were provided to all participants by telefax:

Greed is a dice game played between two or more players. The object of the game is to tally points from the dice rolls and be the first player to score 5,000 points. There are five dice in the game that are rolled from a cup.

To enter the game, a player must score at least 300 points on the first roll of his or her turn; otherwise, the player is considered "bust." If the player goes bust, he or she must wait his or her turn to roll again. If this first roll produces 300 or more points, then the player has the option of stopping and keeping the initial score or continuing. To continue, the player rolls only the dice that have not yet scored in this turn. A player may continue rolling until all the dice have scored or until he or she is bust. With the exception of the entry roll, a bust is when an individual roll produces no points. The player may stop and keep his or her score after any roll as long as he or she is not bust. Each dice roll is tallied as follows:

Threes of a kind score 100 × face value of one of the three dice. If the three of a kind are 1s, then it is scored as 1,000. Three 2s = 200 points; three 4s = 400. Single 1s and 5s score 100 and 50 points, respectively. Examples (for first roll):

```
   44446 = 400 points
           with the option to roll the 4 & 6
   11111 = 1000 +100 +100 = 1200 points
           with the option to roll all five dice again
   12315 = 100 + 0 + 0 + 100 + 50 points
           with the option to roll the 2 & 3
```

Finally, the winner is determined after a player collects a total score of 5,000 or more and all players have had an equal number of turns. If, for example, a player scores over 5,000 points, he or she may still lose if a subsequent player ends up with a final score greater than his or hers.

GREED—IMPLEMENTATION SUGGESTIONS

For design purposes we should assume that the rules, strategies, and scoring algorithms can be changed. For this reason, the design should be cleanly factored. The designer is also encouraged to play the game a few times before beginning the design. The following sections give a suggested basic object breakdown for the design. There can easily be more objects involved.

Game object

The greed game itself can be considered an object. The game consists of players, dice, a cup, and rules. The game object should also know who started first, whose turn it is, and what the rolls are for the current turn. It should be playable "by itself" and independent of the type of interface used. For example, the object should respond to request (messages) like:

- roll the dice
- go to next player
- restart game
- add a new player

The game object should be flexible enough to easily allow for different game parameters, such as:

- different numbers of dice
- different minimum score to enter
- different high score
- different dice scoring rules

Die object

Each die can be considered an object. It should know how to roll and display itself. It needs to randomly choose and keep track of its value. The die object would probably need an undefined state that would represent it being shaken or sitting in the cup. A die in an undefined state would also display itself differently (i.e., rolling or spinning). We will assume the die is a cube, but the design should be flexible enough to account for dice with different numbers of faces (i.e., a die with 11 sides).

Player object

Players participate in the Greed game and keep track of their score. Score tracking should also reflect the scoring history. A player should at least know what his or her score was for each turn of the game. Players have names. This player object expects an external source (user) to make the decisions (i.e., when to continue rolling or stop).

Computer player object

The computer player object is a subclass of player object that makes his or her own decisions about whether to roll or stop. The computer player allows a user to play Greed with the computer. The intelligence about whether or not to roll should be represented by a "degree of risk" or greediness factor. The computer player can also take into account things like how far behind he or she is, is this his or her last turn, his or her history of busts vs. rolls, etc. Any number and combination of players (users) and computer players should be allowed.

Interface model object

This object is determined by your interface design. Its role is to orchestrate the game and players and reflect player decisions and game state. As a minimum, the interface should:

- show the dice graphically for current turn and roll
- allow players to be added and removed
- allow players to provide roll/stop decisions
- graphically display the scoring history of the players (This could take the form of a monotonically increasing curve for each player.)

The designer is encouraged to use creativity when designing the interface. This could be anything from animating the cup and dice to giving the computer players or game a personality.

Many strategies are possible, and the game turns out to be a little more interesting than it might appear at first. It can be played by anyone capable of rolling the dice and learning even a rudimentary strategy. Gayle, my seven-year-old daughter, chooses to roll until she either busts or has only one die left to roll. She wins surprisingly often.

Like any attempt to write a spec, this attempt was not perfect either. It was considered incomplete despite the fact that it had been tested with a trial implementation prior to sending it out to all the implementors. Several days after the initial spec was sent, a modified spec went out with corrections. What is shown above is actually the corrected spec. The changes were so minor that none of the implementors reported any difficulty coping with the differences.

THE DESIGNS

We were intentionally trying to get similar implementations of the same program in each of the object-oriented languages. Nevertheless, it was striking how similar they were. The next most striking aspect of the design process was how each participant chose to elaborate the design based upon his or her own interests. Those interested in rule-based programming elaborated the strategy, those interested in graphics got completely carried away with animation, and several chose to do a lot of work to show off the special strengths of their particular language, development environment, or development tools.

THE IMPLEMENTATIONS

A detailed analysis of all the implementations could represent one if not several Ph.D. dissertations. Space permits only a brief summary of results from the exercise. I hope to do a comprehensive analysis with complete source code examples one day.

BASIC

At OOPSLA '89, I was given an article from the May 1987 issue of *Laptop User Magazine* which described a Greed implementation in BASIC for a laptop computer. That implementation provided a wonderful example of how not to write software. It violated almost every admonition of how to write code presented in *Elements of Programming Style*—gotos, no comments, complex control flow, formatting, etc. But presumably it did run on a 1987 laptop computer. I even found typing the program to be amazingly difficult. A reformatted sample is worth seeing:

```
 5   CLEAR
     DEFINT A-Z
     H=1
     IF MAXRAM = 61104
          THEN POKE 63277, PEEK(61983)
          ELSE POKE 64634, PEEK(63791)
10   CLA
     PRINT @97, "GREED"
     PRINT @131, "A Dice Game by"
     PRINT @173, "Joe Wasserman"
     PRINT @215, "73117,3600"
     FOR Z=1 TO 4E3
     NEXT
15   CLS
     PRINT @164, "Do you want to go first? Y/N ";
     Y$ = INPUT$(1)
20   CLS
     PRINT @70, "This Roll"
```

```
        LINE(176,5) - (235,25),1,B
   25   IF Y$ <> "Y" AND Y$ <> "y"
               THEN PRINT @269, "*"
                      GOTO 235
   30   PRINT #229, "*"
   35   PRINT @230, CHR$(27) + "p" + " YOU " + CHR$(27) + "q"
        PRINT @270, " ME "
        D = 6
        S =0
        R = 0
        X(1) = 0
        X(2) = 0
        L = L + 1
   40   IF MAXRAM = 61104
               THEN POKE 63227, PEEK(61983)
               ELSE POKE 64634, PEEK(63791)
   45   FOR Z = 1 TO VAL(RIGHT$ (TIME$,2))
               DU = RND(1)
        NEXT
   50   V = 200
        GOSUB 410
        O = 0
        F = 0
        N = 0
        T = 0
        FT = 0

   55   IF X(1) AND X(1) <> 1 AND X(1) <> 5
               THEN GOSUB 575
   60   GOSUB 420
        IF C < 6
               THEN 70
   65   FOR Z = 1 TO 6
               IF D(Z) <> Z
                      THEN 70
                      ELSE NEXT
        PRINT @7, "You have a STRAIGHT"
        S = S + 1500
        R = 1
        GOSUB 500
        GOTO 105
   70   FOR Z = 1 TO DO
```

```
75      IF Z <= D - 2 AND D(Z) = D(Z + 1) AND D(Z) = D(Z + 2)
                THEN PRINT @179, CHR$(152) + "Triple"
        T = T + 1
        X(T) = D(Z)
        D(Z) = T + 6
        D(Z+1) = T + 6
        D(Z+2) = T + 6
80      IF D(Z) = 1
                THEN PRINT @164, CHR$(155) + " 100"
        O = O + 1
        D(Z) = 9
85      IF D(Z) = 5
                THEN PRINT @172, CHR$(154) + " 50"
        F = F + 1
        D(Z) = 10
90      IF D(Z) = X(1)
                THEN FT = FT + 1
        D(Z) = 11
        PRINT @172, CHR$(154) + " 50"
95   NEXT
100 IF T + F + FT + O = 0
        THEN PRINT @167, "You have NOTHING"
                SOUND 16000,20
                GOSUB 415
                GOSUB 505
                GOSUB 515
        GOTO 235
220 IF X + Y < 500
        THEN BEEP
                GOTO 110
225 IF O > O OR T > O OR F > O
        THEN BEEP
                PRINT @206, "Are You Sure Y/N ";
                E$ = INPUT$ (1)
                IF E$ = "Y" OR E$ = "y"
                        THEN 230
                        ELSE PRINT @206, SPACE$(16)
                                GOTO 110
230 IF S>0 THEN Y = Y + S
        PRINT @235, USING "#####"; Y
        GOSUB 505
        GOSUB 515
```

```
            GOTO 235
     ELSE 110
```

This example was carefully reformatted to make it more comprehensible than the published code, which looked like this:

```
230   IF S>0 THEN Y = Y + S: PRINT
@235, USING "#####"; Y: GOSUB
505: GOSUB 515:GOTO 235:
ELSE 110
```

As object-oriented programmers, we should never forget that most of the world's software is written like this. As we try to explain to the world why objects help, keep line 230 in mind!

Despite its total intractability, I feel sure that this implementation wins the prize for the implementation that runs at the highest speed on the smallest machine. Even so, it could have been made much more comprehensible.

Capers Jones provided me with another Greed implementation in BASIC that can be thought of as competent, structured BASIC. It is much more readable than the laptop Greed.

Smalltalk

Four implementations were presented in Smalltalk; two from Norway (Else Nordhagen and Trygve Reenskaug), one from North Carolina (Ken Auer of KSC), and one from Oregon (Ward Cunningham).

Trygve did a marvelously literate design for the game using some new tools he had developed for doing simultaneous design, documentation, and development. As he described it, it involves a combination of "design with documentation; implementation with documentation; testing with documentation and exploratory programming with testing; reverse engineering with documentation; testing with documentation."

His result after 27 hours of work was a literate design but he got so involved in the design and documentation that he did not complete the implementation! Later, he not only completed the program but wrote a wonderful article describing his experiences.[1] Trygve's comparison of Max Weber's description of human organizations to object-oriented design is not to be missed. Reenskaug proposes the following seven steps for rational object-oriented design:

1. emphasis on structure
2. a specific sphere of competence

3. hierarchy
4. norms of conduct
5. independence
6. documentation
7. reusability

By contrast, his colleague, Else, took 17 hours to produce a working prototype involving 9 new classes and 132 methods. It was sparsely documented but such a clean design that it was easy to understand. Her class design is shown in Figure 4.1.

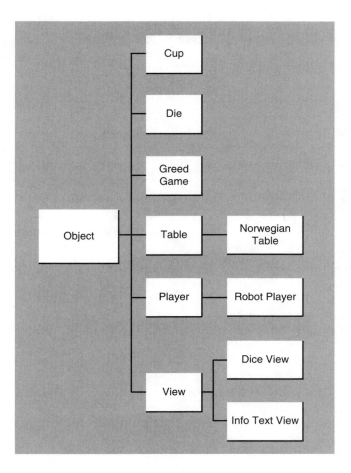

Figure 4.1. Inheritance of Greed classes (rotated 90° for improved readability).

Each Greed Game knows its players, its table, its cup, and which player is currently active. The players know their names, scores, total score, and whether or not it is the first round. The table object contains the rules for the game. Subclasses such as NorwegianTable, can be the rules for a variant of the game known in Norway. The dice have values and are able to spin. The robotPlayer plays based upon a hard-wired strategy that can be changed by altering various methods known to this object.

Some sample code will help us understand the implementation of this design. Let's begin with a look at the Player class:

```
Object subclass: #Player

        instanceVariableNames: 'scores totalScore name cup table nextPlayer playScore
            firstTurn bust '
        classVariableNames: "
        poolDictionaries: "
        category: 'Greed'!

initialize
        scores ← OrderedCollection new.
        totalScore ← 0.
        bust ← false.
        firstTurn ← true.
        playScore ← 0.!

reset
        scores ← OrderedCollection new.
        totalScore ← 0.
        cup ← nil.
        playScore ← 0.
        firstTurn ← true.
        bust ← false.! !

calculateScore
        playScore ← playScore + table diceValue.!

registerScore
        | finished |
        (totalScore <= 0) & (GreedGame PlayStartLimit > playScore)
        ifTrue:
                [finished ← true. "BinaryChoice message: 'You will get no points.
Are you sure you want to quit ?'"]
```

```
    ifFalse:
        [finished ← true.
        scores addLast: playScore.
        totalScore ← totalScore + playScore.
        self changed: #score].
    ↑finished! !

haveCup: c
    self cup: c.
    firstTurn ← true.
    playScore ← O.
    bust ← false.
    self changed: #playing!

putDiceInCup
    | dice |
    firstTurn
    ifTrue:
        [playScore ← O.
        dice ← table giveMeDice]
    ifFalse:
        [table allDiceGiveScore
        ifTrue:
                [playScore ← playScore + table diceValue.
                dice ← table giveMeDice.]
        ifFalse:
                [dice ← table giveMeAllUnscoredDice.]].

    cup addDice: dice.!

rollToTable
    | answ dice |
    cup stopShaking.
    dice ← cup giveAwayDice.
    table addDice: dice.

    table bust
    ifTrue:
        [playScore ← O. bust ← true].

    self noScore
    ifTrue:
```

```
            [table diceValue < GreedGame PlayStartLimit
            ifTrue: [bust ← true].
            ].
      firstTurn ← false.

      bust
      ifTrue:
            [self changed: #bust.
            self stopPlaying.
            scores addLast: 0.
            self changed: #score]!
shakeCup
      | answ |
      bust
      ifTrue:
            [answ ← (BinaryChoice message: 'You are bust !!!!
Shall I give the cup to the next player').
            answ
      ifTrue: [self stopPlaying]]
            ifFalse: [cup shake].!

startRoll
      self putDiceInCup.
      self shakeCup.!

stopPlaying
      | finished |
      finished ← true.
      bust
      ifFalse:
            [self calculateScore.
            finished ← self registerScore].
      finished
      ifTrue:
            [nextPlayer notNil
            ifTrue: [self leaveCupTo: nextPlayer.]
            ifFalse: [self changed: #gameEnd]].! !
cup: c
      c isNil ifTrue: [self halt].
      cup ← c.!
```

```
leaveCupTo: player
    | c |

    c ← cup.
    cup ← nil.
    self changed: #notPlaying.

    player haveCup: c.!

name
    ↑name!

name: aText
    name ← aText!

nextPlayer: pl
    nextPlayer ← pl!

noScore
    ↑(totalScore = 0) & (playScore = 0)!

playing
    ↑cup notNil!

playScore
    ↑playScore!

scoreText
    | str |
    str ← totalScore printString, ' - '.

    scores do:
    [:s | str ← str, s printString, ', '].

    ↑str asText!

table: t
    table ← t!

totalScore
    ↑totalScore! !
```

At first glance, anyone would rather try to understand and modify the Smalltalk program than the BASIC program. Even though there are very few comments in the Smalltalk code, its use of mnemonic names for classes, methods, and instance variables makes it much easier to comprehend. Also, the code is organized as a model of the objects in the application domain. In the Smalltalk code, for example, we have in one place the definition of the data structures and behavior of all Player objects.

Let's scan the code to see what we can learn. Line one tells us that Player objects inherit all the data and behavior of generic Objects as previously defined in the class library. On the second line of the class definition, we see that Player objects contain the following data structures: scores, totalScore, name, cup, table, nextPlayer, playScore, firstTurn, and bust. We can also just read down the list of methods and conclude that Player objects know how to initialize themselves, calculate scores, register scores, put dice in a cup, roll dice on the table, and stop playing. So, even without a single line of comment, we can quickly grasp what this class is designed to do.

As we penetrate each method, we can find how that particular behavior is actually implemented. The initialize method does exactly what we would suspect; it initializes five instance variables. One instance variable, scores, is initialized as an empty instance of the OrderedCollection class. The methods bust and firstTurn are binary variables that are defined as false and true upon receipt of the initialize method.

All Smalltalk code is not trivial, though. When we look inside the putDiceInCup method, we see two levels of nesting of branching statements. But with just a little study we see that we put all of the dice into the cup if it is either the first roll or if all of the dice have scored points on the previous roll. In effect, these branching statements are defining the rules for the game and seem essential. One could imagine an implementation in which the rules were more cleanly factored but maybe not one that could have been implemented as quickly as this one.

The person unaccustomed to Smalltalk should be reminded that one rarely looks at class listings as presented here. In fact, both class and method definitions would be displayed via a browser. Browsers are designed to make it easier to find classes and methods and in the process ensure that changes made to a method or class can also be accessed using such interactive tools.

According to the author, "this implementation in Smalltalk involved 825 lines of Smalltalk code." But 509 changes were made to correct errors after the initial prototype was working. It still only took 17 hours! Thank goodness for efficient development environments.

When I began to analyze the source code, I discovered 170 pages of source listings! Why this discrepancy? The balance consisted of previous changes made by the author to the "standard" Smalltalk-80 classes used in this example program.

Rapid development without tools to manage and control changes creates new problems that also must be solved.

High-performance development environments allow the rate of change of systems to increase markedly. One unsolved problem in our industry is how to deal with such entropy. I really do not want to deal with 150 pages of additional code just to compile and run a new application involving 17 pages.

C++

One pair of implementors, Ward and Karen Cunningham, provided an especially interesting set of examples. They did the design using class, responsibilities, and collaborator (CRC) cards and then did implementations in HyperCard, C++, and Smalltalk-80.

Karen Cunningham did a C++ implementation of the CRC design that she and Ward did together. This implementation required 455 lines of code excluding blanks and comments. The implementation, like the Smalltalk implementation done by the Cunninghams, involved a simple Teletype user interface quite unlike the user interfaces developed by Ms. Nordhagen in Smalltalk-80, Ward Cunningham in HyperCard, Dr. Phil Cox in ProGraph, or the Apple team in Object-Pascal.

Let's see what the C++ implementation looks like. Presented below is the game class:

```
game.h

# ifndef _GAME_
# define _GAME_
# include "globals.h"
# include "player.h"

class Player;

class Game
{
    // Sequences players
    // Creates and distributes the dice as rolls

    int numPlayers;
    Player *players[MAXPLAYERS];
    int current;

public:
    Game();
```

```
        ~Game();
        // Danger! Should also overload assignment and the initialization constructor
        // since this object uses heap allocated storage.
        void begin();
        void add(Player *);
        int gameOver();
        int leadScore();
        void nextPlayer();
        void play();
        Player* player();
};
# endif
```

game.C

```
# include "game.h"
# include "player.h"

Game::Game()
{
    // Create a game with no players

    numPlayers = 0;
    current = 0;
}

Game::~Game()
{
    for (int i = 0; i < numPlayers; i++)
        delete players[i];
}

void Game::begin()
{
    // Start a game

    for (int i = 0; i < numPlayers; i++) {
        players[i]->beginGame();
    }
    current = 0;
    player()->beginTurn();
}
```

```
void Game::add(Player *aPlayer)
{
    // Add a player to the receiver

    players[numPlayers++] = aPlayer;
}

int Game::gameOver()
{
    // Decide if the game is over

    return current == 0 && leadScore() >= WIN;
}

int Game::leadScore()
{
    // Find the maximum score of all players in the receiver

    int max = -1;

    for (int i=0; i<numPlayers; i++)
        if (players[i]->reportScore() > max)
            max = players[i]->reportScore();
    return max;
}

void Game::nextPlayer()
{
    // Tell the next player in the game that it's his turn to play

    current = (current + 1) % numPlayers;
    player()->beginTurn();
}

void Game::play()
{
    // Let the current player play as long as he can without human intervention

    while (player()->canPlay() && !gameOver()) {
        player()->play();
    }
}
```

```
Player* Game::player()
{
    // Return the current player in the receiver

    return players[current];
}
```

C++ requires that we have two files to define a class. The first defines the external behavior of the class, the second the details of its implementation.

HyperCard

Ward and Karen did a wonderful implementation in HyperCard that not only played the game but also provided an image of the current player, voice interaction, and a sound and graphic display of the rolling dice. The design and implementation only required six hours.

```
— Copyright (c) 1989
— Ward and Karen Cunningham
— All Rights Reserved

on openStack
 hide menuBar
 set lockScreen to true
 set lockMessages to true
 repeat number of cards of this background
  put empty into field totalScore
  go to next card of this background
 end repeat
 set lockScreen to false
 set lockMessages to false
end openStack

on mouseUp
 play "clickDice"
 if field turnScore is not empty
 then play "clickScore"
end mouseUp

on closeCard
 put empty into field rollScore
 put empty into field turnScore
 repeat with i = 1 to 5
```

```
    show background button i
    put empty into field i
   end repeat
  end closeCard

  on stop
   global leadingScore
   add field turnScore to field totalScore
   if field totalScore > leadingScore
   then
    put field totalScore into leadingScore
   end if
   nextPlayer
  end stop

  on roll
   global diceInPlay
   rollDice diceInPlay
   if field totalScore is empty
   then put 299 into bust
   else put 0 into bust
   if field rollScore <= bust
   then
    say "bust"
    nextPlayer
   end if
   if diceInPlay is empty
   then
    say "newDice"
    newDice
   end if
  end roll

  on rollDice dice
   put empty into field rollScore
   put empty into dist
   repeat with i = 1 to number of items in dice
    get item i of dice
    put empty into field it
   end repeat
   repeat with i = 1 to number of items in dice
    get item i of dice
```

```
    put random(6) into field it
    put it after item field it of dist
  end repeat
  scoreDist dist
end rollDice

on scoreDist dist
 repeat with i = 1 to 6
  get item i of dist
  if number of chars of it >= three
  then — score triples
   play "triple"
   say i
   repeat three
    hideDie first char of item i of dist
    delete first char of item i of dist
   end repeat
   if i is one
   then scorePoints 1000
   else scorePoints 100 * i
  end if
  get item i of dist
  if i is one or i is five
  then — score singles
   repeat while it is not empty
    — play "single"
    say i
    if i is one
    then scorePoints 100
    else scorePoints 10 * i
    hideDie first char of it
    delete first char of it
   end repeat
  end if
 end repeat
end scoreDist

on scorePoints n
 add n to field rollScore
 add n to field turnScore
end scorePoints
on hideDie die
```

```
  global diceInPlay
  show background button die
  repeat with i = 1 to number of items in diceInPlay
   if item i of diceInPlay is die
   then delete item i of diceInPlay
  end repeat
 end hideDie

 on newDice
  global diceInPlay
  repeat with i = 1 to 6
   put empty into field i
   hide background button i
  end repeat
  put "1,2,3,4,5" into diceInPlay
 end newDice

 on nextPlayer
  visual scroll left slowly
  go to next card of this background
 end nextPlayer

 on say aString
  global startTime
  put the seconds into startTime
  play aString
  wait until the sound is "done"
 end say
```

Their conclusion was that "Smalltalk no longer deserves its reputation as the best tool for experimenting with user interfaces. HyperCard is clearly better."

ProGraph

Dr. Phil Cox of Gunakara Sun Systems provided an intriguing implementation of the Greed game in ProGraph. Even more interesting was an analysis of the strategy that only a competent mathematician could provide.

At a particular point during a turn, it is necessary to decide whether or not to continue rolling. To do this, we need the following definitions:

Let

n = number of dice in the game

k = number of dice in next roll $(1 \leq k \leq n)$

$S(k)$ = expected score from rolling k dice, including scores from subsequent rolls $(1 \le k \le n)$

A   = the current maximum score among preceding players in this round

N   = the current maximum score among following players in this round

C   = my current score before this turn

T   = my score in this turn so far

$q(X)$ = the probability of scoring at least X in one turn for any nonnegative integer X

b_k = probability of a bust in a roll of k dice.

(a) Now, if $A \ge 5{,}000$ and $T+C \ge A$, I should roll because this is the last round of the game and someone else has the winning score.

(b) If $T+C \ge 5{,}000$, $T+C > A$, and I am the last player in the round, I should not roll.

(c) If $T+C \ge 5{,}000$, $T+C > A$, and there are players left in this round, then this could be the last round of the game and I should worry only about the players that follow. Obviously, $T+C > N$ because otherwise $N \ge 5{,}000$ and the game would have ended in the last round. So, $T+C-N$ is a positive integer.

If $q(T+C-N) > b_k$, I should roll, that is, I should roll if the following player with the highest score has a greater chance of getting enough points to beat me than I have of going bust on the next roll.

(d) In all other cases, if $(1 - b_k)T + S(k) > T$ I should roll, that is, I should roll if the expected turn score from rolling is greater than the current turn score. We can simplify the comparison as follows: I should roll if $S(k)/T > b_k$.

This is an excellent example of where mathematical formalism adds some real value during the specification and design of a computer program. Often such formalism is counterproductive.

ProGraph is a visual programming language for doing object-oriented development. As such, it was challenging to do any direct quantitative comparison with textual languages. But it was significant that ProGraph was sufficient to develop this example program with an extremely modest amount of effort.

While I find the ProGraph development environment quite attractive and comprehensible, it was interesting to see what archival output looks like on paper. It seemed almost as obscure as the unstructured BASIC in this form.

Object Pascal

Kurt Schmucker and his Apple Scientific Computing staff decided to do a serious and complete implementation of this game for use as a comprehensive example of Object-Pascal and MacApp. It was a real tour de force—color graphics, n dice, m-sided dice, realistic sound, a complete scoring pad, etc. All this capability was fully Mac-compatible, including the ability to establish preferences for each game and print results.

```
{ The abstract superclass of all players, both human and machine. }
  { TAbstractPlayer inherits 19 methods from MacApp's TObject class. }

        TAbstractPlayer = OBJECT(TObject)

                fName:                  Str255;
                fNumberOfTurns:  LONGINT;
                fCurrentScore:          LONGINT;
                fScoreHistory:          TList;
                fRules:                 TScoringRules;
                fPlayerList:            TPlayerList;
                fDiceList:       TDiceList;

        { Initialization/Freeing }
                PROCEDURE TAbstractPlayer.IAbstractPlayer(aName: Str255;
                rules: TScoringRules;

         players: TPlayerList;

         dice: TDiceList);
                PROCEDURE TAbstractPlayer.Free; OVERRIDE;

        { Inspecting }
                PROCEDURE TAbstractPlayer.Fields(PROCEDURE
                        DoToField(fieldName:Str255;
                                fieldAddr: Ptr;
                                fieldType: INTEGER)); OVERRIDE;
        { Accessing }
                FUNCTION TAbstractPlayer.GetName: Str255;
                FUNCTION TAbstractPlayer.IsQualified: BOOLEAN;
                FUNCTION TAbstractPlayer.GetNumberOfTurns: LONGINT;
                FUNCTION TAbstractPlayer.GetCurrentScore: LONGINT;
                FUNCTION TAbstractPlayer.GetScoreForTurn(turnNumber:
                        INTEGER): LONGINT;
```

```
{ Player actions }
        PROCEDURE TAbstractPlayer.YourTurn;
        PROCEDURE TAbstractPlayer.TakeAction(action: ActionType);
        PROCEDURE TAbstractPlayer.ActOn(action : ActionType);
        PROCEDURE TAbstractPlayer.Roll;
        PROCEDURE TAbstractPlayer.Hold;
        PROCEDURE TAbstractPlayer.PassCup(scoreThisTurn: LONGINT);
        PROCEDURE TAbstractPlayer.Reset;

{ MacGreed "Hook" methods }
        FUNCTIONTAbstractPlayer.DoEnableButton(button: ButtonType):
                BOOLEAN;

END;
```

This implementation required 179 person-hours of effort by a team and involved 20 classes and 123 methods. Many hundreds of methods and tens of classes were reused.

They did make one slight mistake: their final implementation used 10 dice rather than 5 as clearly stated in the specs! They found that a more interesting game. They also misunderstood the rules of play, which is why their game seemed so uninteresting.

I was struck while preparing this chapter by how verbose and difficult it is to read a good Object-Pascal program. While admittedly this was the most exotic implementation, it was also 3,986 lines of code. It was not aggressively documented, either. I found the C++ code easier to read—I never expected that at the outset.

OTHER IMPLEMENTATIONS

Several other implementations were done including Eiffel, Trellis, Actor, C-Talk, a design in IDE, and Complete C. However, the authors provided these implementations in a variety of formats and physical media. Work continues to get them into the agreed standard form readable on a Macintosh. Stay tuned for more information and analysis as these implementations become available.

QUANTITATIVE COMPARISON

As an initial analysis of the various implementations, I counted the words and lines of uncommented code for three implementations that were similar in functionality.

Microsoft Word was used to perform these counts. All comments and blank lineswere stripped out in advance. BASIC and C++ were roughly comparable in size and about twice the size of the Smalltalk implementation.

These three implementations used a character-oriented user interface much like what one would expect on a Teletype connected to a time-shared computer.

	Words	Lines	Branching stmts	% branches	Looping stmts	% looping
BASIC	1,698	470	211	45	31	7
ST-80	720	250	24	10	58	23
C++	904	455	33	7	16	4

While the size of the BASIC and C++ implementations were roughly comparable, they were very different in complexity. A staggering 45% of the statements in the BASIC program were branching statements compared to only 7% in C++. Of the 211 branching statements, 43 were unconditional gotos!

Although I have actually written some fairly complex BASIC programs to control laboratory experiments in the early 1970s, I must admit I found this program totally intractable after hours of study. By contrast, the Smalltalk and Object-Pascal programs were completely transparent and extremely easy to understand. C++ was not too difficult to understand, but was significantly more complicated than Smalltalk and "devoid of ergonomics."

The existence of appropriate class libraries directly affected the user interface design for the participants. Languages like Object-Pascal, Smalltalk, and HyperCard had pleasant, visual user interfaces. Languages like BASIC and C++ presented text-oriented interfaces.

While not much should be made about development time statistics due to a total lack of control over individual differences, some observations are worth noting. It took 10 times longer for the Apple team to develop an application with 123 methods than for a solitary Smalltalk developer to develop one with 134 methods—179 hours vs. 17.

One of the most sophisticated graphical interfaces that involved speech was also the fastest to develop—only six hours. It took more than three times longer to do a comparable job in Smalltalk. A conclusion might be that "less language can be more productive."

What has not been evaluated as yet is run-time performance or memory utilization. We can guess that there will be lots of variation among the respective implementations.[2]

QUALITATIVE COMPARISON

Because the Cunninghams implemented the same design in four different languages, they were able to do a direct comparison of what it felt like in each. They concluded that "HyperCard is quick and easy but not best for complex problems; Smalltalk is easy too, has the best code, but it no longer deserves its reputation for providing the best user interface; and C++ is difficult, even for small tasks, and might be best used for big systems."

It is unclear to this author why something that is difficult, even for small tasks, might be better for "big systems." It is my experience that the larger the system, the more important it is for the design and implementation to be easy to understand, easy to modify, and easy to use. Remember, the larger the system the lower the average quality of developer likely to be involved in its development and maintenance. But all of the object-oriented languages were a dramatic step ahead of unstructured procedural languages! So, "Greed is good." *Wall Street*, the movie.

NOTES

1. See Reenskaug's *Intermediate Smalltalk: Practical Design and Implementation,* presented at TOOLS Europe '92.
2. Ph.D. students, feel free to contact me for some wonderful dissertation data—assuming the suppliers of the code are willing to provide it.

5

Experiences with Objects

I was blown away.

Steven Jobs
(upon seeing Smalltalk at Xerox PARC in 1979)
Fire in the Valley
Freiberger and Swaine, Osborn/McGraw-Hill, New York, 1984, p. 239.

Most of the world's software is written in COBOL, FORTRAN, C, and various assembly languages. It was arduous to produce and is difficult to maintain. But most of it appears to work. Why switch paradigms? Why abandon the familiar for any new technology?

I believe in object-oriented technology because I have seen it work. Objects allow more function of higher quality to be developed with less development effort in less time than any other approach to building software. Let me describe the projects that have convinced me.

COMMERCIAL EXPERIENCES WITH OBJECT-BASED LANGUAGES

Three of the largest telecommunications companies in the world—ITT and GTE in the United States and L. M. Ericsson in Sweden—have built central office telephone exchanges using object-based languages. The three examples from the telecommunications industry described below involve languages or development standards that support encapsulation but not inheritance. They were the precursors of object-oriented programming languages.

L. M. Ericsson

In the early 1970s, L. M. Ericsson used a programming language called Plex to build the AXE telephone switching system. They used "program segments"—data encapsulated by a set of procedures that could access that data; in other words, big objects without inheritance. By 1984, over four million lines of AXE systems were in service in 52 countries.*

The AXE system was estimated to require 1,200 person-years of effort to design and construct. Many times that amount of engineering effort has gone into the system during the 18 years since its inception. It has been the most successful switching system in the international telecommunications industry.

According to John Meurling,[1] the AXE project leader, the modular software architecture of AXE recognized that "software is a living organism, not something stable. Software must be modified and added to, to accommodate new functions and new applications, or to control new hardware. So the most important requirements set for our AXE system software were contained in words like flexibility, manageability, ease of handling, ease of modification, and so on."

When every exchange has to be modified to accommodate local constraints or governmental regulations, flexibility and ease of modification become crucial determinants of success. Program segments in Plex provided just this capability.

In the telephone world, a "line" is not a line of code but rather a telephone line. Each subscriber has a line coming into their home, for example.

ITT

In 1975, ITT began the design and development of the 1240 telephone exchange, a major financial and technological undertaking. The objective was to build the first digital exchange architecture with fully distributed control, able to switch 100,000 telephone calls simultaneously.

I observed this project at close range and even made some modest contributions. My role was to review the software development tools being used on the project and make specific recommendations for improvements. One improvement was to contract for the development of a new and more efficient CHILL[2] compiler for use on the project. I also managed a skunkworks effort to demonstrate the feasibility of an alternative testing environment that was ultimately used by the project.[3]

Looked at in another way, the objective of System 1240 was to build a special-purpose massively parallel computer consisting of 2,000 microprocessors, each with 512 K of memory. Remember, this project was started in 1975, four years after microprocessors had been invented; and at a time when the PDP 11/40 was considered an advanced computer.

The software for the ITT 1240 was designed around the concept of "finite message machines" (FMMs). An FMM has a predefined set of input messages and each produces a finite set of replies. No FMM has direct access to the memory of another FMM. All communication is through messaging. Special hardware was designed to make messaging acceptably efficient.

FMMs may reside on the same or on different machines. The sender of a message does not know whether that message will be serviced locally or will travel across the network to be serviced by an FMM on another node. The message handler determines which FMM should receive the message and therefore, to which processor that message should be sent.

The concept of an FMM is similar to the notion of objects. It also differs in several ways. One was its approach to concurrency. When messages were sent in the 1240, no reply was awaited. Typical object systems today are implemented with a send–wait approach; that is, the sender suspends operation until a reply is received from the receiver of the message. FMMs also had no notion of inheritance, either in concept or implementation.

ITT's 1983 annual report claimed that the 1240 was developed in five years and involved more than 1,300 engineers spanning six countries (Germany, Belgium, Spain, Italy, France, and the United States). The initial development cost was over $1 billion.

Remarkably, the system was delivered on the second major schedule and the software was more reliable than expected. The first time the system carried live telephone traffic, ITT's goal was to keep it operational for 24 hours, regardless of the effort required. Fourteen days later, it was still in operation! The system proved to be more reliable than any other stored program control switching system developed within ITT. The distributed architecture and the FMM concept were identified as the reasons. So, here is a distributed system built with an object-based architecture, employing 2,000 microcomputers, and operating more reliably than expected. Objects must have helped.

COMMERCIAL EXPERIENCES WITH OBJECT-ORIENTED LANGUAGES

Pundits have recently wondered whether real commercial systems have ever been built using objects.[4] Well, maybe real systems have never been built in Austin but they certainly have in other parts of the world. Containers coming through the port of Singapore are controlled using objects; trains arriving into the station in Geneva, Switzerland, are controlled by objects; the paper-making process is controlled by objects; computerized axial tomography (CAT) scanners are controlled by objects; medical information in large hospitals is managed by objects; complex real-time test equipment is driven by objects; commercial system engineering tools have been developed with objects; most iconic user interfaces to contemporary workstations are driven by objects; commercial data processing applications have begun to use objects; and computer-integrated manufacturing (CIM) at the most advanced factories is made possible by objects. These examples are certainly encouraging.

Also, no company I know of has delivered a system with objects and decided to do the next version of that system without objects. A few companies were acquired where the acquisitor demanded that software be written in conventional nonobject languages. Turnover was high in every case. The "turned over" found new places to work, with objects.

Let me share with you what I have learned about commercial projects that have used objects. I will attempt to present these experiences in approximate chronological order. Some readers might prefer to go to the end of the chapter and read only the more recent experiences. On the other hand, don't just read the early experiences and ignore the more recent ones.

Xerox[5]

Evelyn Van Orden, Smalltalk Products Manager at Xerox Special Information Systems, participated in the development of the Analyst, an integrated information analysis environment implemented in Smalltalk-80. The Analyst integrates a number of packages with a uniform user interface, including spreadsheets, outlines, and reports that can include text, business graphics, maps, and images.

Professional information analysts use the Analyst as a set of tools in a working environment they can customize as required. Programmers can also customize the tools to develop sophisticated interactive applications.

Van Orden said that "the Analyst could not have been developed using traditional procedural programming languages—it would have been far too much work, and taken far longer than the customer was willing to wait."

Schlumberger

In 1983 at Schlumberger, I used Smalltalk-80 to build a tiny prototype of an analyst workstation for viewing a diverse collection of data from oil wells.[6] A working demonstration was built with only 220 lines of new code and lots of reused classes provided by Xerox. It provided an interactive interface to data residing on a VAX computer. This interface furnished iconic menus for accessing maps, measurement data, analysis reports, and photographs. It also did simple plotting of measurement data.

I showed my work to any number of software professionals in the company and asked them to estimate how much effort it would have required to develop comparable facilities in FORTRAN, the most commonly used language at Schlumberger at that time. The smallest estimate I ever received was 10,000 lines of code. While certainly not a commercial product, it was a commercial problem, and the leverage provided by objects seemed most impressive.

This project was also interesting because of some important observations about the use of objects. One day, a company Vice President was in my office looking at the small amount of work I had done. He said, "do you mean I paid you a year's salary to produce 220 lines of code?" At first, I felt terrible. Then, I began to realize how inappropriate it is for us to feel obligated to produce bulk in return for our compensation.

How I had actually spent that year was learning Smalltalk-80 as the first commercial user of that system. Much of the year was spent reading source code I thought I could reuse in the prototype application I was building. Documentation for Smalltalk did not become available until the next year!

Apple Computer

Apple Computer was one of the first companies to see the potential of object-oriented software technology and to build tools for their customers to use. In 1984, Apple Computer developed an object-oriented extension to Pascal called Clascal (now known as Object-Pascal). It supports objects, messages, classes, and inheritance. But classes in Object-Pascal are not as independent of one another as in Smalltalk. For example, superclasses must be recompiled if a conflict arises in the method names used for subclasses.

Larry Tesler, an Apple Vice President, said that rewriting a major Pascal application in Object-Pascal resulted in a two-to-one reduction in lines of source code for that application.

More recently, Apple has made it clear to its internal and external developers that object-oriented programming is the approach to building software that will be used at Apple. If application developers want to build software for Apple machines, they must become familiar with objects.

Artecon, Inc.

Dana Kammersgard, vice president of engineering at Artecon, was the leader and architect of a civil engineering design and office automation system implemented in Objective-C. It was developed at Artecon, a Carlsbad, California, startup. This product contains a number of significant innovations such as:

- an object-oriented GKS implementation
- a virtual object management system
- a persistent object manager
- an iconic user interface to UNIX

Artecon has also chosen to sell some of the building blocks of their overall system for use by others interested in building noncompetitive products. Examples of these building blocks include ArteGKS, a full implementation of the GKS graphics standard. The ArteDraft package uses ArteGKS and supports the interactive creation and editing of geometry, text, and dimensions. With ArteDraft, one can generate drawings more accurately and less expensively than those produced manually. ArteBase is a persistent object database that allows objects to be stored in a relational database.

"Object-oriented technology is a major step in the evolution of programming languages," said Mr. Kammersgard. "Object-oriented technology provides inherent organization and discipline in writing software systems. It is a great framework for translation of concepts and ideas to actual implementation. The effort and cost of development and maintenance using object-oriented technology more than offsets the effort and cost of learning the technology."

For example, in developing device drivers for printers and plotters, Artecon found that objects reduce the effort to support a new device by a factor of 10. Once they had developed a set of classes that properly modeled what a printer or plotter does, adding a new device driver was merely a process of describing how this particular device differed from a standard device.

Lawrence Livermore National Laboratory

Peggy Poggio designed and implemented the user interface for EAGLES/Controls, an environment that runs various computer-based engineering tools for control simulation and electromagnetic modeling. Written in 45,000 source lines of Objective-C code, EAGLES/Controls assists engineers with systems analysis and control systems design. "We reused the classes shipped with the compiler immediately, and several months into the project we noticed a payoff in the reuse of our own code," said Poggio. "I estimate it probably would have taken us 25% longer to finish the project if we had used straight C."

Poggio commented on how object-oriented technology offered a lot of power for developing user interfaces for different devices by allowing her to easily hide the device dependencies. For instance, objects that provided generic terminal interactions were used to interact with device-specific objects. In that way, the applications built using this interface only interacted with generic objects.

"Object-oriented languages lend themselves to a higher level of modularity due to objects' real-world modeling capabilities," added Poggio. "Changes and additions later in the development process were much simpler than they would have been in a procedural language. What might take weeks to accomplish in C could take only hours in Objective-C."

ABB Process Automation

ABB Process Automation Inc. (previously AccuRay) manufactures automatic control systems to monitor and maintain quality throughout a manufacturing process. One of their important markets is the paper-making industry.

The ABB engineers studied object-oriented technology extensively for 6 months before choosing Objective-C for its compatibility with the C language and overall system maintainability. Bob Wilhelm was the principal engineer for the project and led the development of the real-time process measurement system they developed in Objective-C. The system, called the *FirstSight*™ Measurement System, includes a scanner, a sensor head, and a series of precision sensors that measure such qualities as the weight of the paper, its thickness, its smoothness, its opacity, and more. It is a distributed real-time process control and information system.

"Object-oriented design is well suited for such a system by virtue of its real-world modeling capabilities," said Wilhelm. "Entities such as sensors, I/O hardware, signals and measurements are readily modeled as objects; and class hierarchies with inheritance are invaluable for promoting software reusability among many models of sensors and many types of signals." The system involves measurements taken as often as 100 times a second from paper moving through the machines as fast as 3,000 feet per minute.

"Our productivity has increased significantly and objects will also help us improve our responsiveness when making changes and updates," Wilhelm added. To prove the point, the FirstSight system has since been replaced by the next-generation *Smart Platform*™, which is faster and distributes intelligence to the sensors.

Much of the object-oriented software survived unscathed, and its modularity contributed to a rapid redevelopment.

Hewlett-Packard Lake Stevens[7]

Richard Jones described the VISTA project, a UNIX-based data acquisition and measurement system implemented in Objective-C, in the August 1989 issue of the *HP Journal*. VISTA is a window-based, interactive measurement environment for signal characterization and stimulus-response testing. It can be used in applications ranging from geophysics and control systems to audioelectronics.

Jones credited reusability, inheritance, and ease in designing user interfaces as the greatest benefits of object-oriented technology. Jones stressed "One has to throw away their previous concepts of design and start over. . . It is important to think of data flow instead of control flow. . . Interactive interpreters are a big advantage."

"We feel confident that the Objective-C environment will definitely save us time on future projects," said Tom Kraemer, VISTA project manager. "We could easily talk about factors of two, and possibly even factors of ten in certain cases. Probably 95% of this code will be reused for our next project—exactly what we need to stay competitive in this marketplace." By contrast, according to Kraemer, their previous reusability with procedural languages such as C was closer to 10%.

Enator Functional Systems

Functional Systems was a UNIX systems house near Stockholm, Sweden, in 1985 when they became involved with object-oriented programming. The founders of the company were Tore Bingefors and Ivar Jacobson, previously at Ericsson building telecommunication systems. They completed their first commercial product using objects in 1986. Since that time, Functional Systems was acquired by Enator and completed 15 different projects using a variety of object-oriented programming languages. They have more than 70,000 person-hours of experience building commercial systems with objects.[8]

The first project Functional Systems undertook was a billing system for a Chinese telephone company. Its function was to read magnetic tapes containing information about telephone calls and extract data used for billing customers. The system ran on a MicroVAX computer under Ultrix. It was programmed in Objective-C.

In their 1992 article, they describe a valuable experience. Some of the developers of this initial product were not impressed with objects because of the immaturity of the programming tools back in 1985. So the company actually stopped using objects. But wiser heads prevailed. They caution contemporary developers to consider development tools and class libraries as well as programming languages. But developers should also be patient.

Prime Computer

Alen Schiller was tasked with developing the next generation of Geographic Information Systems for his company (which until acquired was called Wild Heerbrugg and was a division of the Swiss optical company, Leitz). System 9 was built with Objective-C. It is one of the largest commercial object-oriented products—over 300,000 source lines of code. System 9 is a product for the utility industry that allows utilities to draw a map of their coverage area and display information from several databases on those maps based upon user-supplied queries. The problem is to be able to integrate topologically correct graphic data with non graphic attributes while being able to update everything as required with reliability.

System 9 is sold to different utilities, in different locales, in different countries for use by a diversity of users. These users want a constant stream of new and more powerful features added to the system.

Schiller believes they could not have built what they did using conventional software technology. He also believes that most of the benefits will be downstream. Dynamic binding allows their system to accommodate change while retaining stability within a substantial base of preexisting code.

Ascent Logic[9]

Ascent Logic Corporation is a San Jose, California, company that has delivered the largest product I know built using Smalltalk-80. Their RDD product involves over 1,000 classes and over 20,000 methods. RDD is a system engineering environment to support the front end of the systems development process.

I was a consultant for Ascent Logic for three years, spending several days a month with the company. When I first became familiar with the company and what it was trying to do with Smalltalk, I was concerned. For many months, I encouraged them to move to a more efficient programming language, Objective-C and C++ being the obvious candidates. In retrospect, it is clear to me that I was wrong. For the product that Ascent Logic delivers, Smalltalk is efficient enough and has resulted in amazing productivity now that their staff is fully trained.

They have also achieved substantial leverage from acquired software components. For example, they have purchased and successfully integrated over 500 classes into their commercial product. Dr. Christine Jette, Vice President of engineering at Ascent Logic, estimates that more than 50% of the classes in their delivered product were acquired from the outside.

Dr. Jette comes from a real-time systems background and has managed several C and one C++ language development projects on UNIX development platforms. She is astonished at the difference. "With Smalltalk, we don't lose a bunch of time looking for troublesome errors. Neither does the system crash very often during development. One day it all just seemed to snap together and we have been making steady improvements and enhancements ever since. . . Sure, we have paid a performance penalty, but the value far exceeds the cost. Besides, hardware really is getting cheaper and faster."

GE Medical

GE recently delivered a complete reimplementation of their CAT scan and nuclear magnetic resonance (NMR) system using objects. The project involved nearly 100 programmers working at several sites using Objective-C. It is often featured on GE television advertisements.

Brooklyn Union Gas

Brooklyn Union Gas created the first major mainframe-based MIS system using objects. They have more than one million customers. The Customer Information System (CIS) manages the entire revenue cycle of the company including field service orders, cash processing, credit and collection, meter reading, billing, and general account services.

The CIS consists of over 400 screens servicing 850 users, of which 450 are dedicated. Three-hundred and fifty meter readers are equipped with portable radio terminals that access the system. Normally, there are 330,000 transactions per working day with 10 transactions per second being recorded near busy hour. Forty thousand bills are produced every evening, along with 250 reports.

The third rewrite of this system was done using their own object-oriented extension to PL/1. Designing your own programming language and building your own development tools is a pretty bold move. But the architects for CIS felt that it was a lower risk than trying to construct such a complex system using traditional development methods and tools.

Their high-risk project has been a major success. Today, CIS contains 650 classes and 10,000 methods. Their conclusions, reported in the March 1991 issue of *Hotline on Object-Oriented Technology* (SIGS Publications) included:

- The paradigm scales to projects with more than 100 staff.
- Outstanding end-user response time can be delivered with modest CPU capacity.
- Object development is a more design-intensive process than traditional approaches.

An iterative approach is recommended:

- The packaging of code into small units provides for a high degree of code reusability in a typical business application. This packaging, combined with architecture layers and processing frameworks, provides a much stronger model than current 4GL CASE technology can offer.
- The use of a standard communication technique, messaging, between all application code results in a more uniform and understandable system.
- The system has a vocabulary that is shared by users and technicians.

It is difficult to imagine a more positive set of comments. As I have said for years, objects are ideal for traditional business applications. The technologists at Brooklyn Union Gas provided us with the first major example. I feel sure there will be many more soon.

Applied Intelligent Systems, Inc.

Applied Intelligent Systems (AIS) of Ann Arbor, Michigan, is in the business of building machine vision systems. Their AIS vision processors use sixty-four 512 K parallel processors (SIMD processor) to support up to six cameras. Their products are integrated with other companies' products to perform operations such as scanning parts to guide a robot arm. It can perform whole-image processing on images as large as $1,024 \times 1,024$ pixels.

The company felt a need to reduce the time to market of new applications built for its machine vision products. Productivity has increased approximately threefold using Objective-C. Staff morale is also considerably improved. But the AIS product has little RAM available for each processor—512 K. Objects created too much overhead, because even if just one method in a class were needed, they had to bring in all the methods of that class. As a result, AIS is no longer using Objective-C. In their system, each processor is constrained to 512 K and there is no disk.

To overcome this limitation, AIS developed a style of writing C called Intelligent C. They then built a scanner to scan the comments within the source files and use the comments to build the appropriate data structures. They also built a tool to prune unused methods by developing a list of methods actually used and compiling only those methods. In their application of about 400–600 K, this technique saves about 150 K of space compared to that in Objective-C.

One of the common issues in an object-oriented design is the appropriate level of granularity for each object. AIS found that following the rather conservative Objective-C model of granularity has worked well. For example, they began by representing each lead on a computer chip as an object. Later, they found it more desirable to have the object be a list of leads. The advice once again is to make larger, not smaller, objects.

According to Dave Coupland, "objects were a wonderful way of doing design for a system like this. But objects introduced as many questions as suggestions." He found that Sam Adams's adage was very true: Objects make good designers better, and mediocre designers obvious.[10]

For this project, the time required to do preprocessing with Objective-C was a problem. It took 10–15 minutes to do a build. This "delay" contributed to their decision to revert to C and simply maintain the generated Objective-C code.

Dave also commented that "O-O design seems very desirable for manufacturing systems. But, there is still a lot more talk than action among companies engaged in manufacturing software development." He estimated that "of the 60 sites that use their product, not one was using objects before they became involved with AIS, in spite of the fact that they are all high-tech semiconductor companies."

Hewlett-Packard Clinical Information Systems[11]

Hewlett-Packard has a Clinical Information Systems group near Boston that recently delivered a product called CareView 9000. It is a hospital information system designed to deal with the myriad of forms and reports developed in a hospital and provides near-instantaneous access to this information throughout the hospital. It is specially designed for use in intensive care situations where access to information is critical.

This product was built using C++. They were an early user of the language and had to build many of their own development tools, make some language changes, and develop many foundation classes. Nevertheless, they believe the system could not have been built without objects—it was just too complex.

Note that this was a real-time, high-reliability, high-availability system. Their delivered system involved more than 150,000 lines of C++ code.

Port of Singapore[12]

All containers handled at the Port of Singapore are managed by an interactive program written in Objective-C and Common Lisp. A large container ship can transport thousands of containers. It is a challenge to minimize the amount of handling of these containers as the ship moves from port to port. The goal of the software developed by the port authority and the Information Technology Institute of Singapore is to provide a planning tool for dealing with the containers to be offloaded from a ship as well as for those going on board.

This product involves some particularly innovative integration of technologies. They used Lisp's foreign-function interfaces to load Objective-C libraries into Lisp as a set of Flavors and associated methods. They also used Ingres to store data about the containers and began to treat the tables as classes and the records within them as instance variables. This partially object-oriented view of the database proved surprisingly useful and efficient.

NeXT [13]

NeXT Computer, Inc. has built some remarkably capable development tools, class libraries, and application development tools using objects. Their interface builder product is an especially good example of the benefits of objects and the importance of dynamic binding in particular. It was built with Objective-C.

NeXT offers an application development architecture that integrates programming tools, windowing systems, user interface toolkits, class libraries, database interfaces, and program management tools. The full suite of tools and classes must be object oriented, not just written in an object-oriented programming language or a set of repackaged C function calls.

The development environment cannot be independent of the operating system and must make some explicit assumptions about the underlying hardware. Where one sees weaknesses in the NeXT system, it is often traceable to weaknesses or incompatibilities with Mach or UNIX underneath.

The benefit from this degree of integration is programmer productivity. NeXT users often report factors of two or three productivity effects with little if any loss of efficiency. This productivity comes not only from the development tools but from the NeXTstep Application Kit. This "kit" is a collection of about 100 Objective-C classes. The classes in the Application Kit include Windows, Menus, Scrollers, Fonts, and Text. Three other kits are now available from NeXT: the Sound Kit, the Music Kit, and the DB Kit. Combined, these kits represent more than 200 classes that work together, were designed with a common vision, and are of reasonably high quality.

But it's the Interface Builder that most effectively demonstrates the power of objects, value of dynamic binding, and benefits of a tightly integrated development environment. Interface Builder was designed to assemble the user interface objects and relationships you require in an application, test the interface to verify that it works as expected, then generate and debug the actual code for the application. It is also generalized to allow programmers to add their own objects onto the palette so that more specialized applications can be assembled.

For new functionality, Interface Builder allows the application developer to sketch the external behavior of a new class, designate its superclass, and identify the connections between that class and others within the system. This information is done quickly and easily using a graphical interface. Later it will generate code, but one does not have to deal with code until it's really necessary.

Application developers are quite happy with the performance of Interface

Builder. It is a powerful and useful tool. Behind the scenes, it is also providing a front end to the usual collection of UNIX lower computer-aided software engineering (CASE) development tools such as editors, compilers, debuggers, version control tools, and management tools. Some object-specific tools are also accessible from Interface Builder—class browers and object inspectors.

The weakness of Interface Builder is that once a programmer begins to modify and extend the generated code, he can no longer rearrange the user interface from Interface Builder. While such a "reverse gear" would be incredibly desirable, important lower-level control of the application would have to be sacrificed to make it possible. So, once that "generate" button has been pushed, the programmer should be confident that the interface will not require additional changes.

NeXT "bet their company" on objects. I expect it to be a rewarding bet.

Mentor Graphics

Mentor Graphics is in the business of building computer-aided engineering (CAE) tools, especially tools for electronic design and engineering. Mentor Graphics has made a major commitment to the C++ language and objects. Their bet has been in a lot more jeopardy than that made by NeXT.

Almost all of their new development is being done with C++. Their most recent product involved over 8 million source lines of code or 12,000 classes. Its very size suggests that inadequate attention has been paid to elimination of redundancy and clean design. I would bet that at least 6,000 classes are redundant and maybe many more than that.

Mentor Graphics understands electronic CAD systems. Their prior generation of products was the leader in the industry not because they had the very best functionality but because their suite of products worked together. Objects seemed a natural technology to employ in building their next-generation system.

They adopted a "bet your company" strategy—rewrite all of their products in C++ to produce a revolutionary new set of features for their customers. That was a big undertaking that, to its credit, it has managed to "ship." But that shipment came late, with disappointing functionality and with such large machine requirements that most customers could not use it on existing workstations.

What began as a research project was blessed as a stable building block upon which all products of the company could rely. The Falcon Framework was an impressive piece of software functionality. But as various product groups tried to use it in their challenging products, they found weaknesses. As each weakness was repaired, it affected other products. Software building blocks must be stable, efficient, and easy to understand. The Falcon Framework was just too immature to use for such an aggressive project. In addition, Mentor Graphics developed their own persistent object base as a part of this project—a $100 million, five–year problem itself.

The object community should be grateful for the tireless dedication of many software engineers at Mentor Graphics for getting Falcon and its dependent products out the door. Hopefully, it will buy enough time to make the needed changes. Had they been unsuccessful, objects would have gotten a "large black eye" that would surely have delayed introduction of the technology in many companies.

HP's VEE*

Hewlett-Packard's Instrumentation Group has released a product called Visual Engineering Environment (VEE). VEE lets an engineer select and link icons that control laboratory instruments. The idea was to create a visual object for each laboratory instrument. Then, by clicking on the icon for that instrument, the engineer could adjust the knobs and dials of that instrument to the desired settings. Further, an instrument could be connected to another instrument by simply connecting them on the screen.

Once the engineers had developed this functionality, they realized they could generalize the software to deal with any object. VEE then became much more powerful. I like to joke with them and accuse them of building a "graphical assembly language for objects." Actually, it's an extensible, graphical application development environment. It has the constraint (or virtue) that new classes must be created by programmers.

VEE was built using Objective-C and ICpak 201. It was built by a small development team over a four-year period. It contains a wealth of predefined objects ranging from models of hundreds of laboratory instruments to a full simulation capability, to data analysis, manipulation, and display classes. It is a fully interactive graphical application development environment including programming tools, debuggers, tracing tools, and online help facilities.

As new assemblies of objects are created in VEE, they can be defined as an icon with a restricted interface to the other objects in the system. There is no constraint on the depth of nesting of such icons so there is no fundamental reason why VEE could not be used to construct business applications if some company were to build an appropriate set of business classes for use in VEE.

At Object Expo '92 in New York, Bill Hunt described their productivity on this product as 1.5–2.0 times their previous experience with C language. They averaged about 17 source lines of code per working day on the project. The product required about 350 classes and 5,000 methods.

Undoubtedly by learning from the previous Lake Steven experience, the VEE designers chose to design their system with rather large objects, not small, fine-grained objects. They tried to design classes with 1,000 source lines of code and 50–100 methods. The average is, of course, much smaller than that.

---

* See two articles in October 1992 issue of HP Journal on VEE.

The VEE team understood that designing with objects is new and different. As new members joined the team, they began by maintaining existing code, then worked as apprentices to trained team members, and more than a year later were allowed to do independent design that was reviewed by the team.

One of the truly interesting comments from Hunt's paper relates to memory management:

> Everyone assumes that [memory management] is required for good object-oriented programming. I disagree. It is much more likely that manual memory management methods will result in more reliable code for two reasons. First, the architecture is usually simpler and clearer when every object is 'owned' by exactly one object that is responsible for freeing it. Second, very subtle, but potentially serious bugs can be masked by automatic memory management that become very obvious under manual memory management.

The largest benefit from using objects came late in the project. It was determined that the product needed a major architectural change. Because the system was written with objects, this change could be made without the huge consequences that would have been true in C language.

Aldus Corporation[14]

Aldus Corporation is in the business of building publishing software. PageMaker is a highly successful product of the company. Like many successful companies, customers would like to have the company's products running efficiently on many different combinations of hardware and software. Aldus delivers products for both the IBM PC and Apple Macintosh markets.

In 1988 the company decided to develop a common application development framework for the designers and developers within the company. The primary goals were to be able to accomplish platform-independent development, provide a general mechanism for multiple views of content, and provide a standard way to execute and undo commands. At a technical level, Vamp is a collection of event-driven C++ classes. Classes include Windows, Panes, Canvas, Events, Event Handlers, Commands, and State Machines. Vamp should allow PageMaker to evolve into an interactive compound document processor.

American Airlines[15]

Commercial airlines have one or more centers where dispatchers control the scheduling of aircraft in real time. It is their job to ensure that each flight has the appropriate resources—flight crew, cabin crew, meals, fuel, take-off and landing slots, and flight plan. If a mechanical problem arises or there is a weather-related delay, it is the dispatcher's job to identify what problems need to be solved and to solve those problems efficiently. Solving the problem often involves sending a ground-to-air text message and receiving confirmation from the pilot.

American Airlines built and introduced a new hardware and software system to support dispatchers at their Dallas facility in November 1991. This new system was built in ObjectWorks Smalltalk (Smalltalk-80) and involved 200 classes and 2,000 methods with over 150,000 objects in active memory at a time. There were also about 100 lines of C code used to interconnect the Smalltalk system to the host online transaction processing system. The Smalltalk system downloads and parses 20–30 Kb of data every 2 minutes and more than 24 megabytes per day.

The new system was built with a development team of three people in 8 months. The first month was spent learning Smalltalk. They estimated that the resulting system would be equivalent in complexity to a system involving 116,000 lines of Assembler code. I first heard about a description of the system and the size of the Smalltalk application; then, I learned of the development time and resources. I was frankly amazed.

Because this system shares many of the generic features of business information systems, it is worth describing in some detail. Each dispatch desk is responsible for about 50 flights under normal circumstances. To check the status of any given flight, a minimum of three to four transactions to the host database is required. The computer configuration involves a network of Macintosh IIx machines connected to a Novell network server and a host machine on which the central database resides. Every 2 minutes, the server downloads incremental changes from the host database. Every 10 minutes, a total dump of some 1,500–1,700 flight segment objects is downloaded. There is also a secondary and tertiary link from the workstations directly to the host if necessary.

The workstations present a color textual display of flight status information and a graphical display of dependent flights. Dependent flights are those flights that depend upon another flight for some resource, e.g., pilot. For any given flight, the dependency graph shows two levels of prior dependent flights (those that provide resources to the selected flight) and two to three levels of subsequent flights (those that require resources from the selected flight). These displays are used to do impact analysis. If the flight from JFK to ORD is going to be 2 hours late in departing, what other flights will be impacted? And, what can be done about it?

Not surprisingly, there were some performance bottlenecks to be worked through on this system. The most challenging was created by the original garbage collection approach used in Smalltalk-80. With help from ParcPlace Systems, American Airlines was able to reduce the 10-second user delays to subsecond delays. Also, improvements in the multitasking have made a material impact on performance in this application.

The productivity and quality metrics for this project were also quite impressive. They produced 72–75 function points per person-month. On a subsequent project, their rate has actually increased to 114.1. Productivity did not come at the expense of either quality or availability. Only two errors were reported in the application after deployment. Availability has also been greater than expected.

The most difficult error encountered after implementation occurred because the host computer was generating an undocumented error message that the dispatcher system did not recognize. It was a bit difficult to track down but a snap to fix. Nevertheless, remember that three people designed, built, tested, and delivered this system in eight months!

At American Airlines, management was accustomed to providing a requirements specification and having an application working after a lengthy development process. With this new approach, an operational version of the system existed during the third month of the project. Many changes and refinements were made based upon users' reactions to the system. At the time of the handover of the system, it was already running on the desks of four dispatchers. The system was phased into operation voluntarily with about 80% of dispatchers currently using the system. Management was delighted with this project. "It just blew their doors off," I was told. That's an odd phrase to express enthusiasm in the airline industry!

The next system to be developed will graphically display aircraft positions and weather information in realtime. The development of this system will be done in a combination of C++ and Smalltalk.

SUMMARY

Objects have been used for large-scale commercial development projects in a number of system and application domains. The technology is not perfect; some projects do have difficulties, but the developers continue to use objects on subsequent projects.

The use of object-oriented technology in commercial software development is a reality. The companies and products described here are only a sample of the many pioneers who have made this technology a reality within their organizations. I apologize to all those hardworking developers who have built equally large, equally successful products using objects but were not mentioned here. Hopefully, these pioneer commercial system developers will profit handsomely from their important work. Surely, the software industry has profited from theirs. In conclusion, it is less risky to change to object technology than to remain with the current generation of software technology.

NOTES

1. John Meurling, *A Switch in Time: An Engineer's Tale*, Telephony Publishing, Chicago, IL, 1985.
2. A CCITT standard programming language derived from Pascal.
3. Brad Cox led this project.
4. For example, Scott Guthery, Are the emperor's new clothes object oriented? *Dr. Dobbs Journal*, December 1989.
5. The Analyst is a commercial product available from Xerox and demonstrated on a videotape by the same name featuring Kurt Piersol.
6. Described in *Using Smalltalk-80 for Commercial Application Development*, paper presented at ACM SofFair '83, Arlington, VA.
7. See the August 1989 issue of the *HP Journal* for a comprehensive description of this project, exactly the kind of retrospective we need to see more frequently.
8. See Susan Miller and Lennart Minsson, Success Criteria for Object-Oriented Systems Development, in *LOOK '92 Proceedings*, SIGS Publications, New York, 1992.
9. Dr. Jette is featured on the 1991 videotape distributed by PARC Place Systems entitled *Smalltalk—Big Results*.
10. Sam Adams is a principal of Knowledge Systems Corporation and has been an advocate for object technology since the early 1980s.
11. This project is described in some detail by Rob Seliger of HP on the excellent videotape marketed by SIGS Publications called *An Introduction to Object-Oriented Programming*.
12. See the *Sun Technology Journal*, Winter 1989, for more details on this project.
13. See Bruce Webster's *The NeXT Book* for an excellent introduction to the NeXT computer and interface builder in particular.
14. See Ferrel and B. Meyer, *Vamp: The Aldus Application Framework* in *1989 OOPSLA Proceedings*, 1989.
15. The information regarding this project came from a telephone interview with the leader of this development team on August 14, 1992. I later learned that a two-page brief describing this project had also been developed by the Gartner Group (Report E-700-713, May 15, 1992).

6

Where Do the Objects Come From?

*[In the software industry] we tend to fabricate
each new house from mud, grass, rough lumber,
and prayer instead of from preassembled walls,
window kits, and engineering know-how.*

Glenford J. Myers
Composite/Structured Design
Van Nostrand Reinhold, New York, 1978, p. 4.

Customers arrive at the door of a software house with vivid dreams of the future, but without:

- a clear idea of what they want built
- an understanding of the available construction technology
- sufficient time to accomplish the desired project
- adequate resources to construct their "vision"

In 1625, the king of Sweden faced a similar problem. He knew "exactly" what he wanted, but there was no reliable way to communicate that "vision" to the ship designer. To complicate the problem, there was little understanding of the constraints imposed by the available construction technology. The king also felt that "time was of the essence" because they were at war. One usual constraint was, however, missing—a budget! He was, after all, king.

The ultimate demise of the *Vasa* came from a failure to cope with changing customer requirements. There were no established rules for rejecting change requests. Saying no to the king in 1625 was life-threatening behavior. But, if the consequences of this change request had been carefully and accurately explained to the king, he might have made a different decision concerning that third gundeck.

Our goal here is to prevent customers of software houses from having the same experience that King Gustav had on August 10, 1628, when the *Vasa* sank on its maiden voyage! Enough software "Vasas" have already sunk.

GOALS OF DESIGN[1]

Most that write about software design lament the absence of a standard design representation such as blueprints used by architects or the schematics used by electrical engineers. Yet, these writers show little understanding of the complexity, amount of detail, and number of attachments that actually accompany a set of "blueprints," or all the other "views" of a circuit that are required before a construction company or foundry is willing to provide a fixed-price bid and construction schedule.

Let's look beyond the two or three pages of room layouts and elevations found in "grocery store plan books" to discover what is actually contained in a set of construction plans for a "residential building." Let's also look at the process by which those construction plans were created.

BLUEPRINT FOR DESIGN

Attached to a blueprint is an elaborate set of notes. In these notes, the architect specifies the specific components to be used throughout the house. For example, Peachtree window #CH4848, 6" walnut T&G flooring, clear cedar siding, Alaskan granite floor tile, solid core birch doors, or Tylö sauna #SH354. These notes can dramatically impact the cost to build the house. The impact is not just in direct costs but also in their implications. The particular selection of appliances or toilet fixtures sends an important message to the builder concerning the level of quality the customer expects and for which he or she is prepared to pay. An even more subtle message is provided when exclusive items are specified that are not functionally superior but are currently in vogue or make a particular fashion statement. The message could be that the customer is not sensitive to costs.

The construction plans for a two-story, 3,000 ft^2 house can easily be 30 pages long. As one flips through the pages, important decisions are reflected on each page. Some of the most important pages are near the end, which describe specific components by brand, size, and variety. Good architects understand the full range of materials and components available to construct a house. They know how to impose subtle constraints on the highest level design to minimize the waste of building materials and to simplify the construction process. The best even know how to accurately estimate the financial and schedule implications of each major decision.

I had the misfortune of working with some commercial architects who were amazingly bad at evaluating the financial implications of their design. They managed to design a house that was 325% more than the specified budget. Needless to say, we did not actually build what they designed, nor did we even find it possible to alter their design to accommodate our very real budget. We started over with purchased blueprints and built the house within 20% of the original budget, despite the fact that we added 15% additional floorspace as we were building the house.

It is not required in the United States for architects to have any direct experience with the various building trades. Nor are they obligated by law to satisfy the written specifications provided to them by their customers. I was intrigued to discover that Thomas Jefferson spent almost 40 years designing, redesigning, and building Monticello. Frank Lloyd Wright is said never to have built a house with a roof that didn't leak. One of Wright's most attractive buildings, the Unity Temple in Oak Park, Illinois, has the disturbing feature of maintaining a nearly constant temperature during the month of August—117° Fahrenheit!

Lest you think I am picking on a prior generation of American architects, I should also provide a contemporary example. I once worked in a building designed during the early 1980s by Philip Johnson, an important contemporary American architect. This building was constructed largely of glass. It was gorgeous to look at, impressive to visit, but amazingly unpleasant to work in. For example, almost every office had a computer terminal or workstation, but productivity was significantly affected on sunny days—you simply could not see the screens due to the glare. Summer sun and winter snows presented their own special challenges. An even more interesting design defect was the unisex toilet situated next to the rear entrance of the building. It had a floor-to-ceiling glass wall that was opaque when viewed from the outside. No one was really comfortable using this particular facility. The little-known defect was that late in the afternoon on hazy days the glass wall became completely transparent, according to the person whose office overlooked this outside wall.

Tom Wolfe has written a wonderful book, *From Bauhaus to Our House*, describing the current state of architecture in America. It begins in the following way: "O BEAUTIFUL, for spacious skies, for amber waves of grain, has there ever been another place on earth where so many people of wealth and power have paid for and put up with so much architecture they detested as within thy blessed borders today? . . . Every new $900,000 summer house in the north woods or on the shore of Long Island has so many pipe railings, ramps, hob-treaded metal spiral stairways, sheets of industrial plate glass, banks of tungsten-halogen lamps, and white cylindrical shapes, it looks like an insecticide refinery." Far too much of our contemporary software seems to have come from an analogous architectural design process.

THE DESIGN PROCESS

The process of design is not just to "figure out how to solve the problem" but also to progressively disclose the solution efficiently to others. Once disclosed, the designer must be able to accept and act on the feedback received from customers as well as construction experts. Another crucial characteristic of a good designer is the ability to accurately assess the cost and schedule impact of each design decision. The goal is to understand the customer's problem, propose a workable solution which includes costs and schedule, receive approval with modifications, then communicate the final, detailed design to both the customer and construction crew. What is wanted is a repeatable process that results in a design consistent with the needs of the customer, can be understood in detail by professional builders, complies with the agreed budgets (time and money), and satisfies a variety of externally imposed standards (building codes, bank audit requirements, safety guidelines, or ergonomic standards).

Any design that contains unique elements complicates the tasks of the building trades. Only with a modular approach to design where the modules have been regularly used can costs estimates and schedule be accurately provided.

Understanding the requirements

Most houses constructed in the United States today are not built with the assistance of a commercial architect. Most are built by builders using "stock" plans that have typically been used by that builder before. Nevertheless, let's explore the development process for the design and construction of a single-family dwelling with an architect.

The lucky couple kicks off the construction process by identifying, evaluating, and selecting their architects. But, unbeknownst to the first-time builder, the contract with the architect shrewdly turns them into patrons for the artistic and creative endeavors of the architect. It also removes the architect from assuming direct responsibility for scheduling and costs for the construction project. Often, it even rewards the architect for cost overruns.

When designing a new home, an architect begins by obtaining the basic requirements of their clients: how many bedrooms? how many cars in the garage? how many bathrooms? how much money can you spend on the house? From these basic requirements, the architect develops some sketches of different exterior designs that have been done with the knowledge of the basic requirements. Do you want a contemporary, Georgian, colonial, or prairie school home?

Once the style and basic requirements have been determined, several iterations occur with basic floor layouts. Interior elevations come next to establish more detail concerning ceilings, stairs, doors, etc. Additional elevations[2] are added that begin to include the design of the kitchen; floor, door, and ceiling moldings; built-in bookcases; and stair railings. Next comes the lighting plan, with drawings of the ceilings throughout the house showing the types and locations of light fixtures. Once these fixtures are agreed upon, the electrical plan can be drawn, showing a wiring diagram for the house with the locations and types of all switches. Complementing the electrical diagram is the plan for the heating and air conditioning system. This heating, ventilation, and air conditioning (HVAC) plan shows the location of all duct work, the furnace, the compressor, and fuel tank.

At the end of the plan is a list of specific components, as well as lists of specific instructions to tradespeople. Specific requirements for the heating system may be contained on these lists, as well as details like how to sand and stain woodwork. Major requirements can be written here that dramatically affect the time and cost to construct a house.

DESIGNING WITH SOFTWARE COMPONENTS

At the beginning of the century, Frank Lloyd Wright was experimenting with radically new designs for homes and commercial buildings using new materials (like poured concrete), new subsystems (like forced-air heating systems), and new designs (like flat roofs with skylights). There were many construction challenges, mistakes, and unhappy customers. Even the most innovative contemporary architect has much better science, engineering, materials, and design tools available. New designs for buildings that appear wildly innovative may actually "reuse" 90% of the "modules" from previous projects.

By contrast, possibly 5% of contemporary software systems involve a majority of reused procedures. Without higher degrees of reuse, software design and construction will remain as risky, expensive, and slow as the early days of the prairie school of American architecture.

An engineering process for the analysis, specification, design, construction, validation, and recomposition of software systems can be created and used successfully. Although this process is new, it is built upon years of experience from successful software development companies. The process is different because it requires reusable software components.

This engineering process is tailored to commercial systems that require 100,000 lines of new source code and more than 10 person-years of effort.[3] It assumes that an existing library of several hundred software components is available and that several hundred more will be constructed. While the method is scalable in either direction (thousands to millions), some modifications would be required. For example, giant projects have to be geographically dispersed, and geographic distribution raises new issues that must be addressed explicitly and supported by technical and management controls.

SYSTEM DEVELOPMENT PROCESS

The essence of system development is depicted in Figure 6.1. As system developers, we must define the system to be built (the *what*), determine how we intend to develop the system (the *how*), and then verify that what we developed was what was described (*if* the system built is what is wanted). Depending upon the size, complexity, cost, and risks associated with a particular system, the customer for the system may want more or fewer assurances along the way that the system development is progressing satisfactorily. For a $50,000 system development project, the customer may be willing to "risk all" that the supplier is building what they want. For a $1 billion system development project, no one is prepared to take such risks.

The more often a customer wants to be assured that the system is being developed according to plan, the more expensive the development process. The higher the state of development technology being applied to the development project, the lower the cost of developing the system and thus the less time it should take to develop it. The time needed to accomplish a complete iteration of the system is also

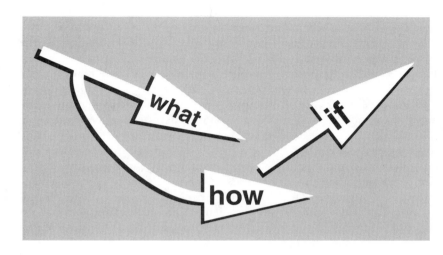

Figure 6.1.
Essence
of system
development.

an important influence on the development process. A pure software system could be specified, designed, developed, and verified in 6 months, whereas a system involving custom hardware, packaging, and software could take 18 months. The greater this elapsed time, the more interim assurances the customer will likely require and the higher the cost per unit of work.

The same process of analyzing a system, specifying a new system, designing that system, building it, and verifying that it was built as specified is required for huge systems as well as for tiny systems. In the tiny system, each step may be small and the customer may be completely uninterested in receiving a "deliverable" representing the outcome of that stage. The designer may never create a single file or piece of paper associated with that stage; nevertheless, the work must be accomplished to progress to the next stage.

One of the challenges of a large-system development project is the need to regularly evaluate the emerging system from a number of different perspectives. Examples include manufacturability, safety standards compliance, maintainability, performance, ergonomics, interoperability, modifiability, dependencies upon suppliers, competitive position, and production costs. These needs contribute to making large-system development so difficult and risky.

The specifications need to be fixed for the designer to design and develop a system that will meet those specs. Yet, specs are always incomplete and often change rapidly. This incompleteness is discovered as the design and development proceed. It is easy for the development to become unstable and nonterminating if servicing the changes to the spec consumes all the development resources.

The most important role of a project manager is to put in place and enforce a development process that controls this inherent entropy in the development

process.[4] Sometimes the project manager must reduce the ambition level of the system to a point where more agreement can be achieved and fewer changes to the specs will be required. Another tactic is to batch the changes, prioritize each one, and layer them according to importance. The prioritization will cause many change requests to go away, eliminate redundant changes, and provide important additional guidance to the developers. Because changes are rarely independent, it requires much less work to service 10 similar changes at once than to deal with each one separately.

Many object-oriented methodologists are now promoting their particular approach to object-oriented design—some have actually built products using objects before developing their design methods.[5] I do not intend to enter this competition. Instead, it is my intention to describe a process that has worked in my experience at Stepstone and with consulting clients. One such example has been published as IBM Technical Report GG24-3566-00, entitled "Object-Oriented Analysis of the ITSO Common Scenario." It is actually a worked-out 220-page design for building a comprehensive information system to support a network of automobile dealers in Europe. It uses the approach described in this chapter.

Step by step

The following pages describe a development process for a large system and offer sample notations that could be used to reflect the results of each step. For developers of small systems or even programs, the reader should review all the steps in the complete process and determine explicitly which are required for his or her particular system development effort. (Note: I am not recommending that every development process produce as much paper or as many electronic files as would be implied by the concatenation of every step that follows.)

The system development process requires nine steps interacting, as shown in Figure 6.2. The four steps in the top row determine the "what"; the four boxes in the lower row determine the "how"; and the verification step is the "if."

While resembling a traditional "waterfall" development model, the process is inherently iterative, with the added recommendation that each iteration be relatively short— say 3–9 months. A system development process must involve two iterations and will most likely require three. Remember the admonition from Professor Fred Brooks in the *Mythical Man-Month:*

Plan to throw one away; you will anyway.

In object-oriented systems, experience suggests it always takes three refactorings of the design before "it feels right." Three refactorings of the design does not

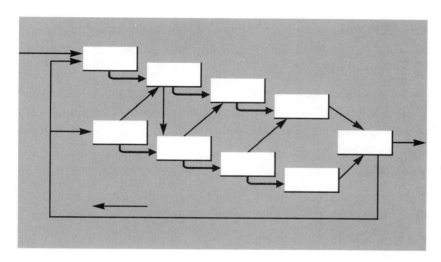

Figure 6.2. Nine steps of the system development process.

mean that two complete development steps need to be discarded. Instead, most of the methods will actually survive from iteration to iteration. What will change is the inheritance tree of classes and data structures within the classes. The following sections describe each of the steps in the systems development process.

Requirements analysis

Narrative description of requirements. Systems development must begin with a written description of the requirements for the system to be constructed (see Figure 6.3). These requirements might be provided by a customer or approved in writing if written by someone else. But the process must begin with a comprehensive narrative description of the requirements for the desired system.

This document will describe:

1. the purpose, mission, and goals of the system to be constructed
2. all known constraints — physical, environmental, financial, etc.

The most common mistake is to hamper the architects and designers by imposing unnecessary constraints. Real constraints have to be known. But all constraints should be critically reviewed, analyzed, and confirmed as early in the process as possible. Is compatibility with existing systems written in a proprietary programming language actually required? Is it really necessary for the system to run on the company's last generation of hardware?

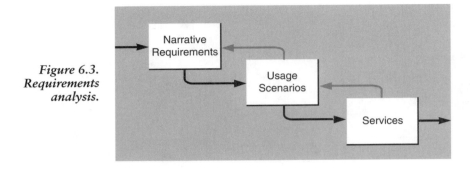

Figure 6.3.
Requirements
analysis.

The process for dealing with constraints should be largely an economic one. It will cost $X million to satisfy that constraint and require an extra five months of development. Is it really worth that additional investment? Be sure that the business decision makers understand the economic consequences of easy-to-write but difficult-to-implement requirements.

The architects and designers should know about the technology available to satisfy the customer's problems. Technology constraints must only be those that are truly immutable, e.g., a preexisting network of 500 IBM 3083 computers.

Never should the requirements deal with issues of how the system will be implemented to satisfy the stated goals or requirements. Great care must be taken to ensure that "how" does not subtly creep into the initial requirements for the system.

This initial step is absolutely mandatory, even for day-long programming exercises. Begin by writing down what you understood as the requirements and have those requirements verified by the customer before doing any further work. It is amazing how difficult it is to accurately communicate simple concepts to another human being. Never underestimate the odds of misunderstandings between people.

Usage scenarios. From the customer requirements, the systems analyst must begin to describe the interactions that various users are expected to have with the system. These interactions, called scenarios (see Figure 6.4), define a specific set of stimuli to the system and the responses expected from each stimulus. Each scenario should describe the intended interaction of a defined user with the system. As we begin to refine and elaborate the definition of the system, scenarios will also be elaborated and refined. Ultimately, each scenario becomes a test case traceable to a specific written requirement.

For substantial commercial systems, analysts and designers must be prepared to develop hundreds of scenarios. Imagine an extremely large wall with each scenario written on a Post-It note. As new scenarios are developed, they are grouped based upon perceived similarity. Quickly, we begin to see clusters of similar scenar-

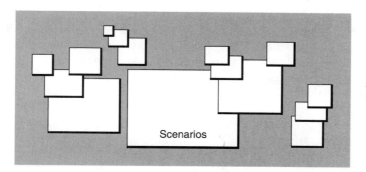

*Figure 6.4.
Scenarios.*

ios emerging.

An important aid in developing scenarios is to think of all the different users the new system will have. For each user, what is the anticipated set of interactions with the new system? For each action by a user, what other types of users will be affected and what are they likely to do in response?

The area of each rectangle reflects the number of scenarios within each anticipated layer. Imagine that we had an automated system that would allow us to click on each rectangle and see a list of the scenarios within that proposed layer. A click on each scenario would allow us to observe the stimulus to the system and the anticipated response. Once collapsed, each layer is given a name that is displayed in a metarectangle. A manual version of this system is equally easy to develop and use. The simplest could be a set of 3 × 5 cards sorted into groups, with the height of the pile indicating the number of scenarios within each pile. Each card must also have a reference to the paragraph where that requirement originated.

Scenarios form the basis of test cases, each of which must be independently verified by the quality assurance (QA) organization. Scenarios will also play a crucial role in formulating the documentation for the system. It will be important to verify that each scenario is adequately documented and documented correctly.

For anything but the tiniest of systems, it will be important that the point of view of each scenario be identified. Consider the example of building a new branch banking system. This new system can be thought of as a large room with a number of doors. Each door represents a class of user who may need to interact with the new system. One door is the automatic teller machine (ATM); others include the teller, branch manager, branch's system manager, and various executives and systems staff at the central office of the bank.

A set of scenarios must be developed for each class of user. A scenario is not a description of the types of transactions a user has available at an ATM, but instead each scenario describes the specific interaction a user has with the ATM - insert your card, type in a secret code, select the type of transaction, etc. No abstraction should be undertaken at this stage, but rather a brute force recording of the intended behavior of the system to be constructed.

The narrative requirements are the user's statement of what is wanted. The scenarios are the system developers' statement of what they imagine they might be able to build to satisfy those requirements. Automated systems are being built to support this activity of describing each scenario, maintaining its traceability to the originating requirement, and identifying its appropriate point of view (class of user).

Ensembles. A scenario describes one sequence of functional behavior through a system. Similar scenarios are implemented by a set of closely related components within the system. Large systems are always implemented with layers of functionality. Think of a scenario as being a vertical thread through the system where this thread touches all the components within the system that must be activated to provide the desired set of responses to the defined stimuli. If we look at a few such threads, we see that the threads activate components on several different levels or layers (see Figure 6.5). But the concept of layers is really inadequate and misleading. What we should be thinking about is ensembles of objects that have a restricted visibility to other ensembles of objects within the system.

Ensembles are named collections of tightly coupled components with restricted external visibility—not all of the behavior available within an ensemble is available externally. Several ensembles will be activated within a typical scenario.

So where do the ensembles come from? They are created by an experienced, creative analyst! Methods, tools, and experience can be employed and can surely help. But in the final analysis this step is quintessentially a creative act involving synthesis of a variety of stated and unstated information. It is not automatable for any interesting system.

Classes of functionally similar scenarios should be implemented by a single ensemble within the system where possible. An analyst might begin with the collections of scenarios in each rectangle and declare each an "ensemble." This "prototype ensemble" must be tested and modified based upon criteria such as:

Coherence	Each ensemble should be describable in one simple sentence.
Model validity	Ensembles should accurately model the physical or logical world of the application or system.
Change impact	Any expected change over the life of the system should result in a change in only one or two ensembles.

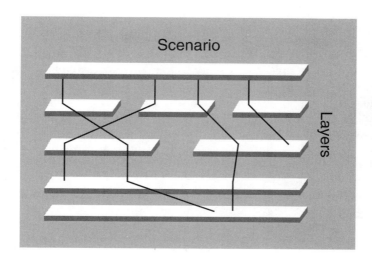

Figure 6.5.
Diagram showing
the threads through
layers for each
identified scenario.

Variety isolation	Standard ensembles provided to all systems should be cleanly isolated from specialized ensembles.
Independence	It should be possible for each ensemble to be developed, tested, and maintained by an independent organization.
Redundancy reduction	Whenever possible, a single ensemble should be used to satisfy a similar set of scenarios.
One point of view	Each ensemble should support a single class of user.
Error recovery	User errors should be isolated and handled within each ensemble.

Each prototype ensemble must be analyzed using the criteria given above. If the proposed ensembles do not comply with the criteria:

- The scenarios within an ensemble might be reallocated to other ensembles.
- New ensembles could be defined to include a series of existing scenarios.
- An ensemble could be partitioned into smaller ensembles.
- The scenarios might be modified to allow for a cleaner, more elegant solution.[6]

This analysis and synthesis process involving scenarios and ensembles is being done in such a way that alternatives that were considered but rejected remain available in the project archives. Each alternative considered is retained along with detailed information testing the viability of the emerging ensembles and their suitability over time.

The goal is to design a system that will be stable and maintainable over its anticipated lifecycle. We can never correctly anticipate all of the changes to which the system will be subjected. But where we can anticipate change, we should design for it. Once we review a complex design trail and reject it, we should leave a record for those who will follow later this week, next month, or in 20 years if we build a truly successful system.

What is great about this approach is that we are doing lots of analysis, but the results of our work will be expressed using the same graphical notation we used in the prior step. No new documentation machinery is required.

The rectangles become prototype ensembles. An ensemble is defined by a set of functionally related scenarios and is implemented by a set of functionally related classes. An ensemble is comparable to a circuit board on which a variety of integrated circuits and connections exist. The interface to the board is well defined and considerably smaller than the collection of interfaces to the individual ICs; the function of the board is more precisely defined than the generic capabilities represented by the ICs; and the board is sold, supported, and maintained as a single unit.

An ensemble should also be able to hide as much implementation detail as possible. Just as the class hides implementation details from the user of that class, the ensemble should also hide implementation details of the classes it contains. At this stage, we will not concern ourselves with which classes will be required to provide a given ensemble. We will only need to be convinced that it is possible to construct such a set of classes.

Ensembles add the constraint that all classes are not available to all users. Such a constraint is a highly desirable feature of a large system. The surface area of hundreds or thousands of classes represents a daunting challenge to the newcomer who must learn how to take advantage of this wealth of functionality. In parallel, the developers of those classes will inevitably continue to make changes to those classes, so the burden on the user becomes magnified over time as well.

Ensembles will be more stable than classes and should have the minimum interface possible to other ensembles within the system. Because current object-oriented programming languages do not have direct support for ensembles, we need to apply management techniques similar to those we have used with subsystems over the years to define and manage this important architectural entity.

Behavioral specification

By this stage in the development process, enough information will have been developed to construct a behavioral specification of the system. This spec could be thought of as the first draft of the user reference manual for the system. It should be complete and all of the system's behavior should be directly traceable to originating requirements or explicitly stated requirements that are derived from the original requirements. The description of each scenario should be as precise as that found in a user's guide or reference manual for the product: "If one performs this exact sequence of actions, the screen will look like this."

Depending upon the ensemble, various descriptive techniques might be used to elaborate each ensemble. Parsers are efficiently described using a BNF grammar, communication systems using state machines, algorithms using flowcharts, generic systems using behavior graphs. But the focus remains on what is to be accomplished, not how it is to be accomplished. Resist the urge to describe how; you'll have a decade or so to deal with how if you succeed in getting the go-ahead to build "what" has been specified. Relish your fleeting freedom.

A major cause of budget overruns is uncontrolled additions of functionality to a system during design and development. Be aware of this risk and resist the urge. If the function is not required and agreed upon by the customer, leave it out for now.

At this stage of the development process, we must begin to make some hard decisions about what will be built and what will be left out. The rectangle diagram provides a natural way to deductively make some of these decisions. For example, it is a useful exercise to rank all ensembles according to criteria such as value, development effort, market priority, technical risk, similarity to other ensembles developed by this development team, and degree of innovation. A variety of techniques from social science research allow for precise rank ordering even when the number of ensembles is large.[7] Once ranked, we can do some simple tallies and decide where to draw the line for version 1.0 and maybe even how to phase later versions.

Observe that we are dealing only with the "what" until this stage of the development. Next comes the "how."

SYSTEM DESIGN

Figure 6.6 shows the four types of diagrams required for system design.

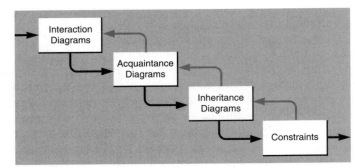

*Figure 6.6.
A system design.*

Interactions

An ensemble is implemented by a set of classes. As a rule of thumb, an ensemble should contain more than 5 and fewer than 30 classes. For each scenario within an ensemble, an interaction diagram should be constructed. This interaction diagram (see Figure 6.7) shows the sequence of messages that must be sent and serviced to satisfy the particular scenario.[8]

The goal is to identify the exact sequence of messages to each object to accomplish each scenario. After several scenarios have been analyzed and their sequence of messages recorded, we begin to get a fairly complete protocol description for each class by simply reading down the vertical lines and recording all the messages that must be serviced by that class. Notice that the time is represented as rows and space is represented as columns or vertical lines.

One particularly effective way to use interaction diagrams is in conjunction with the class, responsibilities, and collaborators (CRC) card approach presented by Ward Cunningham and Kent Beck in the OOPSLA '89 proceedings and also described in a training videotape available from Knowledge Systems Corporation in Cary, North Carolina,[9] and SIGS Publications's *Design Masters* video.

The idea is for several people to sit around a table with a stack of index cards. As classes are identified, their names are written on the upper left corner of each card. Behavioral simulations can then take place as the designers consider what responsibilities or behavior each class will have and which other classes that class will have to collaborate with.

What seems to make the CRC card approach especially effective is the fact that several designers can productively think about the evolving system and dynamically simulate its behavior. CRC cards can be used to design the set of classes that compose an ensemble or could even be used to help identify the ensembles in the first place.

Often it is helpful to construct alternative graphical views of a proposed design. For example, a complete state diagram showing the sequence of messages and the resulting changes in the state of each object could be displayed from the

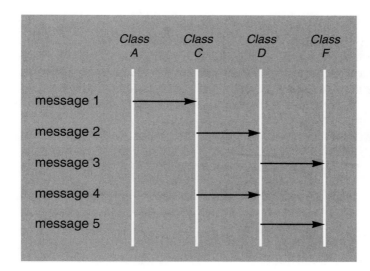

Figure 6.7. Interaction diagram.[8]

interaction diagram shown in Figure 6.7.

Systems that benefit greatly from the use of state diagrams include process control systems, communications systems, and transaction processing systems. Other diagrams could be useful here depending upon the previous experience of the organization, e.g., SDL (telecom systems), Jackson, Yourdon diagrams, or almost any of the "arc and bubble" diagrams. While these traditional presentations of system behavior are not useful in arriving at an object-oriented design, they can be useful in evaluating an object-oriented design.

Systems engineering tools such as RDD-100® from Ascent Logic in San Jose, California, might also prove valuable in their ability to provide alternative views of such a system. If the system is a distributed system, RDD's ability to simulate the dynamic behavior of the system based upon its design will be invaluable.[10]

Method and data definition

A stack of CRC cards has a list of the responsibilities for each class in the system. While generally understood by the participants of the CRC design exercise, it is prudent to more completely record the description of each method for each class. This description should only require a few sentences and can be done as a comment in the programming language of choice.

Similarly, state information will have been discussed during the CRC design exercise. It should be described more precisely and recorded in the programming language of choice.

Dependencies

Classes will often collaborate with many other classes to accomplish their mission. Such collaboration could lead to excessive coupling of classes that would make later changes to the system more difficult. The purpose of the dependency graph (see Figure 6.8) is to make explicit the collaborations that do exist and motivate the designers to maximize the internal strength of each class and minimize the dependencies among classes.[11]

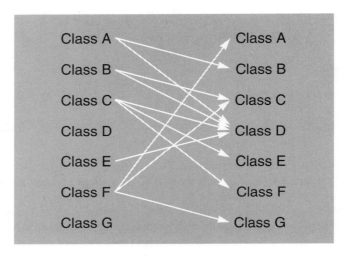

*Figure 6.8.
A dependency
graph.*

When we write a method in an object-oriented programming language, there are several ways in which that method might create a coupling to another class. These include:

- Create an object of another class and send it one or more messages.
- Use an object passed as an argument to that method.
- Inherit an instance variable from a superclass.
- Inherit a method from a superclass.

Each time we create such a coupling, we are increasing the complexity of the system. Changes to one class can no longer be made independently of other classes in the system. Complexity should be reduced by minimizing the coupling among classes—at the class level (e.g., private methods), at the ensemble level, and even between systems. An object should not be able to create any arbitrary object, thus becoming coupled to that object's class. Restrictions should be created and enforced, just as we have enforced restrictions on subsystems within traditional systems.

Classes are referred to as "dependent upon another class" if a change to a dependent class can affect the behavior of the original class. The dependency graph shows the linking of objects within a system. Depicting these relationships graphically is valuable because it allows the designer to see the degree of dynamic coupling among the various classes within a proposed system.

The way to think about graphics such as this is that they can provide you with useful information while standing across the room without being able to read the names of the specific classes. A similar dependency graph should be constructed to show the dependencies among ensembles. Often a brief study of such a diagram will suggest improvements to the basic design.

Another variant of this diagram is a list of messages sent while executing a particular scenario. Count the messages sent from one class to another. Divide the message counts into about five categories. Now, redraw the dependency graph showing the degree of coupling by the thickness of the arrows connecting the classes.

Constraints

Further elaboration of the constraints on each ensemble should be described. This description is a narrative associated with each ensemble. Constraints will differ depending upon the type of system being designed.

System-wide constraints involve processing time, memory space, or the distribution of the system across multiple, heterogenous computers. Other constraints will be dependencies between objects—if object A changes, object B should be notified of that change.

COMPONENT DESIGN

Data elaboration

The data structures (see Figure 6.9) for each instance variable within each class must now be defined explicitly. Often these instance variables will themselves be objects of a pre-existing class. This description of data structures should be done in the programming language directly.

Method elaboration

Provide a detailed, step-by-step description of how each method will implement its desired behavior. Think of this step as writing pseudocode to describe the detailed behavior of each method. Sufficient detail should be provided to allow a "method" engineer to implement the method correctly. Another goal of this method description is to be able to independently verify that the method operates as specified.

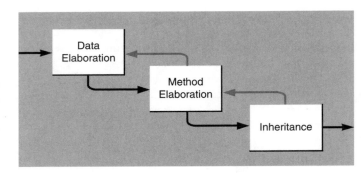

Figure 6.9.
Data structures.

Method elaboration should be done in a pseudocode closely resembling the target programming language.

Inheritance

It is now appropriate to determine the relationships between the proposed and existing classes in the library. Opportunities for reuse should be discovered. One hopes that many of the data structures and methods that have been described above will already exist within the available class library.

Never begin development of classes without having a thorough technical review of the newly designed classes. It has been my experience that designs for new class libraries return from a technical review session with many fewer classes. As other designers review a proposed set of classes, they identify existing classes that have similar functionality, thus simply eliminating the need for the new class.

Designers should take several days out of their design project to do a serious investigation of available class libraries at this stage in the design. Preexisting classes of high quality can save amazing amounts of time, money, and grey hair. Assembling the complete class hierarchy will require "class" engineers to fully understand the existing library of software components, as well as the new classes that are being designed.

The inheritance relationship is typically shown as an inverted tree diagram (see Figure 6.10). For small class libraries, this representation is perfect. For hundreds or thousands of classes, its value quickly degrades. Consider using an indented outline instead. It takes much less paper and is equally informative. For large class libraries that involve multiple inheritance, graphics (and prayer) will be required.

But keep clearly in mind that for even modest-sized systems (100 or more classes) the class is too small a unit of design. You should be thinking and designing in terms of ensembles of classes that have restricted external visibility.

The code skeleton for each class and method can now be generated. The

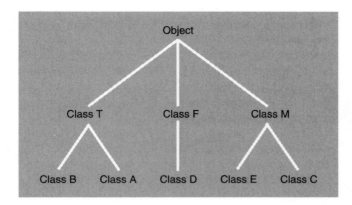

*Figure 6.10.
Inverted tree
diagram.*

method protocol is known, as are the instance variables for each class and a definition of the behavior of each method.

DESIGN VALIDATION

A critical step in the development of a new system is the validation that the design meets the agreed requirements and specifications. Requirements such as maximum allowable response times and behavioral characteristics of the system should be rigorously validated based upon the design. At least there should be the exercise of stepping through each requirement and each functional specification and recording whether or not they are satisfactory.

It will be necessary to build prototypes of portions of the overall system to validate that agreed behavior can be achieved as required. Note how different these prototypes are from so-called rapid prototypes often imagined to replace design altogether.

One aspect of design often most crucial to validate is the interaction among concurrent tasks. Ideally, there should be tools that allow such validation to occur based upon the design notation itself. Otherwise, it will be essential that the design be validated by building a simulation or a prototype to verify the selected concurrency scheme.

DEVELOPMENT

It is now time for the construction to begin. Senior designers should continue in a design role. Their job should be to continuously oversee the emerging system and validate that what is being built is consistent with the described design. If the designers jump into the fray and start hacking code, their more important design oversight role will be lost and that job will not get done.

By the time appropriate design has been completed, reviewed, and validated, the coding should be a straightforward exercise that can be done by developers with significantly less experience.

System verification and validation

It is the job of the designers and Quality Assurance (QA) staff to verify that what was built is consistent with the original scenarios. It is especially important that these two verification and validation steps be accomplished by independent groups. The major difference in their perspectives should be that the designers are doing white box verification and validation whereas the QA staff is working without a detailed understanding of the internal structure of the system under test.

The QA staff at design time has the special responsibility to management to verify that each of the scenarios should work as designed. Later, they will have to also demonstrate that it really works.

Refactoring. A provision is provided in this component design approach for the inevitable discovery that earlier choices for ensembles or classes were suboptimal. The essence of refactoring (see Figure 6.11) is that as the model of the application or system develops, there will come a time when adding the next capability will seem unnecessarily complicated due to a prior decision concerning classes or structure of classes. Once this roadblock is reached, one must carefully consider the implications of making a major change in the names of classes, the inheritance structure of those classes, and also the names chosen for methods. The larger the project, the greater the implications of such a change.

Figure 6.11.
Refactoring.

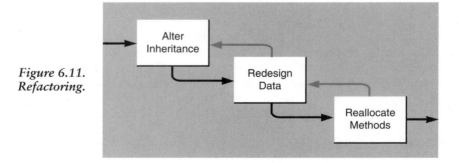

But the experience is that a given design will need to be refactored three or four times before the developers feel comfortable that the design works well and will be reasonable to maintain. The good news is that such refactoring is not terribly expensive in most object-oriented programming languages. C++ is a clear exception. Major restructuring of the inheritance tree in C++ can result in massive amounts of recompilation, as well as changes to virtual functions within a class. It is for this reason that I recommend C++ for use on projects where the design is extremely stable within the project and reasonably stable over the lifetime of the product being constructed. In other words, it is a system programming language, not an application development language.

There is a recommended sequence of refactoring a design. First, the inheritance tree is modified or a new tree created. Then, the individual elements of that class are moved beginning with text description of each class, then the data structures associated with each class, then method and test cases. As each change is made, it should be tested, and that test case should be properly recorded as a part of the class tester for that class.

IMPLICATIONS OF THIS APPROACH

An attractive aspect of the approach described is that portions of the design of existing software systems can be reconstructed from source code that was not built using this method. Also, the complete set of diagrams can be linked and supported within a single design and development environment.

This means that existing components can be integrated into the design environment, thus providing for the reuse of designs as well as their associated code. Fully developed and field-tested components can be integrated easily into the developing systems. Designers will be motivated to find connections between evolving designs and existing designs. It will save work and help produce more reliable systems.

The economic incentive is overpowering. Reusing existing work, rather than designing from scratch, results in higher-quality systems in less time and with less effort.

COMPUTER SUPPORT FOR THE PROCESS

The design and development process being described here can be done manually. However, it begins to gain power as it becomes computer supported. Essentially, the goal is to provide easy and natural mechanisms for recording the design process and presenting different views of the evolving design throughout the lifecycle of the system. Of particular importance is the ability to efficiently alter the design when appropriate during coding and optimization of the system.

A new system of 200 classes and 3,000 methods is far too complex to do *ad hoc* "estimates of its performance." A design method for such a system must allocate a time budget for each method and a space budget for each class. Recording and tabulating this type of information will uncover some major deficiencies in the anticipated system early in the design phase. It will also help the designer discover the actual driving requirements. For example, if you are building a spreadsheet package in a tightly constrained memory environment (say 500 K), managing space is going to be as important a design consideration as functionality. Computer support becomes mandatory to record and analyze issues such as time and space in the evolving design.

Design changes may require the designer to consider the impact of those changes. Change impact analysis is another important role for the automated design tool. Various approaches can be taken to deal with the impact of change. One approach is to simply provide a report that lists the inconsistencies as a result of change; another would be to deal with inconsistencies at the point of origin.

A change cannot be made and committed to the system unless its consequent impacts are dealt with. Design changes will involve not only changes made by an individual designer to that person's solitary design, but must be able to cope with the considerably more difficult issues involving the coordination of changes among a group of designers working in parallel and at high speed.

Let me conclude with a word to the computer-aided software engineering (CASE) vendors. Many of the readers of this book will be sitting in front of 100 MIPS of processing power, a few gigabytes of local storage, and a high-resolution color monitor. Stop writing CASE tools using static black-and-white line drawings. We want color, animation, and pleasure from our tools. Also, as good object-oriented designers we never start from scratch. Instead, we typically begin with 500 or more previously written classes. We want to be able to express them in your tool quickly and efficiently, in at least a semiautomatic way.

SUMMARY

The goal of a design and development method is to improve the odds of customers arriving at the door of a software development shop. Reuse is the key to their ultimate happiness. But providing a development team with a warehouse full of undocumented, untested components is no help. Effective reuse will require object-oriented languages, but it will also require a design management system that will facilitate the design, development, and reuse of quality components. Such a system is not just a suite of CASE tools; it is also the set of management procedures required within the project and the organization.

Hopefully, this chapter has planted seeds to stimulate serious investments and motivate experiments to ensure that such a comprehensive environment will be in common use by the beginning of the next century. Let's also hope that these systems provide both design and implementation support for ensembles of classes.

Building such an environment is a large undertaking but is much easier than putting astronauts on the moon. It will also be worth much more to business, technology, and society.

NOTES

1. Two people played an influential role in the development of the ideas presented in this chapter: Ivar Jacobson of Objective Systems, Stockholm, Sweden, and Mack Alford of Ascent Logic, San Jose, California.
2. An elevation is a drawing of a vertical cross section through the house.
3. If we assume a modest productivity effect due to the application of preexisting components, such systems should be equivalent in capability to traditional systems with 200,000 – 500,000 source lines of code—about the size of major applications or small commercial operating systems.
4. See Chapter 1 of Brad Cox's *Object-Oriented Programming* (Addison-Wesley, Reading, MA, 1986) for an excellent description of some approaches for dealing with change in software systems.
5. See Patti Dock's article in the July 1992 issue of the *Hotline on Object-Oriented Technology*, SIGS Publications, New York, for some metrics on design methods.
6. Modifying the scenarios amounts to changing the requirements based upon further analysis.
7. F. Kerlinger, *Foundations of Behavioral Research*, Holt, Rinehart and Winston, New York, 1973.
8. Thanks are extended to Dr. Anatole Holt, who first described interaction diagrams to me in 1981 at ITT Corporation.
9. These guys are good; give them a call at (919) 481-4000.
10. Call Ascent Logic at (408) 943-0630 for details on their products.
11. For some metrics on module coupling and strength, see Glenford Myers's classic book, *Composite/Structured Design*, Van Nostrand Reinhold, New York, 1978.

7

Pickled Objects

Presumably, man's spirit should be elevated
if he can better review his shady past and analyze more
completely and objectively his present problems.

Vannevar Bush
Atlantic Monthly, 1945

Most object-oriented programming languages were designed with the implicit assumption that objects are activated and deactivated during the execution of one "program" under the control of one programmer. While these assumptions are likely to be true for most objects during the program development process, they are explicitly not true for most objects in delivered commercial systems. Commerce depends upon the creation of durable objects of value.

The intent of this chapter is to explain the relationship between objects and databases. It will begin with the idea of persistent objects—storing an object onto a permanent media and retrieving it. Second, it will discuss how traditional data management systems can be used to support some object-oriented applications. Then, it will describe object-oriented databases (OODBs) and how they can be utilized to construct important new classes of applications. We will conclude with a look into the future at an even more powerful approach for designing durable applications and systems.

The intent of this chapter is not to provide a comprehensive tutorial on any of the topics presented here; that would require another book unto itself. Instead, the intent is to cover the basics for professionals involved in the design of innovative new object-oriented applications and systems.

MOTIVATIONS FOR DATABASES

Programs written in the 1940s had the interesting characteristic that it was difficult to tell what was program and what was data. As we began to develop higher-level programming languages and mass storage devices, we began to create data files and program files. The physical media undoubtedly influenced our thought process about the work we were doing—data processing meant reading a data deck, processing it, and printing a report.

As the scale of what we attempted began to increase, the sheer numbers of people involved in the collection of data and the writing of programs to process it increased dramatically. It was inevitable that we develop a strong need for middlemen. The professional middleman provides a valuable service by understanding work going on in two domains and building a bridge between the two. In commercial data processing applications, a middleman automaton was conceived to solve the problems that arose when too many people needed access to the same data for too many reasons. Programmers needed to make changes in the interrelationships among the data records, users of the reports needed up-to-date access to the information for business decision making, and those involved in acquiring the data needed to continue to add incoming information to the data repository. These needs were not without their conflicts.

Database management systems (DBMSs) were introduced into organizations to solve an organizational problem, not a technical problem. In the beginning, databases' primary role was to resolve this inherent conflict by removing the responsibility for data management from the programmers. DBMSs were pieces of software that provided facilities for defining the structure of data, controlling access to that data, and providing a variety of other important data services such as security, backup, and concurrency control.

The initial problem to be solved by DBMSs was not to provide more efficient access to data within a broader range of applications. The original goal was much more prosaic: "I don't want to discover a horrendous error in the monthly balance sheet because some programmer has changed the record layouts without telling everyone." Efficiency became a growing concern, but it was surely not the motivation for the introduction of databases in the first place.

Neither was it ever a major concern of database designers to cope with high-entropy, complex structure applications. Their model was spreadsheets where every cell was a number—typically a dollar amount.

Because much of what got stored in databases was financial information, the security and availability of that information became a paramount consideration. Computers have never been perfectly reliable devices. When they crash, they should not destroy the businesses that bought them. The recovery goal would be to be able to "roll back to the last transaction" and start from there. Controls also had to be designed in to provide consistency checking and update control so that what was in the database was what its users expected.

Another key problem was the need to be able to store vast amounts of information as efficiently as possible. Disk space was still expensive in the 1960s and tapes were slow and awkward to cope with. A companion problem was the early discovery that if the same chunk of information was stored in two places, one would be out of date. Data needed to be stored nonredundantly wherever possible.

One of the first approaches taken was to organize the information hierarchically with the constraint that there was a one-to-many relationship between nodes and subnodes. For example, a branch office would have certain identifying information associated with the branch office, but it could also be connected to several employees working in that branch office - one office, many employees. The information about the office is stored once and can be ensured to be the same for all employees within the office.

While an amazing number of applications can be successfully modeled by a hierarchical approach, there are enough that can't be to motivate the construction of a network data model. Such a model provided a many-to-many relationship among specified data entities.

Some brilliant information theorists realized that an even more powerful possibility was to create a set of tables that were linked by a common column. Queries that were not answerable from within a single file could be answered by joining these files or relations to discover the correct answer. To the surprise of many, such relational databases provided considerable power and acceptable performance.

THE NEED FOR PERSISTENCE

For years, smart engineering managers have asked, "Why can't we use a commercial DBMS rather than building our own in this new computer-aided design (CAD) system?" Let's take a look at some of the challenges of data management in this specific application area, namely, VLSI design.[1]

Databases for integrated circuit/computer-aided design

It takes several months, many people, and a host of highly specialized tools to design a modern microprocessor. One can think of this process as involving the progressive refinement of a model of the integrated circuit (IC). At various stages during the specification, design, and fabrication of that IC, the designers need to see different "views" of the evolving IC and perform a variety of checks to ensure that the IC functions correctly and can be produced reliably. In fact, seven different views of an IC are used:

- geometric (rectangles)
- electrical (transistors/resistors)
- logical (boolean)
- behavioral
- test
- mathematical
- natural language (English)

Microprocessors now contain millions of electronic components. A designer of an IC is not interested in seeing everything all the time. Instead, he or she needs to view the evolving chip at differing levels of granularity and to "see" the same information in different forms. In fact, there is a need to generate, analyze, and modify all seven views at multiple levels of abstraction while ensuring that all views remain consistent. Servicing this demanding requirement is both an application design problem and a data management problem.[2]

Traditional database technology is not in widespread use in IC/CAD applications. Database technology has been found inadequate due to the complexity of IC/CAD applications, the amount of data involved, the rate of change of the data, the need for interactive performance, and the inherent complexity of the data structures involved. Complex data types like polygons, lines, pins, capacitors, and resistors need to be represented, manipulated, and stored. Also, multilevel composites of lower-level components need to be represented as blocks with predefined functional behavior, physical space requirements, and defined logical behavior.

Relational databases are inadequate for IC/CAD applications because relational database management systems (RDBMSs) assume a small, simple set of basic data types that are relatively static and also assume short discrete transactions. RDBMSs also assume that the data types are relatively static and the data dynamic. In the IC/CAD example, both the data and its structure are dynamic. The typical transaction is of extremely long duration, possibly months! These challenges are complicated by the sheer quantity of data required[3] and by highly paid users who demand smashingly fast performance in doing their interactive design. Essentially every decision made by designers of relational database systems proves invalid for VLSI design applications.

CAD—the tip of an iceberg

IC/CAD applications are one example of a class of applications for which relational or hierarchic data management systems have proven inadequate. One of the first object database companies attempting to build OODBs, ONTOS, Inc. provides the diagram in Figure 7.1 as a way to sort out the applicability of various data management approaches.

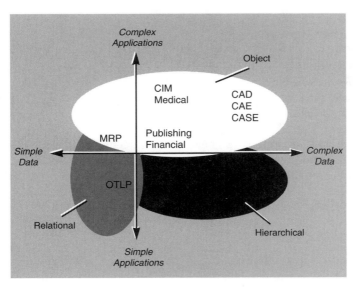

Figure 7.1.

The diagram is missing a third axis-response time required. For example, if a complex application with complex data needs to run overnight, any of several data management schemes might be appropriate. By contrast, if that same application has to run on a workstation connected to a host machine via a local area network (LAN) while a human awaits the result, many fewer options will exist. The particular point shown above is one where the requirement is for fast, interactive response time.

In the IC/CAD example, the need is not to store objects onto disks and retrieve them as required. Rather, the need is for all the capabilities of a commercial DBMS. These capabilities include:

- *Backup:* goal is to ensure a minimum loss of data in the case of an unpredictable and catastrophic failure of hardware or software.
- *Restart/recovery:* ability to recover and restart a database after a major failure.
- *Concurrency control:* control for multiple users attempting to modify the same data at the same time.
- *Data distribution:* data files may be distributed across multiple systems and disks.
- *Query facilities including standard query language (SQL) compatibility:* ability to do *ad hoc* queries against the database using SQL commands if the user chooses.
- *Security:* ability to limit access to selected data within the database as required.
- *Integrity:* a change to the database cannot cause other data in the database to be left in an inconsistent or incorrect state.
- *Schema modification:* as changes to the data definitions (schema) are made, facilities are provided to allow data to migrate as easily as possible to the newly defined database schema.

Let's look at four options for dealing with persistent objects, some of which will assist IC/CAD designers.

FOUR RECIPES FOR PICKLING OBJECTS

Persistent objects

If an object knows its class at run time, that class information can be used to store the object and its dependent objects onto permanent storage. In effect, the class definition is a schema that defines the physical structure and semantic content of the data contained within an object. Because classes are also defined as objects, the procedural content or methods for a given object can be permanently stored using the same machinery.

If all objects in a system know their class at run time, some especially powerful capabilities become available. For example, an application or system can be halted at any arbitrary point and the state of that application or system preserved without prior planning. In other words, a snapshot of a system can be taken by simply commanding all the objects in the system to store themselves onto disk. The process can easily be made reversible so that information loaded from permanent storage can be used to recreate the running system or application.[4] Even more interesting is the prospect of designing systems that routinely maintain shadow objects in one or more physically separate computers and physical storage devices.

This ability to passivate and activate objects critically depends upon the fact that objects know their class or type at run time. Not all object-oriented languages have this feature. Also, in hybrid object-oriented languages one cannot guarantee that any data structure defined in the base language can be deactivated correctly. See the respective language reference manual for more details.

It is surprising how many commercial applications have been built using activation/passivation of objects instead of a full-fledged data management system or object management system. This is an excellent approach to take for newcomers to objects, even if query, redundancy, and security are important requirements for the system later. Let the application drive the object management choice, not vice versa.

Once we have a mechanism in place for storing and retrieving objects from permanent storage, entirely new system building opportunities arise. For example, we are no longer required to think of all the objects for a given system residing in main memory. Nor do we need to think about the names of objects as being unique to a single machine address space. Nor are we obligated to think about single CPUs. Said differently, objects that know their types at run time are key to distributed processing.

While dynamic objects enable the construction of distributed systems, they alone are hardly sufficient. Other important issues related to distributed systems must be solved. The "send, wait" messaging semantics will not work. A global naming scheme for objects must be developed. Consideration must be given to the traffic bottlenecks created as a result of interprocessor messaging. Concurrency controls must be established to cope with conflicts arising when two or more messages are sent to the same object at the same time. With dynamic objects, this myriad of problems becomes tractable. Without objects, they are not.

So persistent objects are themselves extraordinarily valuable to the contemporary system builder. But persistent objects alone do not have some important facilities, such as query, backup, integrity control, security, and redundancy.

Objects with a RDBMS

Why couldn't we use a relational database as the back-end store for objects, thus combining the strengths of the two worlds? You can, but don't expect magic.

A relational database is optimized to deal with atomic data stored as tables (relations) of small, fixed-sized values (attributes). A table can be thought of as a structured file, a tuple or row within the table as a record, and an attribute as a value or field within a cell of the table. The information contained within relations varies over time; the structure of the relations should not vary often.

Database systems separate the storage of data from the schema that describe the logical relationships among the stored data. It is considered crucial that the database schema be stable. Database designers advise, "the conceptual schema should not have to be changed unless some adjustment in the real world requires some definition to be adjusted too, so that it may continue to reflect reality."[5] Extending the conceptual schema to reflect a larger reality is well supported and is not considered a change to the conceptual schema.

Objects involve complex data structures of variable size. Objects combine data and procedures. Class objects describe the data structures within an object and the object's relationship to other objects (data structures and procedures). Procedures can be stored as data.

From the start, then, we see that databases are hardly optimized for dealing with objects and assume a much simpler data model. Nevertheless, commercial databases have important facilities that are not easily duplicated, such as re-start/recovery, support for multiple users, data redundancy, and data security. Despite these differences, we might be better off using a commercial database than trying to hack one together or even to rely upon a very new object-oriented database.

In particular object-oriented applications, it might be appropriate to store and retrieve certain objects using a commercial database. The criteria might be any stable objects that can easily be mapped to a relation (table with small, fixed-size values), deactivated, and stored in a relational database with acceptable efficiency. I know of an example where a computer-aided software engineering (CASE) company was using an entity-relationship-attribute (ERA) model for their designs. Despite the fact that their system was built entirely with objects, it was appropriate to store ERA objects in a relational database instead of trying to use rather immature OODBs or, worse still, build their own. This approach worked because the objects were uniform in structure and easily mappable to relations.

This CASE company also did not design their system with the assumption that the instant a change is made by one designer it will be immediately available to all other designers. Rather, they assumed that a designer would check out an evolving design, work on it for a period of time, and release it back to the database. If it was checked out and being worked on, other users would be notified but still had the opportunity to check it out and work on it simultaneously. If conflicts arose during check-in, tools were constructed to identify those conflicts and allow the respective participants to resolve them.[6]

As the structure of the data begins to change and the dynamics of its use increase, the requirement for an object-oriented database becomes more compelling. But many important commercial applications do not have such requirements and can use traditional databases to support object-oriented applications perfectly adequately.

OODBs

Let's take a deeper look at what we can really expect from OODBs, attempt to state some underlying principles, and address the practical issue of how these new databases relate to those we already have.

Introduction to OODBs. The recent applications in office information and knowledge-based systems and electronic and mechanical CAD environments, made possible by the developments in personal computers and workstations, require capabilities like the creation of novel data types— such as documents, graphic images, and sound—that are not adequately supported by current DBMSs.

Object-oriented programming has become popular in the design and implementation of these data-intensive applications because, as we have seen earlier, it offers a number of important advantages over traditional approaches toward design and implementation, such as:

1. the modeling of conceptual entities with single elements, objects, that completely define the semantics of the entities
2. the inheritance of properties from one or more classes to which the object may belong
3. the ability to accomplish far more efficient updates to databases based upon dependencies among objects rather than enormous numbers of rerun transactions

Current object-oriented programming language models only consider objects as residing in random access memory and ignore a number of typical "database issues," such as additions, deletions, persistence, dynamic changes, queries, versions, and integrity. This works if the number of in-memory objects to be manipulated is relatively small and the objects do not need to be used beyond the system's boundaries.

However, most commercial applications require thousands of objects and large amounts of working and virtual memory. Moreover, these applications need to easily communicate with objects or their classes across system boundaries. To access the created persistent objects, stored in mass memory easily, safely, and efficiently, an object base should have its own management system analogous to DBMSs that is based upon an object model.

Existing object-oriented language systems exhibit significant differences in their support for such a paradigm, and persistent object bases (POBs) are still in either a developmental or early application stage. This leads to differences in the underlying models and the terminology and to rapidly evolving capabilities within the different OODBs.

All OODBs more or less adopt the following concepts:

1. Objects represent entities and concepts from the application domain being modeled. Their behavior is defined by their associated methods or procedures that are also stored in the OODB. In this way, relationships or operations that span applications are kept with the data, thus enhancing their availability compared to having them as procedures in certain programs.

2. Hierarchies of classes inherit behavior and structure from their superclass(es). If every object is stored as a separate entity, the amount of information to be specified and stored could become unmanageably large. To avoid the storage of redundant information and improve conceptual simplicity, similar objects are grouped together into a class, inheriting their generic behavior and structure from their superclasses.

In addition, a number of OODBs provide the capability to define and manipulate a set of objects as a logical entity. Such composite objects consist of either an unordered collection of objects (**Sets** and **Bags**) or a hierarchical structure of dependent objects. For example, the composite object *Vehicle* contains a *Vehicle-body* object, which has a set of *Door-objects*, and each *Door-object* has a *Position-object* and a *Color-object*.

The relationship expressed by this dependent hierarchy is different from the one expressed by the class hierarchy. The subclass-class-superclass hierarchy mentioned earlier implements the IS-A relationship: The Irish Setter "Johnny" can be characterized as an object, identifiable as "Johnny," belonging to the class Irish-setter, which belongs to the superclass Domestic-dog. This relationship reads as "Johnny" IS-A "Irish Setter," IS-A "Domestic dog." As an Irish Setter, Johnny is different from a German-shepherd, another subclass of Domestic-dog. Both dogs inherit their dog-like characteristics from this common superclass. The hierarchical structure of the composite object implements the IS-PART-OF relationship. A *Door* IS-PART-OF a *Vehicle-body* IS-PART-OF a *Vehicle*. The constituent objects of Vehicle are dependent objects; their existence is dependent upon the existence of the object they depend on: If there is no *vehicle*, there are no *Doors* for the vehicle.

Other features of OODBs include:

1. Version control - extremely important for systems such as CAD systems, business systems, office information systems, and software engineering environments. In these applications, users often need to generate and experiment with multiple versions of objects before selecting one that satisfies their requirements.

2. Dynamic schema modification - allows a user to (dynamically) modify class definitions and inheritance structures.

3. Handling of (predicate-based) queries.

Underlying principles. The basic premise of OODBs is that object languages are complete enough to handle database design, database access, and application development. These languages also provide a user-extensible data typing facility. In contrast, traditional DBMSs are restricted to a small, finite set of data types and constrained in their usage because of the heavy costs of schema modification.

We could describe the goal as being able to have full database capabilities available to any object that can be created in any object programming language. The object can be created and stored in the database with a minimum of additional work; the database provides a query language, security, integrity, backup, concurrency control, and appropriate redundancy. It also must provide all these capabilities with very nearly the performance of a hand-tuned object manager specialized for this particular application or system.

This cannot be done. It violates several of the natural laws of data storage and retrieval:

- The more I know about the data, the more likely and the faster it can be found.
- The sooner I know what you want, the faster you will get it.
- The less variety in the data you have, the more opportunities for optimization.
- The less often you restructure the data, the less overhead in keeping track of it.
- The more people from more places who want access to the data, the tougher the problem of serving them.
- The more often you want to ask the same questions, the easier it will be to optimize for those queries.
- It will be much faster to "give you what you stored" than to find some new pattern contained in several "things" that you stored.
- The more complicated the pattern you search for, the longer the search will take.

Objects have the potential for infinite variety. They can be of nearly any size and may change in size often and structure occasionally. The structure of the object could change just before it is committed to the object base. Many objects are composed of other objects. You can never achieve maximum performance with a system designed for maximum flexibility.

Structure-intensive or multimedia applications, where the requirement is to deal with a substantial variety of information types and the complexity of the basic data models is high (such as in engineering, geographic, or software engineering databases), often require OODBs.

Transaction-based, performance-intensive systems, such as airline reservation or banking systems, where speed is essential and data complexity is modest, will not be good candidates for OODBs in the near future.

Compatibility of OODBs with RDBMSs

As stated earlier, applications that have successfully been developed using a RDBMS can probably use a RDBMS to store and retrieve objects successfully, whereas applications such as CAD systems that have not been able to successfully use RDBMSs cannot all of a sudden work successfully because an object-oriented application has been developed.

The open question will be the degree to which OODBs can displace traditional databases. We should expect that OODBs will follow a similar trajectory to that followed by relational databases. As the technology matures and the products become increasingly optimized, we can expect the performance differential between OODBs and RDBMSs to become sufficiently small that system designers will begin to employ OODBs in applications that were previously considered the eminent domain of one or another of the traditional database models. The small loss in efficiency will be adequately repaid by gain in value to the end user by virtue of having additional capabilities previously unachievable.

Just as pure object-oriented programming languages are being used for applications that would have been unthinkable even five years ago, OODBs will enjoy an ever-widening domain of application. But even objects have their limitations, as we will see in the following section.

COORDINATION

Constructing new objects is much easier than storing those objects in some repository where they can be properly retrieved by someone else from another computer at another location. As much or more work may be involved in storage and retrieval strategies as in developing the original system or application. In most cases, the solution will not be as simple as buying an OODB and using it within an application or system.

A well-known example: CASE

One image always arises when I hear people discussing the need for a database or a persistent object base. That image (see Figure 7.2) shows a database surrounded by tens of application programs that can store and retrieve data from that central database.[7]

Think about a system built according to this design. How much online data can it store?[8] How many users can it support? How many applications can use a

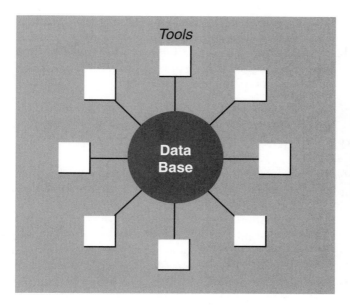

Figure 7.2. The classic spider diagram used to show how tools could all interact with a single centralized database. It does not work.

single data repository? How do we structure the data to provide the information required for all those applications while still ensuring subsecond response time to users? What is the effect on performance if the development group using this common data repository is geographically distributed with poor communications? Who has permission to change what data? If a change is made to data and some failure results, who is responsible and how is that responsible person identified? What happens if the data repository is damaged or lost? What risks exist due to unauthorized access to centralized information?

Any system designed with a single central data store has some important constraints. By analogy, I think of a human information processing system designed according to this scheme. The organizational analogy would be creating a central filing system within an organization. All manila folders that are not being changed must reside in one place. With even a small-scale organization, the central filing system simply breaks down. It takes too long to access important information, critical information gets lost, and workers spend far too much time trying to devise a filing system capable of supporting the needs of their users.

Once the design is expanded beyond a single data repository, new complexities are introduced. If two copies exist of the same data entity, which is the "correct" one? How can the structure of the two repositories remain consistent as changes are made to each?

If a data item in one data repository is dependent upon an item in another, how is this dependency recorded, and how efficiently is the proper update accomplished? Suppose one repository fails; can the other remain operational? Instead of 2 data repositories, suppose there are 200.

The problem is that we often ask technology to solve inappropriate problems for us. I don't believe a general-purpose distributed DBMS can be built that solves all the needs of a typical company. We must rethink the problem and redesign our solutions.

PEOPLE IN THE LOOP

Trying to solve business-critical information management problems without having "people in the loop" is simply a mistake. There is no "system to take care of it"; there are only people who sometimes use machines. Let's consider some real examples.

If I want to find out how much cash a corporation has available, I want the chief financial officer to find the answer and take the responsibility for the accuracy of that answer. If I want to find out how many software trouble reports have been filed in the last six months, I want the quality manager to determine the answer and certify to me that it is correct. If I need to develop a monthly report for a board meeting that involves input from each department within a company, I want the desired information to be collected, scrutinized, and then reported to a person who has the responsibility for assembling the information and presenting it to me for review prior to distribution. I do not want complete automation of these tasks; I want a human being accountable for the answers they provide!

Of course, I want all the respective individuals working with the most economic and productive information system that we can afford. I do not want the maximum degree of automation. I want correct answers, provided promptly and economically.

The scheme that seems most general and applicable for large-scale information processing tasks is one proposed by Anatole Holt and described by Holt, Ramsey, and Grimes.[9] Any information-processing system can be decomposed into activity centers with defined roles and interactions. An activity center (think office) contains private data (think filing cabinet), specialized tools (think software, computers, and support staff), and a person (think manager) responsible for that activity center. At any point in time, a designated person has assumed an operational role in a particular activity center. As a part of the overall organization design, both the mission and scope of an activity center are defined along with their interactions with other activity centers.

If a responsible individual would like to delegate routine requests for information to a computer program, he or she is capable of doing so. But that individual retains the responsibility for the quality and accuracy of the information provided. A responsible person remains in the loop, supplying and verifying the supplied information.

Note that many activity centers will be supported by one or more databases or persistent object bases. Complex queries will often require multiple activity centers to accumulate information, report it in agreed-upon formats, and allow it to be analyzed in another activity center. This model of information processing scales to an arbitrarily large problem—the Pentagon's war room, IBM's strategic planning group, an oil field reservoir modeling problem, or a three-person software company.

If we step back and look at coordination systems from the perspective of a book on object-oriented programming, we can think of them as a natural evolution of object technology. Activity centers are organizational objects that interact by sending messages to other activity centers. Both data and procedures exist within an activity center. An important change is that a human being sits at the interface between activity centers and is responsible for sending and receiving messages. That person is responsible even if he or she has fully delegated their responsibility to an electronic device using software.

In coordination systems, we see encapsulation, dynamic binding, and message passing fully implemented. Even a type of inheritance exists in that certain procedures and forms become agreed upon as standard within a particular subset of an organization. Everyone uses the same expense account form, but salespeople have a time card that includes more detail about customers visited, miles traveled, entertainment expenses, and status of evolving sales. Another important difference is that message passing is asynchronous and occurs in parallel.

To apply this coordination thinking near term, ask yourself how accountability is preserved in the particular system you are involved in designing and developing? In other words, suppose something goes terribly wrong and someone loses a lot of data, money, or lives. How do you determine the individual responsible? Can responsibility still be determined in the case of catastrophic failure? Could you be responsible without realizing it?

COORDINATING COMPONENT EXPERTS

Coordination technology may become an important enabling technology for the creation of a business in reusable software components. As we have seen throughout this book, one of the major challenges to widespread use of existing software components is the effort required to study and understand components, to be able to reuse them. With interesting applications requiring hundreds if not thousands of components, the study time can become immense—literally years.

An alternative model is to partition the component library so that each person is responsible for a manageable set of components, say 50. Learning 50 components should only require a few months of effort, and a person should be capable of being absolutely current with any internally generated or externally supplied changes to those components. For larger projects, we can add more people even though there will be some loss of efficiency for every new person added to the project. The prudent manager would always assign at least two people to each set of components.

To secure the right component involves a process of consulting an expert in a defined area of expertise. That person then provides the best-known component along with a suggestion of how it might be used in the particular application or system. Such an approach scales rather well and can work successfully on the largest of systems. It is almost certain to be more effective than hypertext, associative retrieval, relational databases, or artificial intelligence solutions to the component retrieval problem. Vannevar Bush summarized this chapter perfectly when he said, "*For mature thought there is no mechanical substitute.*" What more can be said?

NOTES

1. The author extends thanks to his friends at Philips in Holland for helping him understand the software challenges facing the IC/CAD developer.
2. For a description of one of the first serious attempts to apply objects in the VLS1 design domain, see Pieter S. van der Meulen, *Proceedings of OOPSLA '87.*
3. It is often hundreds of megabytes per transaction and hundreds of gigabytes for a single design.
4. For more details on the filer mechanism, see Brad Cox, *Object-Oriented Programming*, Addison-Wesley, Reading, MA, 1986, pp. 127–130.
5. C. J. Date, *An Introduction to Database Systems*, Addison-Wesley, Reading, MA, 1977, p. 427.
6. This approach is called optimistic concurrency control in the technical literature.
7. For a classic example, see figure 2 on p. 14 of *Software Magazine*, March 1988, devoted to CASE.
8. It is important to know that for any instance of a CASE system there are answers to each of these questions. Unlimited is never an answer.
9. A. Holt, H. R. Ramsey, and J. D. Grimes, Coordination system technology as the basis for programming environments, *ITT Electrical Communications* 57:307–314, 1983.

West
Portico

Monticello Floor Plan
*The shaded portions indicate
the outline of the first house*

Parlor

Porticle

Cabinet
(Study)

Jefferson's
Bedroom

Dining
Room

Tea
Room

South Terrace

Mezzanine

Gallery

North Ter

South
Piazza
(Greenhouse)

Library

Passage

Passage

North
Piazza

Porticle
(Aviary)

Library

Hall

South
Square
Room
(Library)

North
Square
Room

Chamber

East
Portico

Floor plan of the second Monticello.

8

*Providing
an Environment*

*Graphical excellence is that which gives the viewer
the greatest number of ideas in the shortest time
with the least ink in the smallest space.*

Edward R. Tufte
The Visual Display of Graphical Information

In the early 1980s, I assembled and managed a group of capable technical people responsible for designing and prototyping the 1985 Advanced Programming Environment (APE) for ITT. Our objective was to design and build a next-generation programming environment for internal use in building commercial telephone switching systems at ITT. The stated objective was to achieve a 10-fold increase in programmer productivity.

In preparing to write this chapter, I reread the documents we produced for this project. It was striking how desirable our imagined 1985 environment would still be in 1992!

Our 1980 specification for a programming environment is still an appropriate place to start. Let us begin by describing what we meant by environment and what kind of hardware and software is required to support such an environment.

THE 1985 APE

The purpose of a programming environment is to provide automation for the full variety of activities involved in developing a commercial software product. The emphasis should be on the word *environment*. A programming environment includes not only the computational but the physical, social, organizational, and cultural aspects of one's environment. It should be "a total facility that enables programmers, their managers, and support personnel to accomplish the programming function efficiently."[1]

The humanistic aspects of the development environment are the most difficult to design, measure, or change, yet they may be the largest single determinant of the organization's productivity. A newly painted wall may increase productivity more than any new programming tool. We will not spend much time talking about these issues, but it would be a total mistake to discount their importance.

TYPES OF TOOLS

The most important aspect of a development environment is its ability to facilitate work among a group of individuals. We labeled tools that support communication among individuals "contact tools." By contrast, "solitary tools" are tools used by an individual to accomplish private work. The result of that private work is communicated to others using a contact tool. A compiler is a solitary tool; electronic mail is a contact tool.

Another important insight was that solitary tools may themselves require contact tools. A compiler is a perfect example. As typically used, a compiler is a solitary tool, one per programmer. But compilers change. A different group is responsible for supporting and evolving the compiler. How is the compiler upgraded? A set of contact tools is required to coordinate the operation.

At ITT, we realized that most builders of programming environments had focused on building solitary tools. Far too little effort had gone into the design and construction of contact tools. Our idea was, therefore, to buy the solitary tools and build the contact tools.

Actually, this idea was new only to us. It was a very old idea to Dr. Douglas Englebart, then of SRI. In the 1960s, while working under contract to ARPA (now DARPA), he designed and built an incredibly capable office automation system, called NLS (for oN-Line System). NLS was the first system to use a mouse, split the screen into windows, support collaborative writing, and provide an outline processor. And it worked perfectly well for two users separated by a continent connected by both a voice and data link.[2]

ACTIVITY CENTERS

Dr. Anatole Holt, who began as a consultant to the ITT/APE project, suggested that we think of an environment as a collection of activity centers communicating in specified ways. One person within each activity center is designated to be responsible for the center's work. This person is supported by a specialized set of solitary tools, information, and procedures. Contact tools support the interaction among activity centers.

Dr. Holt used "organic diagrams" to describe his notions of environments and activity centers (see Figure 8.1). The lines circumscribe the activity centers, the circle denotes the responsible individual, and the dots depict the resources available within a center to accomplish work.

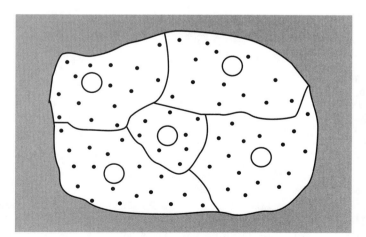

*Figure 8.1.
An environment
and its activity
centers.[3]*

An individual can fulfill different roles within different activity centers. A first-line software manager might sometimes take on the role of team manager and at other times perform the role of programmer. These two capacities require different information, different solitary tools, and different contact tools.

The beauty of these ideas is that they can be used to describe both manual and computer-assisted work. From such a description, one can begin to propose new solitary and contact tools to support the ongoing work of professional software developers and related support personnel.

What we were really doing was applying the object-oriented concept of encapsulation of data and methods to model organizational behavior.

Let's now turn to more prosaic issues associated with programming environments, such as the hardware and software they require.

Hardware and Software Capabilities

In December 1980, we estimated that a 32-bit CPU with 1 Mb of memory, 100 Mb of disk storage, a 1,000 × 1,000 pixel display, and voice input and output would cost ITT $10,000 in 1990.

Table 8.1. Estimated vs. actual 1990 hardware costs for a software engineering workstation.

Item	Estimated cost ($)	Actual cost ($)
32-bit CPU with 1Mb of RAM	2,000	2,000
100-Mb disk	3,000	1,200
Large-format graphics display	3,000	1,500
Voice input/output	2,000	1,200
Total	10,000	5,900

As you can see from Table 8.1, we were pessimistic. An Apple Macintosh SE with a large-screen display and 1 Mb of RAM is considerably less expensive than the estimated $10,000. (However, few developers in 1990 would actually have been satisfied with only 1 Mb of memory.) Voice I/O is also available for well under $2,000.[4]

In 1990, most software developers working on a Macintosh would require at least 8 Mb of RAM and would want 16 or 32. So, it turns out that our estimates of hardware costs were more accurate than our estimates of "hardware desire."

We imagined a software development environment that included the following:

- comprehensive coordination tools to support all members of the development organization that included voice messaging and annotations
- language compilers, interpreters, and debugging tools
- project management tools that not only allowed for estimation but also did real-time project tracking based upon up-to-the-second information from developers
- analysis and design tools that allowed for dynamic system simulation and comprehensive traceability of requirements
- powerful desktop publishing tools to allow for the publication of numerous documents required by customers and end users of the target software products
- comprehensive real-time testing tools for distributed systems

Our software estimates were wildly optimistic. The estimates were optimistic in terms of costs and availability. We estimated that a typical software developer would spend $5,000 on software for this 1990 software engineering workstation. That is a substantial underestimate for the amount of functionality envisioned. The software cost estimate was off by a factor of five.

A machine such as the NeXT is a better model of what we actually envisioned. It has more processing power, a lot more memory, a higher-resolution display, a tremendous amount of bundled software, and substantial audio capabilities. It sells for a price near the estimated $10,000. It has no voice recognition capabilities, although such a capability would be easy to add because all the required hardware is in place.

We can see from this experience that hardware costs and functionality can be reasonably accurately predicted, even a decade in advance. By contrast, software demands on that hardware and the rate of producing the envisioned software capability were not accurately predicted at all.

In trying to understand software development environments, let's start by looking at what exists today. Then, let's decide where we should be and determine how we can get there.

WHERE SHOULD ENVIRONMENTS BE?

A proper software engineering environment should make the software engineer more productive and retain the corporate software components in a standardized form that can be accessed by others within the company as required.

We must provide a software development process and environment in which rigorously characterized, definitively tested units of function are available for integration into new systems. These units of function must be reusable across many systems and applications; they must also be accessible through electronic catalogs. The development process must lead to components that are properly specified, designed, tested, and indexed. Each component must provide a specified margin of safety in its use. Tools must also link diverse components with a minimum of hand-crafted code.

The environment and the development process should be seamlessly bound together instead of disconnected. Such a seamless connection would provide both a forward and a backward link between any line of code and the relevant specification and design documents.

SOFTWARE AS AN ASSET

From a business perspective, the software environment belongs to the corporation; it must support the business interests of the corporation. A proper environment should stimulate a continuing stream of innovative new products and lead to higher corporate earnings. It must also be designed to obtain and retain the software assets acquired, developed, and supported within that environment. For this reason, better environments are actually more important for the survival of software engineering companies than they are for software engineers.

One of the fundamental responsibilities of a manager is to create and preserve the assets of the corporation. A software manager must build software such that the asset represented by that software is preserved independently of the original developers.

Software is a corporate asset and should be thought of that way. Every subroutine, tool, documentation aid, training manual, and test case generator, no matter how small, represents an investment that the company has made either to acquire or develop the capability. A software development environment is that set of tools, facilities, methods, and procedures that supports the development of new software and, more importantly, retains the software assets of a company.

Looked at in this way, it becomes clear that environments will take time to be developed, will cost real money to construct, and must be highly customized for each organization. Software tools and components can be bought as required to support this customized development.

Imagine a system supporting a team of developers designing and developing software in the fashion described in the previous chapter. It would offer a great improvement because it would create reusable code and designs. Systems that reuse designs and code can involve real innovation, not just a reimplementation of the subsystems and functions built many times before. Reusability leads to more functionality and a higher level of innovation.

Solitary programming tools

Present solitary programming tools include the standalone workstation and programming environments, both of which have been optimized for individual programmers. A solitary tool has one user and operates strictly within one activity center.

Workstations have created an image of individual autonomy and independence. "I can do whatever I like on my machine," programmers typically feel. Well, certainly they can unless a group assigned to building a new product must coordinate its efforts —the usual case!

The programming environments available to leading researchers today are a far cry from what exists on the desks of production software developers, data processing organizations, or universities. InterLisp and Smalltalk are considerably more advanced than VM/CMS or UNIX. What computer-aided software engineering (CASE) companies sell as programming environments are equally far removed and yet still incomplete.

Most computer scientists have been uninterested in the problems of large-system specification, design, and maintenance.[5] Research environments built at institutions such as MIT and Xerox PARC work spectacularly well for the individual and would be absolutely horrendous for use by a team of 100 programmers. I don't buy the argument that all important software can be built by a small team. We need systems that cannot be built by a small team, and we must provide environments to support large-scale system building. This is not to say we should use large teams to do small things. That is a terrible mistake in the software business.

For an excellent review of mid-1980s research into interactive programming environments, read Barstow, Shrobe, and Sandewall's *Interactive Programming Environments* (McGraw-Hill, New York, 1984). It includes papers by the developers of InterLisp, Smalltalk-80, the Programmer's Assistant, EMACS, UNIX, and Ada/Stoneman. Sandewall, Strömberg and Sîrensen's chapter "Software Architecture Based on Communicating Residential Environments" deserves special attention because it focuses directly on the issue of coordinating work flow within a programming or office environment. After reading this book, you will understand the magnitude of the job ahead for environment builders.

Contact tools

From a productivity standpoint, the most critical characteristic of an environment is that it supports group work. The world has built enough solitary programming tools; let us now begin to construct tools that support group endeavors.

CASE companies should supply contact tools that address the following development concerns:

- How can I acquire the most recent version of an evolving system?
- Who can alter the original design?
- Whom do I invite to my design review?
- How do I schedule the conference room?
- What happens when I find a bug in a software component?

A contact tool is a tool that involves more than one activity center. Electronic mail, configuration control systems, and group scheduling tools are examples of contact tools. If the tool environment is changing due to frequent releases of new software, solitary tools become contact tools. Contact tools will augment the database management systems that software environment builders have mistakenly assumed to provide the coordination within a development project.

Reusable components

Successful CASE companies must integrate components built by others, certify their own components, furnish documentation, and provide full service to their customers. CASE companies must provide not only the glue between the individually supplied tools but also the organizational glue required to support teams working with those tools.

Finally, we must remember that the humanistic aspects of the environment can never be forgotten. Without motivated, dedicated software engineers, a new system cannot be built regardless of the quality of the tools lying around in the workshop.

COMPARING ENVIRONMENTS

Any object-oriented programming system can be analyzed from three points of view: language, environment, and component library.

Languages

Object-oriented programming languages can be considered in three categories:

- *Pure:* any language that includes only objects and messages. A pure object-oriented system views everything as objects, even files on a disk or packets on a network. The most mature example is Smalltalk-80, whose development began at Xerox PARC in 1970. Smalltalk-80 creates a pure object-oriented environment by means of an interpreter, which translates the object view of the system to one that can be manipulated by the underlying operating system and hardware. Another example is Actor, developed by The Whitewater Group.

- *Extended:* a base language that adds objects while trying to follow the rules of the base language. Examples include Object-Pascal, developed at Apple Computer, and C++, developed at AT&T Bell Laboratories.

- *Hybrid:* a base language that adds the full semantics of objects and messages by adding an object level to the base language. A hybrid environment provides full access to object-oriented semantics and simultaneously to the traditional base language and its operating environment (operating system, file system, networks, and databases). Examples include Objective-C from The Stepstone Corporation and Dylan from Apple Computer.

Traditional systems programming languages such as C and Pascal have been used as base languages for extended or hybrid languages. However, there is no fundamental reason that languages such as FORTRAN or COBOL could not be used in the same way.

Pure object-oriented languages have the disadvantage that translating their simple message/object language into operational code results in some significant memory and performance penalties. The simpler the environment and the language, the easier it is to build powerful development environments.

Extensions to base languages provide a natural way for programmers accustomed to the base language to begin using objects and methods. Often, however, some important capabilities of pure object-oriented languages are omitted because they are incompatible with the underlying language, or the extensions are just poorly designed. The hybrid approach provides access to the lower-level procedural language while allowing a high-level object language to be used both for system structuring and higher-level applications programming.

Both extended and hybrid languages let you operate within traditional operating system environments and freely make calls to existing code written in other procedural languages. However, important environmental support for memory management and debugging becomes considerably more complex.

Extended and hybrid languages must confront another issue as well. Some argue that objects should look and feel different from the underlying procedural language, while advocates of extended languages feel no such need.

Both hybrid and extended languages allow an object's encapsulation to be violated from the procedural language. This can be an advantage during the optimization stage of a project. Later in the lifecycle, however, it can become a disadvantage if such optimization has created some subtle side effects or, worse, major distortions in the overall system structure.

Some object-oriented languages will prove much more difficult to debug than others (Smalltalk, for example, provides spectacular debugging facilities). When using pure object-oriented languages, if the bug occurs within the interpreter or external to the object-oriented environment, it can be nearly impossible to uncover.

Below, I attempted to provide my own assessment of five object-oriented programming languages. I have chosen a particular implementation because there can be a lot of variability across platforms or compiler vendors. The languages are rated on a 10-point scale, where 10 is a high score.

	Eiffel on Sun	Borland C++	Dylan	NeXT Obj-C	ST-80
Purity	7	1	8	5	10
Typing	10	8	8	4	1
Dynamism	10	5	10	10	10
Exec. Speed	3	10	8	8	1
Env. quality	3	6	2	8	10
Classes incl.	5	6	2	8	10
Memory mgt.	6	1	10	4	10
Copies sold	2	10	1	4	6

You should be careful not to automatically conclude that a high score is a good score. Whether memory management might be a real virtue or a major liability depends upon the type of system you are building. Similarly, execution speed may not matter, as long as it is fast enough for your particular application or system. Also, remember this chart may have to be updated based upon changes to these languages by the time you are reading this.

Environments

The environment for software development includes all computers, software, methods, buildings, furniture, and people required in the construction of a computer program. The environment includes the host environment on which software is developed and the target machine on which the generated software will run.

Aspects of the environment can be either personal or shared:

- *Personal:* An individual programmer has available various tools that are used in isolation to design, develop, test, and document software.

- *Shared:* A team of programmers requires complex development environments that combine traditional personal environments with others on the same network or networks. For example, it may be appropriate to use Smalltalk-80 as a front end to an IBM mainframe for developing a prototype of a new database query facility, or an Objective-C development system to generate C code that will run on a numerically controlled machine tool.

Isolated environments can be a pure delight for building prototypes, yet their "features" can become real bottlenecks when trying to build real-time distributed systems.

Component packages

Component libraries contain predefined classes. As the component library grows, it raises the level of the language used to solve the current problem. Assuming that a component can be found that exhibits the desired behavior, system building can become amazingly efficient.

As we enter the '90s, it is remarkable how few component libraries actually exist in the commercial market. The ones that do exist vary considerably in their quality and robustness. Most component libraries available today are much closer to prototypes than commercial components—especially Smalltalk components.

Some language and development environment suppliers also supply component packages. The Smalltalk-80 library from ParcPlace Systems (version 2.1.1) is one of the larger component libraries currently available; it contains 350 classes and 5,600 methods. Stepstone's ICpak 101 and ICpak 201 represent 78 classes and 2,000 methods. But more is not always better. The NeXT class library is regarded by some to have functionability comparable to ParcPlace's library, but required less than 100 classes.

GUIDE TO AVAILABLE ENVIRONMENTS

There can be no clear choice of an object-oriented programming system for all software development projects. Further, any statements about the capabilities of a particular environment that you are not reading over a 9,600-baud link are sure to be out of date by the time you read them.

SUMMARY

Software development environments are at least as complicated and expensive to assemble as a new fabrication facility for integrated circuits. To suppose that a development environment can be assembled by two or three people in a couple of months is naive. I have used a simple motto for years to describe the environment construction process—"buy the best and build the rest." Whenever possible, buy a tool rather than develop it.

As any professional knows, it is not possible to provide a small shopping list for software engineers. The particular demands of the project will determine which particular support tools are required.

Providing comprehensive development environments that effectively use high-performance workstations for improved productivity will be an industry-wide project for at least the next decade—just as the recent transition to computer-aided engineering systems has been for engineers. A single company cannot provide all the required capabilities—compilers, debuggers, configuration control, design, testing, and documentation tools will come from many vendors.

As the electronic computer-aided design industry has demonstrated, truly capable development environments will require 3–5 years to build and 8–10 years to become comprehensive, mature, and widely available.

Plan to wait for it.

NOTES

1. A. W. Holt, H. R. Ramsey, and J. D. Grimes, Coordination system technology as the basis for a programming environment, *ITT Electrical Communications* 57(4):307–314, 1983.
2. For a description of NLS, a complete reference to articles written by Englebart, and a description of other similar projects, see Ted Nelson, *Computer Lib/Dream Machines,* Microsoft Press, 1987.
3. From ITT *Advanced Programming Technology Monograph 8101*, December 31, 1980, p. 70. This document was prepared while Dr. Holt was at Massachusetts Computer Associates under contract to ITT.
4. For example, a product called Voice Navigator from Articulate Systems is a trainable voice recognition product that can recognize 700 words in a speaker-dependent fashion. It can be used for voice-driven menu commands and sold for $1,200 in 1990.
5. There are important exceptions to this statement, and some of those exceptional people are likely to be friends of mine. Please understand that you are the exception, not the rule.

9

Educating Your People

*The best education is to be found in gaining
the utmost information from the simplest apparatus.*

Alfred North Whitehead
The Aims of Education

T his chapter presents guidelines for developing software engineers who can use object-oriented tools and techniques for commercial development projects. I make a distinction between education and training. Education is the process of learning general knowledge for use at some unspecified time in the future. Training is the process of learning a skill for specific applications. Learning object-oriented software engineering is education; learning to program in C++ is training.

LEARNING TO LEARN

Learning software engineering is more analogous to learning the piano than to learning physics. With an instrument such as the piano, it is necessary to understand the concepts, learn the notes, learn the physical actions, and practice, practice, practice. Practice over many years is essential to becoming accomplished.

A friend of mine, Johnny Maddox, is a professional ragtime pianist who has practiced several hours a day for more than 50 years. He can play over 5,000 pieces from memory and claims to have learned every piece from sheet music. A list this size contains some really obscure tunes, like "Barney Google," "Lamberth Walk," "Minnie the Moocher," or "Mussel Schoals Blues."

Professional software engineers also require a large vocabulary of algorithms and designs, each of which must be reconstructed quickly and flawlessly.[1] All too often we reinvent when we should be using what already exists.

Hundreds of years of experience in teaching people to play musical instruments may help our young software discipline to more efficiently train our professionals.[2] As with learning a musical instrument, software engineering requires a structured approach and is heavily influenced by practice and experience. To become a truly skilled software engineer, one must study programs, analyze existing designs, and write programs of one's own devising.

Two well-developed learning systems provide some useful analogies:

- The Suzuki approach to learning a musical instrument strongly emphasizes listening, practice, and mastery of even the smallest details before progressing to the next level of study.[3]
- The classic master–apprentice relationship in fine woodworking shops assumes that years of progressive understanding and practice are required to become a true artisan.

Maybe academic computer science curricula, which provide only 3–5 years of part-time training, cannot produce software engineers capable of designing and building complex commercial systems. Woodworkers and concert pianists require 10 or even 20 years of training and practice before they are considered accomplished. There is a lot to learn.

Neither do we teach new engineers as efficiently as we could. Most educators in the software industry comment that we get it all wrong in the beginning—we first learn to write, then learn to read. When I taught FORTRAN programming at the University of Washington in the early 1970s, I found that most instructors never got to the chapter in the textbook on subroutines. I saw one of these students years later suffering through a 700-page program that did not have a single subroutine! As an engineering student, he only took one programming course.

We haven't figured out what the equivalent to musical scales should be in the software business. Undoubtedly, software engineers should be expected to know a certain basic set of algorithms, design approaches, and style guidelines. Maybe some time should be allocated to memorizing these basics so we will have them immediately at hand when the occasion arises.

Some additional lessons may be learned from the woodworking professionals. Woodworkers must learn how to use and respect their tools. They also must learn the consequences of using different raw materials.

Master programmers I have watched are distinctive in the way they use their tools. To begin with, they know their tools intimately. They understand the power of the tools available to them and spend serious amounts of time perfecting their skill with the various tools. In all cases, they also know how to fabricate a tool on the spot to do a better job or to do a job more efficiently.

Master programmers also understand their raw materials. These materials include reusable components, compilers, operating system services, communication systems, and the underlying hardware system. Masters know that "pure design" results in slow, inefficient programs. Good designs take into account the system within which they will operate.

SETTING THE CONTEXT

Since 1981, I have helped introduce object-oriented technology into organizations throughout the United States, Japan, and western Europe. These organizations include large computer, telecommunications and electronics firms, data processing shops, automobile manufacturers, and some small entrepreneurial companies. This chapter outlines what I have found to be the most practical means of training a development staff in object-oriented technology.

Assume you are a manager in a large (over $100 million) electronics firm responsible for building an ambitious next-generation system for your company. This project is expected to take three years and require 30 professional software engineers. The engineers have an average of five years' experience; they know two or three programming languages (such as Pascal, C, and Assembler); they have B.S. or M.S. degrees in computer science or related disciplines and are working on their first or second significant system.

SETTING THE GOALS

As in woodworking, the skills and abilities of masters, artisans (or engineers), and apprentices are required for large software projects. A woodworking master not only is an experienced artisan, but is capable of designing projects that will require many others to implement. The artisan knows the craft well enough to work with a minimum of supervision. The apprentice is still learning the trade and needs direct hourly supervision.

Software engineers can be grouped into three skill levels analogous to those of woodworkers:

- The architect has substantial prior experience, has successfully completed two similar projects of similar complexity to the current project, and is capable of understanding and designing the overall system architecture.
- The engineer has completed one similar project using the same technology and is capable of designing subsystems.
- The apprentice is skilled in the use of traditional programming languages, such as C or Pascal, and is working on this type of project for the first time.

In introducing a new technology, the challenge is not to find the apprentices but rather to find the engineers and trust the masters. For a 30-person project, 1 architect, 8 engineers, and 16 apprentices will be required to build the software (see Table 9.1).

**Table 9.1. Resource allocation in a
30-person development project.**

Title	Number
Project manager	1
Architects	1
Engineers	5
Apprentices	9
Test engineers	3
Test apprentices	3
Toolmakers	2
Technical writers	5
Administrative support	1
Total	30

Fifteen of the 30 people are designing and developing operational software. The other 15 are support staff. Building quality software products requires such a staff. It is critical that experts in testing be used to design and administer the tests independently of the original developers. It is equally critical that technical writers be assigned to the project early and in sufficient numbers. Remember, there will be more text documentation for a typical software system than code. If we don't staff this activity, we will certainly fall behind schedule or deliver less than the expected functionality. I would also devote two engineers to toolmaking. Their sole job is to increase the productivity of the team.

Finding the apprentice

Apprentices are an increasingly scarce resource due to overall demand within the industry. The objective is to find a person with considerable intellectual talent who has a high energy level and excellent communication skills.

I would search for apprentices at the best universities within 200 miles of the office. Don't just look in the computer science department, either. Some of the best projects have multidisciplinary teams that surprisingly often contain cognitive psychologists, philosophers, graphic artists, and musicians. The big secret is to look for jugglers with a good grade point average! I will leave it as an exercise for the reader to figure out that recommendation.

Some of the best companies test their incoming programmers in an unexpected way. They have them spend half a day solving a software design problem and then writing an English language description of their design. A few top companies actually have programming recruits demonstrate their prowess by writing and verifying a program during the interview. Shouldn't this be required as the norm? Musicians must demonstrate their ability, and woodworkers must bring along a portfolio of completed projects.

But most important, leave the big egos, introverts, and scientists for the competitors to hire. They are too expensive, no matter how cheap.

Creating the engineers

To "create" object-oriented software engineers, preparation should include amassing competence in the areas set forth in Table 9.2. Times specified are important as building skills is imperative to solidifying proficiency, competence, and confidence in the professional engineer. Productive prototyping can start in about three weeks. Real engineering can begin after 4-6 more weeks under the guidance of an engineer.

An effective approach for learning both the language and the component library is to use an interpreted object-oriented language. The flexibility and immediate responsiveness of the interpreted environment allows beginners to learn more efficiently than they would using a compiled environment. The slow and tedious

Table 9.2. Educating object-oriented software engineers.

Skill	Time
Learn the concepts of object-oriented software engineering—typically by attending a training course and reading available technical papers and books.	Approximately 1 week.
If the project will use a hybrid language, get a thorough understanding of the traditional base language (C, Pascal, Forth).	Two weeks or more, depending upon specific prior experience.
Learn the object-oriented language and component library by developing a prototype system and sample programs. During this phase, it is vital to have at least telephone support from an artisan.	Approximately 4–6 weeks for the prototype. Time to learn the library depends upon the number of components and the number of methods associated with each; 20 components seem to require about 2 weeks; larger component libraries cannot be learned linearly—familiarity will increase over a long period of using the library.[4]
Plan a more sizable project. All those involved should attend a training course; this includes management.	One week or less.
Develop the first system under the guidance of a master and with the assistance of apprentices. To accelerate the development process, the master must participate in the initial design and subsequent code reviews. The master may be a consultant, but must be personally present. Telephone support will not suffice.	Approximately 20–40 weeks.

edit–compile–link cycle places an additional layer of complexity between the programmers' actions and their results. It is even more advantageous if the prototyping environment has a component library identical to the one in use by development. That way, prototyping can serve the function of teaching object-oriented programming in general and the specifics of the components in particular.

Creating the architect

An architect needs the knowledge and experience of the engineer plus additional insights concerning structures and components that might be useful to the new project. Obviously, the architect must be familiar with other object-oriented programming languages and environments from which new ideas can arise.

Architects can be obtained in three ways: You can spend a few years to develop one internally; hire one—buy the best!—by raiding another organization; or hire one as a consultant. Just as kings used to purchase a master shipbuilder to design their warships, systems houses often use exactly the same tactics to secure local architects. A common mistake is to choose the person who best understands the previous-generation system but has never built such a system from the start. Those people should be engineers, not architects. An architect must have designed and built successful systems before.

Smalltalk-80 is an important language and environment for architects of object-oriented systems to study. More than 20 years of experience is embedded within the Smalltalk-80 system.

The Smalltalk-80 environment makes it easy to get started. It has built-in text editing and graphics systems, and it works with mouse-driven pop-up menus and windows. Smalltalk-80 is a pure object-oriented environment: Everything is an object. It therefore forces the user to think in terms of objects. The library includes 350 classes that will take many months to understand.

Smalltalk-80 gives budding architects the chance to work in an environment made for prototyping. Such experience is valuable before working in a hybrid environment. After all, every pilot should spend time in a flight simulator before jumping into the cockpit.

Typical management questions

Following are my answers to questions that managers most often ask at this stage.

Q. How long will it take my C programmers to learn the object-oriented extensions and become productive?

A. Professional software engineers have reported they are productively developing new software using object-oriented technology in as few as 3 weeks. For example, Objective-C requires the C programmer to learn only four new syntactic devices:

- objects
- messages
- classes
- inheritance

Syntactically, these are trivial; they can be learned in one morning. Meaningful ways to use these devices—design heuristics, quality assurance techniques, and a large component library—take months to learn.

The first time you implement an object-oriented system, expect reduced productivity. Things will move slowly because people are learning and experimenting. Ultimately, productivity benefits will compensate for this time. The time needed to develop a first object-oriented system is approximately equal to the time the project would take with more familiar traditional tools. Later, when object-oriented software engineering becomes familiar to your teams, the real productivity gains will be significant.

Q. How long does it take to create object-oriented software engineers?

A. Qualified object-oriented software engineers can be created in a year—less time than that required to learn calculus (and much less than that required to learn cabinet making!). Qualified object-oriented architects, like traditional system designers, require specific knowledge and considerable experience—which is not gained overnight. Native talent also helps.

Sam Adams of KSC once said, "good designers become great designers with objects, and mediocre designers become obvious."

Q. But I can't afford to wait half a year to begin this critical new project! How long does it take to learn just the new programming language?

A. Object-oriented software engineering does not involve learning just the new programming language. Learning the language is not what's important—it is learning how to design, develop, test, and document using existing components. If you can only learn the language, don't bother. If it were just another programming language, the productivity benefits of modularity and reusability would not be there.

Q. How should component libraries be managed and controlled at a corporate level?

A. Some companies have already created corporate support centers for software components to facilitate their internal software sharing. Each center is responsible for receiving all components, verifying their quality, documenting them, maintaining them, and shipping them where they are needed. Each component has a formal corporate part number, and its use ultimately results in internal charge-backs.

But with yet more experience, companies come to see that reuse does not come free. Components must be designed for reuse, supported, optimized, and ported as required. That is the kind of work commercial software companies perform. So I expect more success from companies who work with their component suppliers than from those who try to do it all in-house. Few in-house markets are large enough to justify an appropriate level of investment in a profit-center components shop.

Q. Can this new technology help us on large, innovative system development projects?

A. A system that would take 60 programmers three years to write 600,000 lines of code using traditional programming techniques could be completed using experienced object-oriented software engineers in two years with 10 experienced programmers (writing fewer than 100,000 lines of code). "Experienced" means they are building their third commercial object-oriented product.

If you include the learning curve for inexperienced object-oriented engineers, such a project may be finished no more quickly than with conventional languages and tools. It will require fewer software engineers, but the size of support staff will increase to a level equal to the development staff.

IMPLICATIONS FOR EDUCATION

Object-oriented software engineering will change the education needs of software professionals, just as the semiconductor changed the education of electronics professionals. In 1960, few people knew how to design complex circuits; today, few people really know how to design complex object-oriented systems. The changes in our profession resulting from this major technological advance are profound and will take a decade or more to fully digest.

The development process must change to recognize the inherently iterative nature of object-oriented development. Design standards must be rethought to take into account this fundamentally new technology. Performance optimization strategies must change. Quality assurance procedures and standards must be completely revised, and documentation practices cannot remain the same either. For example, as we generate more raw functionality per unit of work by software engineers, we are also generating more work for technical writers. Thus, the ratio of technical writers to software engineers will need to change as the productivity of software engineers increases. Even the heuristics of software management must change—the techniques developed by professional managers over the years to make the progress of traditional projects more visible must be modified.

Educators as well as managers must have the courage to experiment and innovate. My experience in visiting a number of top-flight universities suggests that computer science departments are stuck in the mud of the 1970s. Terms like objects, reuse, components, software engineering, and team development do not appear in the curriculum. Lisp and data structures remain more common.

We must modify existing approaches to building systems. None of us should be waiting for someone else to show us how it should be done. We have to find out—just as the customers of Fairchild and Texas Instruments found out how to design using semiconductors in the early 1960s.

NOTES

1. For a study establishing that memory and programming performance are related, see Thomas Love, Relating individual differences in computer programming performance to human information processing abilities, *Dissertation Abstracts International* **38**(3), 1978.

2. For a review of the last 300 years of experience in training instrumentalists, see Stanley Schleuter, *A Sound Approach to Teaching Instrumentalists*, Kent State University Press, Kent, OH, 1984.

3. For a description of the Suzuki approach to learning musical instruments, see Shinichi Suziki, *Ability Development from Age Zero*, Ability Development Associates, Athens, OH, 1981.

4. This fact suggests an important management strategy. Do not insist that all developers learn or use all available components. Instead, the architect should partition the library into sublibraries, each sufficient for one team to learn and use. Because component libraries can quickly reach several hundred components, such architectural partitioning is critical.

10

Software Construction Management

*Even with the most detailed planning and
the greatest alertness there is always the
unexpected. The margin of safety is the
ability a party retains for meeting extra trouble.*

Mountaineering: The Freedom of the Hills
The Mountaineers (a Seattle, WA, climbing club), 1982, p. 286.

Falling down is part of growing up.

old saying

Our avocations are often remarkable sources of new ideas for our vocations. An especially risky avocation—mountain climbing—provides some unusually thought-provoking guidelines and experiences for managers of complex software development projects.

Rocks and glaciers present unpredictable hazards, challenges, delays, and complications. Time is short and the resources available to a climbing team are finite. In addition, the weather will change and unexpected hazards are commonplace—icing, wind shear, injuries, or hypothermia.

Mountain climbers learn on the first day of instruction that they must always create a *margin of safety*. Rock climbers must decide how long a lead to take before security is required—a piton driven into the rock or a block wedged into a small crack. Climbers must always ask such questions as: If we fall, will it hurt me or others? If we fail on this route, how can we recover? Are alternative moves or routes more forgiving? With such calculation, risks are taken routinely. The more experienced climbers take risks after analyzing the failure modes and effects of microdecisions—each hand placement—and macrodecisions—which route to take. Older climbers are those whose techniques have worked!

The software business, like mountain climbing, requires macrodecisions and split-second tactical decision making. We must decide which system to build, estimate how long it will take, and determine the amount of energy it will consume.[1] Then, as the ascent progresses, hundreds of tactical decisions must be made without undue deliberation or dispute. Literally, the careers of a development team hang on every decision.

LEADING A SOFTWARE TEAM

Software team leaders should think of themselves as leaders of a rope team ascending a rock- and glacier-strewn mountain with all available supplies on their backs. The rope team is tied together; a fall by one person can cause everyone to fall.

Large software projects (over 500,000 source lines of new code) have a higher risk of failure than do assaults of the world's 10 highest peaks. Yet, even if the consequences of software development are not as dire as those of mountain climbing, software managers might do well to plan complex development projects with more regard for their margin of safety.

The rapid proliferation of inexpensive, powerful microprocessors has created a seemingly insatiable demand for new software in all aspects of business and government. This demand is so large that many large companies now estimate their backlog of software in units of person-centuries of effort.

Some software projects are never completed; others are completed but have too many errors to be delivered; and some are delivered but prove too difficult to adapt to changing customer requirements. We must learn how to increase the chances that committed projects will be completed successfully.

While object-oriented technology can make significant changes in the costs and risks of software development projects, any project must be properly managed to succeed. Objects create the possibility of success but hardly ensure it. Using any new technology for the first time also creates risks that must be accommodated.

Commercial software development projects are large, complex construction projects, similar in price to constructing a large building or a new airport.[2] The construction industry has recently changed its techniques for planning, designing, constructing, and managing large projects. Adopting such techniques may provide just the margin of safety the software industry has been searching for. A description of these construction management techniques may be useful to understanding how to change the way in which software projects are structured and managed.

BUILDING "REAL THINGS"

Let's begin with a look at the traditional methods for constructing large buildings. Then, we will see how the construction industry has modified this process to reduce the risks and increase the odds of delivery on schedule and within budget.

Traditional methods

The traditional construction of a building follows a sequential approach not unlike the way in which large software development projects have been traditionally structured.

Decision phase:
- Customer requirements are recorded, reviewed, and analyzed.
- The customer's budget is determined.
- The customer's schedule is determined.

Design phase:
- The architect develops a set of alternative designs from which the customer must select.
- The architect and engineers develop a solution satisfying the customer's requirements.
- They express the solution as
  1. detailed engineering drawings
  2. a book of specifications

Bid phase:
- General contractors give competitive bids or the customer negotiates with the builder.

Construction phase:
- The general contractor subcontracts 80% or more of the work.
- The general contractor controls the flow of materials and workers to make a profit.
- An architect inspects the evolving work.

While this process works, it is not a process that results in the highest-quality building with the most predictable cost and schedule. The reasons are:

- The process is sequential. Everything is on the critical path.
- The customer has little control but still pays the bills—typically, each bill is larger than anticipated.
- The process assumes that the designed solution was expressed faultlessly in paper documents and that the documents transmitted the customer's demands and desires perfectly to the general contractor.
- Architects lack the expertise to estimate costs and construction schedules or improve efficiency.
- No incentives exist for the general contractor to reduce costs. The fee structure is often costs plus a fixed fee. Moreover, the general contractor's relationships with subcontractors are often more durable than the relationship with the customer.
- The general contractor's management control system optimizes the general contractor's profit. It often fails to provide information and control to the owner. It creates an inherent conflict of interest, with the owner being the loser.

When these traditional construction techniques are applied to large or especially innovative construction projects, the typical result is a considerable expansion of both construction time and budget. If either of these crucial variables hits a real limit (for example, the customer runs out of money), the project may never be completed or may be finished in a way quite different from the original architect's design.

New methods: construction management

The construction industry has introduced a professional middleman responsible directly to the customer. These professional middlemen, known as construction managers, are master builders with detailed construction knowledge and experience. Their particular strength is their expertise in successfully managing construction projects similar to the customer's—be it a bridge, a skyscraper, an office park, or a condominium complex.

Once engaged, the construction management firm supplants the traditional prime or general contractor. Instead, the customer contracts for each segment of the construction process separately, with the advice of the construction management firm. This results in many more contracts, each bid on a fixed-price basis. If the suppliers are unwilling to make a fixed-price bid, the tasks are subdivided until fixed-price bids can be supplied.

As a result, designs are divided up until much of the traditional risk is removed from the project. Another advantage is that building components turn out to be quite similar from project to project. Two corporate headquarters may not be particularly similar, but their fire escapes or elevators may be identical. With experience, a construction management firm can provide remarkably accurate estimates of the overall costs and schedule for a project based upon this component analysis.

Complex construction projects can also be scheduled using a degree of overlap among the separately contracted phases that would have been unheard of 20 years ago. There are examples of basements being constructed after the steel framework for the top floor of a building has been set in place.

The benefit of the construction-manager approach is that most projects are completed within the allocated budget and schedule. Their track record seems amazing to anyone with personal experience in traditional approaches to construction, either software or buildings. Major office buildings are consistently completed within 5% of both budget and schedule (the budget includes the flat fees paid to the construction management firm).

Other important benefits are:

- The general contractor's knowledge is added to the critical early stages of design.
- The owners retain direct management control over contracts.
- Buildings are decomposed into components that:
  1. involve less risk
  2. are easier to estimate
  3. become more familiar
  4. therefore allow more efficient management of the construction process

Such construction management techniques used on a project at the State University of New York's Stonybrook campus allowed the completion of a building in 9 months; the estimated schedule was 3.5 years! The resultant savings came to $7.8 million—$4.25 million in direct savings and $3.55 million in early lease income.

Obviously, this approach has worked to improve the predictability of construction projects. It is certainly worthy of analysis by the software industry.[3]

BUILDING SOFTWARE

Now, let's look at the traditional process and approach for constructing large software systems.

Traditional software construction methods

Software systems are currently built using a sequential development process not unlike the traditional construction approach described above. Software projects typically involve the following phases.

Requirements phase:
- Customer requirements are recorded, reviewed, and analyzed.
- The customer's budget is determined.
- The customer's schedule is determined.

Design phase:
- The architect and engineers develop a solution satisfying the customer's requirements. The solution frequently involves a small number of subsystems with a high degree of interdependence within each. Each subsystem is large enough to be unique.
- They express the solution as:
  1. detailed engineering drawings
  2. a book of specifications

Bid phase:
- General contractors give competitive bids. The resulting price is high and the resulting schedule long.
- Negotiation is conducted to resolve discrepancies.

Construction phase:
- The general contractor directly manages the work.
- The general contractor controls the flow of materials and workers to make a profit.
- An architect inspects the evolving work.

Many software systems have been built using this approach, but the disadvantages are manifold:

- The process is sequential. Everything is on the critical path.
- The customer has little control, but still pays the bills (typically more than anticipated, each bill slightly larger than expected).

- The process assumes that the design was faultlessly specified in paper documents and that the documents transmitted the customer's demands and desires perfectly to the general contractor.
- System architects are thrust into the role of quality assurance. But they typically lack the expertise to estimate costs and schedules or improve efficiency.
- No incentives exist for the general contractor to reduce costs. The fee structure is often cost plus a fixed fee, and the general contractor's relationships with subcontractors are often more durable than the relationship with the customer. Instead, the general contractor's major concern is to get the next contract from the customer.
- The general contractor's management control system optimizes the general contractor's profit. It often fails to provide information and control to the owner. Instead, it can create an inherent conflict of interest.

If this list of disadvantages looks familiar, it should. When these traditional construction techniques are applied to large or especially innovative software system projects, the typical result is a considerable expansion of both the schedule and budget. Again, if either of these crucial variables hits a real limit (for example, the customer runs out of money), the project may never be completed or may be finished in a way quite different from the original architect's design.

New methods: software construction management

In this section, a new software project management technique analogous to the construction management process described earlier in this chapter will be proposed. It would be wonderful if, at this point, I could give a long list of successful projects that used this management technique. However, these techniques are being described here for the first time.

A major software project should be run by a small group of master builders who have detailed knowledge of software construction and management. No single individual should be responsible for a project. Each segment of construction must be contracted with the customer separately, with advice from the software construction managers.

A large number (tens if not hundreds) of contracts should be bid, each at a fixed price and on a fixed schedule. Every estimate must be based upon a direct reference task from a previous project. The idea is that two recently constructed systems are not likely to be similar—but several software tasks (components or classes) within the last five systems must be!

Projects can now involve overlapping phases with commensurate cost and time savings. Predictability is much higher; the risk of overall failure is reduced.

Software construction management has three benefits:

- The general contractor's knowledge is added to the critical early stages of design.
- The owners retain direct management control over contracts.
- Systems are decomposed into components that:
  1. involve less risk
  2. are easier to estimate
  3. become more familiar
  4. These components are smaller and more tractable than are traditionally designed megasystems.

This approach has some interesting implications. It means, for example, that a project must be decomposed into smaller and smaller entities until the subcontractor can provide a fixed-price estimate for each entity. This process is sure to uncover the real risks in a new project. Also, development standards and quality guidelines must exist prior to requesting bids from development teams. Initially, the size of each subcontractable entity should be constrained, using the guideline that even if this particular subcontract is a complete failure, the project could still be successful—the project's margin of safety.

With the assistance of a professional software construction manager, the software project manager negotiates contracts with internal or external teams. The construction manager's job is to work with the development manager to get the highest quality for reasonable costs. The construction manager devotes full attention to the problem of constructing the desired system within the allocated budget, resources, and schedule.

Teams are measured based upon their ability to deliver quality products according to the contracts. Teams that twice fail to complete their contract may not continue; they are "fired from the job," which is given to another team. Team members are randomly assigned to new teams.

As an initial rule of thumb, no contract should last longer than two months or involve more than five people. This ensures an appropriate degree of modularity. The customer (who may be internal general management) receives a weekly status report for each contract. Overall project status is displayed on a wall visible to all team members. Nothing can be removed from that wall. Major changes may result in another project plan being displayed, but it must be placed over the prior plan. Write-only plans create important management information despite the loss of readability.

A SPIRAL APPROACH

Barry Boehm, while chief scientist at TRW Defense Systems Group, advocated a spiral approach to software construction and enhancement.[4] The key to this approach is to:

- plan to develop the software iteratively, typically employing three or more iterations for a new development project, each iteration typically involving the commitment of more resources
- clearly identify the objectives of each iteration and identify alternative approaches to accomplishing each objective
- identify the risks inherent in each iteration of the spiral, and determine how they can be reduced and what else can be done to acquire existing capabilities

Unlike the waterfall model, the iterative development process is not document driven, but driven by the need to reduce risks and control engineering costs at each step. The use of small fixed-budget contracts that can be independently monitored by knowledgeable software construction managers allows us to implement Boehm's spiral approach.

GUIDELINES FOR SOFTWARE CONSTRUCTION MANAGEMENT

The software manager's function is to lead, manage the resources, and retain a margin of safety. The software manager's job is every bit as complicated and challenging as that faced by the leader of an expedition to K2 or Everest. It is more risky. Plan for software projects as though your professional life depends upon it—it often does.

Some useful rules of thumb to keep in mind include:

- **Remember three lessons from *In Search of Excellence*:**[5]
  1. Remain close to the customer.
  2. Be value driven.
  3. Stick to the knitting.
- **Track by services, use cases, and classes.** The design process described in Chapter 4 identified these three traceable elements, which are associated with any project. All project status reports should refer to each by name and version number.
- **Use early warning indicators.** Inaccurate estimates and delays imply lack of understanding of the customer's problem, the tools, or the

basic technology. Long training delays cannot be incurred, so staff changes may be required—preferably within the company and even within the project.

- **Use the team to manage.** Teams are a strong motivational and management force. Strong teams should be allowed to transcend a given project.
- **Use the contract mechanism to allow for the following important attributes:**
  1. no surprises
  2. accountability
  3. zest to accomplish
  4. joy in success

Apply the lessons learned from traditional software management. Troublesome and error-prone as the software development process has been, some important lessons have nevertheless been learned.

- *Bulk is bad.* The larger a program grows, the harder it becomes to develop, verify, and extend. A software manager should search for solutions involving a minimum amount of code to develop or maintain.
- *Reusability is the key to real productivity.* Innovation and creation are the norm in the software industry. But, unlike the king of Sweden, let's ensure that the ship can remain upright in a breeze before carving and gilding a few hundred lion's heads.
- *Quality must be built in from the start.* Quality can come only from detailed technical reviews by competent, independent engineers at every stage of the development process.
- *Coding represents at most 20% of the overall development effort.* Barry Boehm and Capers Jones[6] have demonstrated repeatedly that real programmer productivity results from improvements in the entire development process.
- *Managers must manage knowledgeably.* The best environment, the best people, and an open checkbook cannot guarantee success; ironically, it can be a harbinger of disaster. Managing software projects requires a detailed technical understanding of the software management business and the software technology itself. Having simply read Brooks's *The Mythical Man-Month* is inadequate. Managers must be able to read and understand every line of code. Content-free software management has been a common cause of failure.
- *Integrated environments are critical.* Such environments cannot be

built with glue or databases. The 1970s idea that a morass of tools could be assembled around a database management system to produce an integrated environment has been repeatedly attempted, and has just as often failed — although new attempts are commonplace. Environments foster productivity as much by coordinating the flow of work among organizations as by providing powerful solitary productivity tools.

- *Time and space always matter.* Any technology that claims "it's a little slow but machines are getting faster" is a good technology to avoid. The economic incentive to do more with less will remain strong.

SUMMARY

> *"The lower you are in a corporate hierarchy, the more time you have to verify the facts upon which you were acting, and the less likely you are to do so; and the higher you rise and the greater your responsibilities, the less time you have to check your facts, and the more important it is to do so."*
>
> *Harold Geneen*[7]

We must check our facts when we plan, while we develop, and as we engineer. Facts should be unshakable. What margin of safety exists within the schedules? Are there any alternative routes? Has anyone considered the failure modes and effects of each route?

Successful construction of software systems requires managers to understand:

- how to build things
- how to plan such construction
- how to analyze and deal with high-risk situations
- how to lead bright, highly motivated professionals into uncharted domains

Above all, it requires a desire to win, balanced by enough know-how to eliminate undue risk.

NOTES

1. Software managers will find it unusually valuable to read The climbing party and its leadership, *Mountaineering: The Freedom of the Hills,* 4th ed., The Mountaineers, Seattle,

WA, 1982, chap. 16.

2. I thank my friends at Åke Larson AB in Stockholm for stimulating the idea for this chapter, as well as for supplying me with details concerning their business. Åke Larson is a successful international construction management firm. They typically complete projects in 25% less time than do general contractors, and within 5% of the original budget—a record those in the software industry would envy!

3. *Harvard Business Review* article describing construction management.

4. Barry W. Boehm, A spiral model of software development and enhancement, *IEEE Computer*, May, 61–72, 1988.

5. *In Search of Excellence: lessons learned from America's best run companies.* T. J. Peters and R. H. Wateman, Jr., Harper and Row, 1982.

6. See Boehm, B. "Software Engineering Economics," Prentice Hall, 1981, New Jersey, and Jones, C., "Applied Software Measurement: assuring productivity and quality." McGraw-Hill, New York, 1991.

7. Harold Geneen, *Managing*, Doubleday & Company, New York, 1984, p. 205.

11

Building in Quality

A quality tool is one that pleases me every time I use it.

Donn Combelic

I am an amateur woodworker with a passion for quality woodworking tools. I experience a strong sense of joy every time I use my Japanese saws and chisels, German planes, American workmate, English screwdrivers, and Swedish chain saw.

Quality tools do a defined job accurately, predictably, and efficiently. A quality tool communicates to its user a sense of respect, an obligation to care, and a feeling of having been served a little better than expected. Many tools communicate exactly the opposite message.

Tools must be properly cared for and maintained or their quality will quickly degrade. Woodworking tools must be kept clean and razor sharp. Software tools must work with the current releases of operating systems and compilers.

But cleanliness and sharpness do not ensure quality. A foot adze (Figure 11.1 is a poor-quality tool in my opinion, even when it is perfectly sharpened. It is a poor-quality tool by design. Swinging a four-pound steel blade through your legs to strike a hardwood log inches away from your ankles is "unsafe at any speed." The odds of injury are just too high.

Figure 11.1.
A foot adze.

Professionals need and demand sharp tools for many jobs. Occasional users should have tools with more protective devices attached.

Software tools *communicate* to their users, as do woodworking tools. Most of us remember our first experience using powerful new tool sets like UNIX or Smalltalk. "Gee, that's great," we said as we felt a new sense of power over problems we were being asked to solve. Software tools also require regular maintenance. They get used in a constantly changing environment comprising new releases of operating systems, databases, and application software, as well as hardware upgrades.

This view of quality challenges some of the current lore being preached by corporate quality organizations throughout the computer industry. Quality cannot be defined merely as "compliance to written specifications." A foot adze can be correctly built according to a specification, but it will remain a poor-quality tool because it is inherently unsafe.

I recently used an electronic mail system with terrible ergonomics, many apparent errors, and lousy performance. The developers told me that it was documented as it actually worked, that the *specs* said distribution lists and file folders could not have the same name, and that 95% of the response times were within defined limits. I did some checking and discovered they were right. But it was still a poor-quality mail system.

It is not acceptable to build a software product and proclaim attributes of high quality just because it works the way the user document says it works. Neither is it right to specify a product that is difficult or even dangerous to use and declare that it is of high quality because it meets its specifications.

Quality is more complex than mere compliance to written specifications. Important quality issues are subjective but are nevertheless real and must be explicitly handled. Ergonomics and public reactions to products matter.

Other industries have recognized the importance of subjective issues for years and regularly design for and measure this dimension of their products. They employ focus groups routinely to assess the reactions of the target market. The restaurant industry knows that a grilled steak cannot just be sanitary and nutritious—it must also be served sizzling hot, smell like charcoal, and have distinct grill marks. This subjective dimension of software quality must be taken into account to produce more GTGs—"gee, that's great."[1]

THE SOFTWARE QUALITY CHALLENGE

Software has become such a fundamental technology that it could determine whether our lives, our countries, or even our civilization continues. Software is now central to all medical, financial, and military defense systems throughout the world. Most of this software is not particularly reliable.

A retired senior official from the U.S. Department of Defense (DoD) made the following statement in a public forum in January 1987: "Large DoD systems do not work. We should be happy that the people who use them understand that their systems don't work."

For example, a bug was once discovered that resulted in the arming of nuclear warheads just *after* the warhead was separated from the booster rocket containing the computer! By reversing the calling sequence of two subroutines, hundreds of operational missiles were actually duds. Testing was never an option available to the developers.

The warhead error was an objective error—the program did not work according to its specifications. As programs and systems of programs get larger and larger, it becomes increasingly difficult to exercise these programs and assure that they are objectively correct. And objective quality is never sufficient.

Building substantially higher-quality software will require changes in the ways software is designed, built, assured, and supported. This chapter suggests some of those changes.

UNDERSTANDING QUALITY

Philip Crosby, author of *Quality Is Free*, is probably the leading advocate of quality workmanship in the United States today. Prior to founding the Quality College and building a successful consulting practice based upon quality issues, he was vice president of quality at ITT. At ITT, he spent 14 years developing his notions of quality and creating techniques for managing it.

Crosby defines quality as "conformance to requirements." He says, "requirements must be clearly stated so that they cannot be misunderstood. Measurements are then taken continually to determine conformance to those requirements. The non-conformance detected is the absence of quality. Quality problems become non-conformance problems, and quality becomes definable."[2]

Crosby got it right, but many people who claim to be using his quality management techniques get it completely wrong. Let's revisit the electronic mail system. That particular piece of software was developed without a requirements analysis or detailed functional specification. It was "hacked together," then documented. Neither the software nor its specifications were ever subjected to a technical review. Measurements of compliance to requirements were not possible.

The requirements for an interactive computer program must contain response times (mean and variance) and explicit ergonomic requirements; otherwise, they are incomplete. The functional specification can be thought of as a complete draft of the user manual. This specification should be reviewed not only by other developers but also by representative users from the anticipated user community. Having properly developed and reviewed such a requirements document and functional specification, you can now build a quality product that conforms to the agreed-upon requirements.

Once built, a software product must be rigorously tested not only to determine if it works as specified, but to test the specifications themselves. The unexpected is the norm in the ergonomics business—two commands that seem perfectly clear to the developers will be perpetually confused by users. New users will make different mistakes from experienced users. Users with experience using different products will expect different behavior from the system and like, or dislike, different aspects of the system. Issues of this type must be uncovered and documented, and a business decision concerning them must be made.

I vividly remember my first encounter with an automatic teller machine (ATM) in Seattle in 1971. The man in front of me was also using the machine for the first time. (Remember, this was before hand calculators and touch-tone phones had become commonplace.) The man put in his card and was asked to "key in his personal identification number"; he did so without apparent error. Then the machine asked him to "select the type of transaction," and he pushed the proper button below. Next, it said "enter the amount of the withdrawal," and he paused before taking out his pen to enter the amount on the plastic window of the ATM! When it was finally my turn, I looked more closely and discovered that the plastic was nearly worn through from pen scratches made by other people "entering the amount of withdrawal."

Both objective and subjective measures of quality are required to make a good business decision concerning a new product.

What is software quality anyway?

Quality does not imply a more expensive product, or an overengineered one. It requires that we know what we want in advance, can describe it precisely, and can reliably build what was specified. One test of the process is whether we can define objective measurements to determine if the product being built was the product originally specified. Another equally important test is to determine if the original requirements and specifications were correct. This second test is routinely forgotten, ignored, or mislabeled "beta test."

Software quality cannot be determined by simply counting the incoming software problem reports (SPRs). SPRs are but one measure, and a tricky one at that. If only one SPR was ever received, but that one report said "program failed to execute," no further SPRs would ever be received. The count would be low, but the quality would not be high. Software defects can prevent huge sections of code from ever executing; once these defects are repaired, a raft of new SPRs may be generated.

Formally evaluating the ways in which human beings learn how to use a new product is essential for interactive computer programs. Ergonomics and computer science are not sufficiently mature to allow us to design interactive computer programs guaranteed to be correctly, efficiently, and reliably used without a "live test" with real users. This test should be measured objectively and subjectively—objectively by recording and analyzing every keystroke to identify common patterns of usage or misuse. Subjective measurements are just as important. It does not matter if a product works absolutely correctly if its users *perceive* its performance to be intolerable or its functionality worthless. Videotaping the experiences of new users receiving the boxed product in their office is highly recommended.

Achieving software quality is above all a management process. It is "a systematic way of guaranteeing that organized activities happen the way they are planned. [Quality control] is a management discipline concerned with preventing problems from occurring by creating the attitudes and controls that make prevention possible."[3]

Measuring software quality

The software industry must begin to establish a culture of quality measurement, consistent with all mature engineering disciplines. Software quality measurement will involve objective and subjective measures.

Measuring the pleasure experienced by our users will never be easy. However, it can and must be done. The ultimate users of our software products are human beings whose reactions determine our success. Waiting to measure the financial success of our products is too risky and somewhat foolhardy.

Let me suggest a diverse collection of information sources related to software quality and/or subjective measures of quality:

1. C. Jones, *Applied Software Measurement*, McGraw-Hill, New York, 1991.
2. T. Gilb, *Principles of Software Engineering Management*, Addison-Wesley, Reading, MA, 1988.
3. D. Norman, *The Psychology of Everyday Things*, Basic Books, New York, 1988.
4. J. Adams, *Flying Buttresses, Entropy, and O-Rings: The World of an Engineer*, Harvard University Press, Cambridge, MA, 1991.
5. C. Alexander, *The Oregon Experiment*, Oxford University Press, Oxford, UK, 1975.
6. M. Cusumano, *Japan's Software Factories: A Challenge to US Management*, Oxford University Press, Oxford, UK, 1991.
7. Grady, Robert B. *Practical Software Metrics for Project Management and Process Improvement*, Prentice Hall, 1992.

The keen observer will note that these are not your classic references on software quality measurement. Anyone who approaches this topic from a purely analytic perspective is doomed to fail.

QUALITY AND OBJECT-ORIENTED SOFTWARE ENGINEERING

Object-oriented software engineering produces software of higher quality because:

- Objects accept only a finite number of messages as inputs. One object cannot access the data within another object. This encapsulation simplifies both debugging and testing. This fundamental structure makes test scripts relatively easy to develop and to use—tests are developed for each class at the same time the class is being developed.

- In languages that support dynamic binding, a message replaces numerous branching statements required to accomplish a desired behavior. This can significantly decrease control flow complexity.
- Classes are stable chunks of methods and data structures that can be reused in a variety of systems and applications. Thus, their reliability can improve steadily. Reusability ratios between systems will increase from their current levels of 5–15% with traditional procedural methods to 60–90% with object-oriented technology. This means that a lot of code will be exercised again and again.
- The size of systems decreases due to dynamic binding and inheritance, so errors are easier to find.
- The model in the designer's head is directly expressed in the software itself. Unlike procedural languages, designs are actually preserved in the source text of the software, making the code more comprehensible to later maintenance engineers.

Previously unattainable levels of quality are possible through the combination of these factors. But these gains remain only theoretically possible unless we apply to our workaday world what we know about quality assurance (QA) in general and software quality in particular.

Developing software for potential reuse by many organizations creates some new quality challenges:

- The specification, testing, and documentation requirements of reusable software components are significantly greater, because the software under development may well be implanted into the core of a key customer's system or major application.
- Documentation style and comment format have by tradition been considered discretionary issues for each development organization. But when libraries of Software-ICs from different companies are combined into a single system and can be browsed on-line, such issues are no longer a local option. Standards will be required.
- The dynamic behavior of a system can be difficult to understand as the number of objects involved in a single use case grows. New types of tools are required to help users understand the dynamic behavior of large object-oriented systems. These tools will involve animation rather than ever more complicated "bubbles and arcs."

A higher level of development technology implies that we will attempt to tackle hitherto unachievable objectives. Every technology has its limits. Finding them requires failure. Object-oriented technology will rise to its limits as well.

BUILDING QUALITY COMPONENTS: A CASE HISTORY

Theoretical approaches to improved quality are interesting; they may convince you. Actual experiences in improving the quality of component libraries are a lot more interesting and convincing to me. I will present such an experience now.

In 1987, under the guidance of Donn Combelic, we took a completely new approach to improving the quality of ICpaks at Stepstone. Donn was not your typical QA manager for a start-up company. He learned to program on the Whirlwind computer at MIT in the early 1950s after being rescued from three sinking ships in World War II. During the 1970s, he was ITT's senior software technologist in Europe. He has lots of experience in designing and verifying complex, real-time systems. Donn now programs, finds bugs, and designs QA strategies for start-up companies as entertainment during his retirement. He also routinely works the *New York Times* crossword puzzle in less than 15 minutes, using an ink pen.

ICpak 201 was the second class library developed at Stepstone, and the first to be sold as a standalone product. The quality approach described here was used by a team of four people to assure the quality of ICpak 201—a product involving 50 classes, nearly 1,200 methods, and about 800 pages of documentation.

The QA team was led by Combelic and consisted of two young, bright, and aggressive software engineers (Jeff Fiducia and Rob Sanvido). In addition, a senior systems engineer (Ken Lerman), who spent most of his time trying to optimize the performance of ICpak 201, worked closely with the team. What is described below was a team effort with material contributions from all its members.

Role of QA

QA was thought of as "customer support before the product is shipped." The QA group also had the additional role of apprising management of the state of the developing product, so that a decision could be made concerning release. The approach involved quantification of both the objective and subjective aspects of quality.

One can approach this problem by assuming that at any point in time there are N errors in a software product. Theoretically, all should be removed. But if we could remove only one, which one should we remove? We should remove the error that would most annoy the user if it remained in the product.

Stated another way, errors should be removed according to the priority of their user annoyance rating (UAR). Suppose we rate each class based upon its UAR, where UAR is a subjective rating of annoyance given the existence of an error in that particular class. Each class has a UAR ranging in value from 1 to 10.

Because testing time is always finite and the number of tests is always infinite, we wanted to concentrate our testing effort on those classes with the highest UARs. If time ran out, we might not even have time to do any testing on classes with very low UARs. (In fact, we were able to test every class.)

Testing should be efficient; every other test should detect an error. The goal of QA is not to maximize the number of tests executed, but to maximize the number of errors found.

As with most products, there was a set of demonstration programs that had been constructed by the developers to demonstrate the product's capabilities. We used a standard UNIX utility, tcov, to evaluate the number of times each "one entry, one exit" code sequence had been executed. This utility was modified to provide a similar measure for Objective-C programs. With this modified utility running, we then ran each demo extensively to "pile up execution counts." We then postprocessed the resulting information to determine the test coverage for each method of each class.

In the meantime, we constructed a list of every method of every class. We could now scan the output of tcov on a method-by-method basis to determine how comprehensively each method had been exercised with the demonstration programs. Each method was marked N or R. N meant there was no need to test because enough of the method had been executed. Also, simple one-line methods were assigned an N if they appeared to be correct, even if they had not been executed. R meant that the code should be read because the method had not been executed at all or insufficiently.

About 80% of the methods were marked by an N on this first pass. Please note the amount of time that we saved by this approach. We saved having to write additional test cases for over 900 methods!

Each of the methods marked with an R was inspected or read. During this process, the following rule was applied:

> If it is estimated that an explicit test of this method will have greater than a 50% probability of demonstrating the presence of an error, test it; otherwise, do not.

About one third of the methods that were inspected were then tested. More than 25% of the methods marked for testing did, in fact, reveal errors during testing. Unfortunately, we did not keep adequate records to later determine the number of errors found in the code that was not tested. During the code reading itself, a number of errors were discovered and promptly fixed by the developers.

The RAT, Testers, and TestDroid

A mission of the QA group was to create an efficient, reproducible test whenever the presence of an error appeared to have been demonstrated. The problem is that when errors show up during an interactive session, it is often difficult to reproduce such an error exactly.

RAT. To remedy this problem, another tool was constructed to record all the user input events during an interactive test session in such a way that the session could be "played back" on demand. This recorder of *ad hoc* tests (RAT) proved unusually valuable. Because we were dealing with an object-oriented product, we could record the messages generated from every user input event. When played back, the session could be reproduced exactly.

This user event recording was also processed and refined in some useful ways. For example, by setting all the time intervals to zero the session could be reproduced at high speed—often very useful. Further, we converted the binary record to ASCII so that user events could be edited, concatenated, speeded up, or converted back to binary form. In this way, long sessions could be constructed and run automatically. This was unusually helpful when trying to diagnose memory leakage errors, for example.

RAT was especially valuable as a safety net for limits testers. As a tester began to test some particularly unstable portion of the system, the RAT was turned on and the tester moved ahead aggressively. If a problem showed up, the testers knew that they could always go back and replay the session using the RAT. Often, the developer or tester could discover what was wrong the first time they replayed the session. For difficult errors, the session would have to be replayed many times, but it still proved an invaluable tool to testers and developers alike.

As developers constructed sets of classes, they were simultaneously compiling recordings of many user sessions. These were handed over at the time the code was released for initial QA. Essentially, the developers used the tools for their own unit tests.

Class tester. A test case generator was built to scan all classes in the system and construct a test class for each class, and a test method for each method. Each class tester was generated in Objective-C, along with the appropriate superclasses to be tested. The result was a parallel hierarchy of class testers that mirrored the original inheritance tree of the software under test. These class testers were also organized so that *ad hoc* tests could be added within the appropriate class tester at any time.

Method tester. The class testers also had method testers embedded within them. Each method tester was automatically provided with arguments of the correct type. Where appropriate, the method tester would also generate random numbers to insert as arguments within each method. The method tester had provisions for verifying that the return value was of the correct type and that the method had no memory leakage. Additional tests were generated to verify polymorphic and inherited behaviors.

The tests for inheritance were exhaustive: for each class, it was verified that every method in all its superclasses was executable and gave correct results.

With an object-oriented language one must verify that:

- all inherited methods used by the class are correct
- all arguments that are subclasses of the specified argument type are correct
- all methods by the same name perform the same logical operation
- the documentation is accurate and sufficient for an isolated user to use the components

Allowances were made for manual intervention when interactive behavior needed to be verified. If the display was correct, the user could so indicate and the test would continue.

The TestDroid. As one would expect in a good object-oriented language, the TestDroid was just another class in the system. It was actually a dispatcher that concatenated the class testers and method testers while incorporating the RAT as an integral part of all tests. It also found the appropriate log from the previous similar test and made sure that the logs were set up properly and recorded. It recorded the date, time, name of the tester, version being tested, etc. It also provided control of the actual running of the test, the interaction with the tester, etc.

The Testing Process

Each tester was instructed to spend about one hour per day just running demos (with the RAT turned on) to try to "break" the demo or to notice new errors in difficult, complex or unlikely sequences. These exercises not only served to give the testers a little relaxation, but turned up a certain number of errors, which came with a ready-made reproducible test case.

From the starting point of more than 1,200 methods, only 255 needed full test cases developed for them. Each of the 255 methods was tested until one of five conditions was met. These conditions were recorded using the following codes:

TOK	Tests okay.
COK	Code reading shows okay.
USED	Used adequately by execution of demos.
50%	Less than 50% chance of a test revealing an error.
TRT	An automatic minimal test was generated for this method.

Four progress codes were also recorded:

TNG   Demonstrated no good by test execution.
CNG   Code reading shows probable mistake.
DNG   Code reading shows probable faulty design.
READ   Code was read but the result was indeterminate.

A progress sheet was made to record progress for each class. A sample sheet is provided below.

Class Name

Date/Code	Date/Code	Date/Code	Date/Code	NO ML	OK	Method	File

The objective is to have a check mark in the OK column for each method of each class. For OK to be checked, one of the five termination conditions had to be reached, with no observed memory leakage.

For ICpak 201, the objective was to check each of the 255 OK boxes before the work of the QA group could be considered complete. That objective was achieved for ICpak 201 before it was shipped to the first customer.

Throughout the day, new date/code information was recorded on a master progress sheet. At 4:00 p.m. each day, a copy of the master progress sheet was made for each member of the group, and the results were discussed at the daily QA meeting. The meetings usually lasted only 5 or 10 minutes, but occasionally lasted longer to resolve problems or to discuss solutions. The meeting always concluded with a calculation of the number of OK boxes checked and the day's progress as computed by subtracting the prior day's count.

These daily meetings were also helpful in achieving steady and rapid progress in a start-up entrepreneurial environment. The public recognition of daily progress seemed to provide a real psychological lift for the group.

Results

One of the most striking moments in this project came when the development manager stood up in a company meeting and said, "ICpak 201 is shipping and it has no known errors." There was a firm basis for making that statement, and later experiences proved it to be essentially accurate.

About 80% of the product code was found to be essentially error-free by running the demos and using the tcov execution counts. Approximately two thirds of the remaining 20% of the code was determined by code reading to be probably bug-free. That left about 7% of the code suspect and requiring careful attention.

About 40% of the errors were found as a result of analyzing execution counts made available by the use of tcov, by code reading, and by testing dictated by code reading. About 40% of the errors were found by the TestDroid. The remaining 20% were found by "ad hoc" testing, serendipity, and good luck.

In the first year after ICpak 201 was shipped, only five reproducible errors were reported by customers. Five errors in more than 30,000 source lines of code is an honorable number. The industry average is 10 per 1,000. Fewer than 2 errors per 10,000 source lines of code is about as high as we ever get in the software industry. Please keep firmly in mind that this was a cash-strapped, start-up company working on an innovative product with a fixed delivery schedule.

Where this work really paid off, however, was when we ported the product to a new hardware and software platform. As soon as the code would work at all, we immediately had almost 60,000 lines of test code we could run against the ported software to determine what worked and what did not.

Years later, the QA manager was working on another project where he overheard a user of ICpak 201 say, "We have almost a hundred programmers using ICpak 201. In nine months we have yet to find an error."

Documentation

About 800 pages of documentation were generated for ICpak 201, most of it being the user's guide. The initial documents were prepared by engineers who preferred writing computer programs to preparing user documents.

As portions of documents were received by QA, they were read by one QA team member. Corrections and notes were made on the physical documents; then, the marked document was passed on to the next team member, who also read the document and added new notes or corrections. That doubly edited document was returned to engineering for rework. When the document was reworked, QA repeated the double-editing process before returning the final draft to engineering.

Because customers had access to the source code of ICpak 201, we wanted the code to appear to have come from a homogeneous group within one company. Including comments, there were about 45,000 lines to review. The QA group read every line of code and every comment. They submitted a critique on its style, format, and comments to engineering. There were few arguments.

SUMMARY

Introducing a new technology creates new opportunities for improving the process by which work is done. Where quality is concerned, some important changes are overdue.

In essence, we have learned from this chapter that:

- Both objective and subjective quality must be considered.
- Testing is done to estimate the actual quality of a new product and to assist management in deciding when or if the product should be shipped.
- Because the number of tests are always infinite, careful thought must be given to the testing strategy so that every test results in the maximum improvement of the product.
- Objects reduce the probability of many kinds of errors and provide an extremely convenient unit of testability within a system.
- Developing the test strategy and rigorously managing the testing process every day is essential for producing great-quality software.

But surely the greatest quality challenge of all is to create a culture in which quality (both objective and subjective) is routinely measured at every stage of development. Only with detailed measurement can we know that we have achieved superior quality.

> *Discovering cracks in a completed structure enables the designer to learn the weaknesses of his knowledge and thereby to improve upon future designs.*[4]

NOTES

1. At software symposium held at Ontologic Corporation, January 20, 1987.
2. Philip Crosby, *Quality Is Free*, McGraw-Hill, New York, 1979, p. 17.
3. *Ibid.*, p. 22.
4. Henry Petroski, *To Engineer Is Human: The Role of Failure in Successful Design*, St. Martin's Press, New York, 1985.

12

A Road Map for Change

A great product is deep, indulgent, complete, and elegant.

Guy Kawasaki
The Macintosh Way
Scott, Foresman & Company, 1990, p. 50.

I have been involved in several major software technology change projects in sizable companies ($100 million to $25 billion in annual sales). Our clients know they have a problem, and they believe the problem is a technology problem. Rare is the company where everything is working so smoothly and efficiently that all we need to do is change programming technology. The success of any organization depends upon a lot more than software technology.

The purpose of this chapter is to put technology change in its proper context. I will do that in a realistic way. This chapter began life as a report developed for a mid-sized company interested in improving organizational productivity. I led a team of consultants hired to diagnose the company's software problems, suggest solutions, and assist in the change process.

This chapter will provide a practical view of technological innovation to help you avoid some of the pitfalls of a "technology first" approach. We begin with a statement of the problem to be solved, then review the diagnosis, and finally describe the therapy plan.

After doing a diagnosis and determining the right therapy for a patient, doctors must also consider the sequence of presentation of the diagnosis, the style of presentation, the possible side effects, and the appropriate bedside manner. You can't just walk in and announce to a patient that he or she has cancer, a major operation is required, and there is a fifty–fifty chance of survival. Before you suggest major technology changes for your organization, spend time understanding the broader issues within your company.

PROBLEM STATEMENT

> Econo-Metrics collects, processes, analyzes and reports econometric data for its customers. The company expresses a need to update its computer-based systems. Their traditional batch information systems are years behind the state of the art. They "must" be replaced with interactive systems. Management is convinced that technological changes can help increase the company's overall productivity and improve its market share.

ASSESSING THE STATE OF THE COMPANY

A workshop was held for two and a half days to assess the current state of the company and develop a strategy for achieving efficiencies in the use of information systems throughout Econo-Metrics. A dozen key managers and technologists involved in delivering and using computer systems participated, along with two consultants serving as facilitators.

The workshop began with each participant describing one wish—the single new information systems capability they felt would most benefit the company. On the first day, these desires were listed and recorded publicly. As the discussion diverged into discussions of near-term issues, each issue was publicly recorded but not dealt with on the spot. On the second day analysis and synthesis began, as participants developed mission statements for the business and specific proposals for addressing those issues. On the evening of the second day, the participants presented their mission statements to Dr. Bennett,[1] founder of Econo-Metrics. During the final half day, they worked with Dr. Bennett to refine the mission statement and develop a plan for achieving it.

Information needs of the company

Econo-Metrics feels pressure from its competitors. It knows it is possible to analyze data more efficiently and appear more technologically advanced to its customers. Dr. Bennett challenged Econo-Metrics' managers to provide "visual access to client data *instantaneously*."

Data access

Emerging technologies make it possible to dramatically improve both the quality and quantity of econometric data. The result is an exponentially growing quantity of data from a similarly growing number of sources. Simultaneously, customers demand nearly immediate access to data integrated from many sources.

Data reduction

The same technologies that make data collection more pervasive also enable new options for analysis, report development, and data presentation. Data reduction must be accurate and timely. Customers require answers to queries within 24–48 hours.

Data integration

The value of a database increases geometrically with the amount of additional data that can be accurately integrated with it. Users want to be able to fuse data from an ever-widening variety of sources before performing their analysis—data fusion, they call it.

Modeling

Econometric modeling is becoming increasingly important. Regression analyses are no longer adequate; customers now want specialized simulations, allowing them to play "what-if" games.

More normative data

"What is your experience with . . . ?" is an increasingly popular question from a new client company. Proper answers require access to all previous information on the topic at hand, but with sensitive or proprietary data reliably screened out.

More knowledge of the customer

The consumers of econometric data have changed over the years and will continue to change. Directing the business only toward its traditional customers could be a costly mistake, because it might only represent a tiny fraction of the real market. Yet, ignoring the traditional customer base could prove equally hazardous.

Reporting

Customers are beginning to acquire powerful personal computers. They are beginning to ask why it takes so long for Econo-Metrics to produce a simple report. Laser-printed reports with professional graphics are expected today. Color graphics combined with 3-D images would be even better.

Current information technology

You can estimate the overall complexity of information systems within an organization by simply counting the variety of:

- computers
- operating systems
- programming languages
- database systems
- communication systems

Econo-Metrics has three types of computers, three operating systems, four programming languages including SAS (a statistical programming language), five database systems, and one corporate data communications system—a complexity rating of 16.

Econo-Metrics can be grateful—some large companies have ratings in three digits! Nevertheless, incompatible programming languages, operating systems, and computer systems clearly complicate the company's efforts to integrate more data and provide more rapid access to that data.

Software

Proprietary analysis software is as precious an asset to Econo-Metrics as data; it represents an encapsulation of corporate knowledge. The more analytic abilities that are captured within software, the better Econo-Metrics can serve its clients. Therefore, Econo-Metrics must be in the business of developing and maintaining software for internal use.

Analysts within the company have the predictable difficulty trying to use software tools such as TSO, SAS, and FORTRAN. With more capable tools, analysts might perform their own statistical analyses rather than communicate those needs to a "data junkie," who then works to express those needs as cryptic incantations to a remote host computer. With even better tools, analysts might do their own graphics.

The existing Econo-Metrics system consists of the following distinct items, which we will discuss separately:

- user interface
- operating system
- programming languages
- statistics packages

User interface. The terminals at Econo-Metrics operate over a remote line to a time-shared IBM 3083 running MVS/TSO. A full-screen text editor is used to edit the text of a program for batch submission. It took about 10 minutes to submit and process a simple job.

However, it often took over 45 minutes to determine the meaning of a particular error message. No manuals were available to learn TSO or even to look up error messages. To find the meaning of an error message required a telephone call to the remote computing services vendor and a follow-up call to their expert in another city 1,000 miles away. Even the expert had no reference manuals, but "had the impression" that the error was "x." On the basis of that impression, a change was made and the "job" was resubmitted.

A few hours later, it was discovered that the impression was wrong.

Operating system. Econo-Metrics uses the MVS/TSO operating system; it serves as the development environment as well. This classic mid-1960s software technology is reputed to be the most complex, difficult to use, and difficult to repair in the industry. A famous computer scientist once said, "Using TSO is like trying to kick a dead whale down the beach."[2]

Econo-Metrics is also using at least two other operating systems—MS-DOS on IBM PCs and VMS on VAX. These three systems are essentially unconnected.

Programming languages. Internal Econo-Metrics software has been developed in either FORTRAN or COBOL — programming languages developed in the 1950s. Such languages are sadly wasteful of precious human resources. Better choices exist.

Econometric modeling applications should be built with programming languages that are good at data modeling and computationally efficient. FORTRAN is efficient but is just terrible as a modeling language. COBOL was designed for first-generation business application development. It is largely out of date for building the types of business applications users want in the 1990s.

One choice would be to use a more modern procedural language, such as C, that has sophisticated lower-level computer-aided software engineering (CASE) tools available and is a more powerful data modeling language. These tools include interpreters or incremental compilers, powerful debuggers, testing tools, documentation tools, and optimization tools.

An even better choice would be a hybrid object-oriented programming language based upon the known language. An object-oriented extension of FORTRAN or COBOL might prove ideal. Objective-C with a Smalltalk front-end would be my choice.

Statistics packages. SAS is a batch-oriented statistical programming language being used at Econo-Metrics. Graphics are generated with SASGRAF. Quality interactive packages such as interactive versions of SAS, S, DataDesk, SPSS, and others exist but are not being used, because the current generation of hardware is inappropriate for their use.

Hardware

An expensive, overloaded mainframe computer is the primary workhorse for data analysis and presentation. Hundreds of users are queuing up for its CPU. To supplement the mainframe, five standalone minicomputers (VAX 11/780s) were acquired several years ago. Custom software was developed to transport data from a tape written on one machine to a disk on the other.

An MIS organization is responsible for managing the data center: the mainframe, network, and minicomputers. Isolated IBM PCs have been purchased and are connected to the mainframe. Most commonly, they sit with their power off.

Prospective PC users were easily convinced they should invest in a personal computer. But when the machine arrived with a stack of application software, a set of DOS manuals, and a terminal emulation package, the thrill wore off in a great hurry.

Communications

There are two types of communications: between computers and between people. Econo-Metrics needs help with both.

Between computers. Terminal controllers connect remote terminals to the IBM host. No direct communication exists between the VAXs and the IBM 3083. Files can be moved between systems using magnetic tape or floppy disks, but moving a program is a major task, possibly requiring a substantial fraction of the original development cost.

Between people. No electronic mail exists within Econo-Metrics today. Telephones and overnight couriers are used instead—an expensive and time-consuming alternative.

Organizational dynamics

An information-processing company such as Econo-Metrics is not unlike a manufacturing organization; raw data is processed in several steps, ultimately leading to a finished, packaged product. And, at any given time, a number of products are being produced by different people for different customers.

In any such process, there will be bottlenecks both obvious and surprising. With a simulation model of the organization's work flow, analyses could be done on the effect of selectively removing a bottleneck or optimizing some process. Note that a simulation model is more than the typical information model, or even enterprise model. It must be sufficient to model the dynamics of the work flow within the organization.

Econo-Metrics needs a model to analyze the costs and benefits of selected modifications to their internal "report manufacturing center."

Summary of findings

Management support will be mandatory to catch up with and surpass the information systems available to competitors. Considerable management, technical, and financial resources must be dedicated to such a project. Typically, such upgrade projects take 18–30 months to achieve their initial objectives and cost between 10–15% of yearly sales for their duration. This project is not just a project to upgrade computers but also to redeploy human and organizational resources. It will be expensive.

The project will require many professional employees to make measurable changes in their daily work practices and tools. More than one task may require fewer workers. Managing the human process is as important as selecting the appropriate technology.

VISION OF THE FUTURE

It has been said that management is the process of determining where you are going and ensuring that you get there. A portion of the workshop was devoted to creating such a vision: Where should Econo-Metric's systems be in five years? We needed a clear strategic vision against which to evaluate near-term tactics.

Data collection

Econometric analyses can be no better than the data being analyzed. To the extent that a particular kind of data can be collected at its source without the need for manual data collection and manual data entry, substantial improvements in the quality of data can be achieved as well as improved timeliness of the analyses.

Inexpensive and infinitely patient microprocessors can be deployed to collect raw data. They can even perform some basic data cleaning at the same time.

Data reduction

Up-to-date equipment should be provided for information workers; modest capital investments can yield extraordinary benefits.

Analysts earning $60,000 a year can easily have enough computing power in their offices to achieve 90% of their data analyses and graphics needs for a capital expenditure of $10,000 to $20,000—the equivalent of one to two months' worth of their cost to the organization. As a result, turnaround times would be reduced from hours to seconds or minutes.

Data integration

Econo-Metrics collects data from a variety of sources. The quality of this data depends upon the quality of the design, precision of the measurement instrument, accuracy of the data collection and handling process, and accuracy of the analysis and reporting process. The goal is to integrate the data thoroughly so that accurate analyses can be performed across a number of data sets.

Data storage and retrieval

Customers are requesting faster and faster analyses of increasing quantities of data. This calls for better systems overall—hardware, software, and communications.

Communications

Computers are often more important for their communications capabilities than for their computing capabilities. Computers are typically used to support a single analyst performing a statistical analysis. But the same computer and the same peripherals could be used to send electronic mail, schedule meetings, access remote databases, and support the process by which analyses are reviewed for accuracy and then delivered to customers.

Reporting

Customers want easy access to all data within Econo-Metrics' proprietary databases, and they want the results presented quickly and professionally. Current workstations can prepare such presentations more quickly, more easily, and with higher-quality graphics than can the antiquated batch systems.

SYNCHRONIZING THE VISION WITH THE COMPANY MISSION

Any major organizational change effort must be designed and implemented so that the changes are consistent with the skills, culture, resources, and business objectives of the company. As the inevitable inconsistencies arise, senior management should be informed and involved in the change process. The easiest way is to have all key decision makers involved in each checkpoint meeting.

Econo-Metrics' corporate culture is that of a service organization. As someone said in the workshop, "If a customer asks for apple pie and we don't have it, we say, 'we don't have the pie, but we have planted an apple tree to be sure that we have apple pie the next time you ask for it.'" A supplier of standard products cannot customize each product and must be prepared to reject some requests from even their most favored customers.

It is hard to develop standard products in a company with a strong services culture. Management must make a decision: to create a separate software products company, to create a separate products division, to design and price software products as a service, or to stay out of the products business altogether.

Standard software is difficult enough to build, validate, document, modify, and evolve. Customized software for every customer, every computer, every workstation, and every product line must be paid for on a time and materials basis. Given the fundamental differences in culture, Econo-Metrics should consider forming a separate company or division to provide standard software products if it decides to go into the software products business.

IMPLEMENTING THE VISION

A statistician friend of mine has a sign on his desk saying, "If you didn't come into this office before you collected your data, don't come in now!" Econo-Metrics is essentially trying to move from second-generation computer technology, developed in the 1950s and 1960s, to fourth-generation technology. It is going to require requirements analysis, design, verification, and quality assurance, just like an econometric study. The quality of the results depends upon the quality of the original design and the attention to details during implementation.

The change process unfolds as follows:

1. hire a technology general contractor
2. appoint a productivity coordinator
3. establish checkpoints
4. grow internal champions
5. establish a process for acquiring new technology
    a. develop requirement
    b. design the system with purchased components and glue
    c. acquire appropriate technology
6. provide training
7. measure and report results

Let's discuss each step in more detail.

The technology general contractor

Starting and controlling any fundamental change within a sizable company is not easy. An approach that works well is to acquire an external, technology general contractor to lead the technology change process. It must involve a long-term contract—say, two years duration. Hiring an external contractor publicly commits management to the change process while providing a critical new resource to the organization. The technology general contractor has no day-to-day responsibilities other than to focus on the change project. Working with dedicated resources from within the company, the technology general contractor helps initiate, track, and direct the change process.

Appoint a productivity coordinator

One experienced, competent individual should be given the full-time job of scheduling and managing the set of tasks and subtasks to be accomplished within the next 18–30 months. This productivity coordinator has the assignment of coordinating corporate actions, working with the technology general contractor, and measuring the results of the projects.

Establish checkpoints

The technology general contractor must get prior agreement that meetings with executive management will be regularly scheduled and held to review the project's progress. Initially, reviews should be held monthly; as measurable progress occurs, they can be held less frequently.

The productivity coordinator will lead these reviews. He or she will meticulously record progress and develop plans for the upcoming period. All persons with the authority to implement these plans must be present at the checkpoint reviews. A few days after the review, a summary face-to-face presentation will be provided to senior management. These meetings will keep management in the loop and help maintain their interest and support for the change project.

Grow champions

"No ordinary involvement with a new idea provides the energy required to cope with the indifference and resistance that major technological change provokes. Champions must display persistence and courage of heroic quality," according to Edward Schon of MIT.[3]

The popular business book *In Search of Excellence* studied successful corporations. One attribute they shared was that each had developed a process for finding and supporting champions of new ideas. The better developed the support system for such champions, the more profitable the companies. This support system always involved appropriate protectors—in particular, an executive champion and a godfather. Let's examine the role of these individuals in a little more detail.

Product champions. Product champions are zealots, even fanatics. They may well be egotistical, cranky, and difficult. But product champions know what they want to accomplish and will let nothing stand in their way.

Executive champions. An executive champion is typically a former product champion who knows what it takes to implement a successful idea and is willing to provide appropriate resources.

Godfathers. The godfather is commonly an older individual who provides the corporate role model for the product champion. Bill Hewlett (Hewlett-Packard), An Wang (Wang Laboratories), and Thomas Edison (General Electric) are examples of successful godfathers.

For technological change to become a part of the corporate culture, the company must find a way to cultivate and retain product champions, executive champions, and godfathers. If they are not a part of the corporate culture, then during the initial change process, efforts should be made to create these roles and support them organizationally.

Establish a process for acquiring new technology

Develop requirements. Any engineering project must begin with a clear and understandable description of the needs of its intended users. This statement must address needs, not solutions—the "what," not the "how."

But people often cannot tell you what they need, because they don't know what is possible. Nontechnical staff in particular may need assistance; therefore, demonstrations of pilot systems or other technology demonstrations may be required to provide examples of what can be done. These demonstrations need not be fully functional or connected to any other systems for users to get an idea of what contemporary technology can accomplish.

When more comprehensive computing and communications capabilities are introduced to a company, new and different kinds of users emerge to exploit them. The Lotus 1-2-3 programmer provides a classic example; most cannot satisfy their computational needs using a traditional computer language and would not use a computer if they had to. Anticipate the needs of these new users as well as your traditional users.

As we begin a technology introduction process in a company, we must document in writing what is currently being done within the organization. From there comes the giant creative leap—the proposed solution.

Proposing solutions. The proposed solution or proposed options should also be documented and reviewed. But it is critical that this be a separate document from the requirements document. The proposed solution or solutions will have to address the "how" questions.

The most common mistake in major development projects is to converge too quickly on a particular solution without having seriously considered competing alternatives. I have often suggested to companies that they not only allow competing solutions to be described in detail but that they continue with competing designs. Internal competition is healthy and should be encouraged.

Design the system with purchased components and glue. In a previous chapter, I introduced my motto: "Buy the best, build the rest." Building software is too time consuming and risky to justify the reinvention of any purchasable components. The tough part is determining how compatible new software must be with existing systems. The stronger this requirement, the fewer real options exist for making changes.

Carefully analyze how each component will integrate with existing components. Give priority to integration over basic functionality—the ultimate power of the overall system depends more upon its being fully integrated than upon the functionality of its individual components.

Other goals should be a high degree of component integration, a better tool set, and a consistent user interface. To some degree, these can be achieved with many off-the-shelf packages. However, to thoroughly integrate all computational resources, Econo-Metrics must expect to build some specialized software.

The seemingly simple goal of providing one common user interface to all databases and tools within the company has rarely been achieved; it is fraught with technical challenges. Another way to state this goal is that the system should be built entirely of reusable user interface components.

Acquiring appropriate technology. Both hardware and software should be acquired, not built, whenever possible.

Hardware. Electrical components now need to be separated by less than one micron on the semiconductor surface, thus providing very powerful computing capability on a single chip. Ten-year-old mainframes can often be replaced by more powerful desktop computers. As microprocessors begin to be used in parallel, this statement is even more compelling.

Software. Develop new models and components using objects.

Object-oriented software engineering can benefit Econo-Metrics in the following ways:

- Models of the problem domain (that is, econometrics) can be easily extended as understanding deepens.
- Generic components or products can be specialized for the needs of a particular customer without altering the standard products.
- A generic user interface for a variety of applications and databases can be created with economy, flexibility, and power.
- Toolsets exist to develop iconic, direct manipulation user interfaces to applications and databases.
- Objects can be passed naturally across dissimilar computers without concocting specialized formatters or parsers. Among other things, this means that text, graphics, and statistical data could be freely accessed throughout the company on heterogeneous computers and operating systems.

Provide training

Valued employees must become a part of the technological change process. After all, their daily working environment and habits must change as a result of introducing new technology. To maximize the new technology's effects and minimize the risk of its being rejected by the rank and file, acquire or develop proper training programs.

If you buy software components, you should buy installation and appropriate training for all users at the same time. On-the-job training is both expensive and error prone.

Report results

The technology general contractor is responsible for providing detailed and unbiased reports of the project results to executive and project management on a monthly basis. Reporting should be organized item-for-item by comparing developments against the original project objectives.

CONCLUSIONS

Object-oriented technology is not a silver bullet. No single software technology is sufficient to fix a company's fundamental problems. Success depends upon a host of business, human, technical, and organizational issues that must be successfully managed — issues that are more important than any software technology. Before considering any change in software technology, be sure to consider the context within which such a change is being suggested. Is this the right treatment for the patient? Is the patient healthy enough to withstand the treatment?

Moving from second-generation computing technology to fourth-generation technology can be done. But such a change must stem from a fundamental business motivation and must be done with knowledge of other near-term demands on the business. The costs of such a rapid transition will be considerable and the risks are significant. The larger the transition being attempted, the more expensive and the higher the risks.

If your organization does not need to take a huge step, don't take it. There are lots of injured (and former) companies that tried to take an unnecessarily large step and failed.

REFERENCES

I recommend the following books to anyone pondering the development of a software products business or software products company:

- *Silicon Valley Guide : A Guide to Financial Success in Software*[4]
  A comprehensive handbook (over 300 pages) for creating a new software business. It deals with financial, legal, and business issues related to the software business.
- *The Mythical Man-Month: Essays on Software Engineering*[5]
  The classic guide to the traditional issues in developing software products and managing software projects.
- *A Practitioner's Guide to Software Engineering*[6]
  Just as the title suggests, this is an excellent guide to the practical application of software engineering practices in a commercial development project.
- *The Psychology of Computer Programming*[7]
  Since the 1960s, Jerry Weinberg has written a series of important books describing the software business, often from a humanistic perspective. This classic has been one of the best-selling books in the computer industry.
- *Walkthroughs, Inspections and Technical Reviews*[8]
  An excellent description of how to conduct reviews of technical material, and even how to conduct a technical meeting.

NOTES

1. I use this hypothetical name in honor of Dr. Carl Bennett of the Battelle Memorial Institute, the best statistician I have ever had the pleasure to work with.
2. A statement made by Steve Johnson in the Murray Hill cafeteria of Bell Labs in the early 1970s.
3. As quoted in Modesto A. Maidique, Entrepreneurs, champions, and technological innovation," *Sloan Management Review*, Winter, 60, 1980.
4. Daniel Remer, Paul Remer, and Robert Dunaway, Microsoft Press, Redmond, WA, 1984.
5. Fred Brooks, Addison-Wesley, Reading, MA, 1975.
6. Roger Pressman, Prentice Hall, Englewood Cliffs, NJ, 1981.
7. Jerry Weinberg, Van Nostrand Reinhold, New York, NY, 1971.
8. Dan Freedman and Jerry Weinberg, Little, Brown, Boston, MA, 1980.

13

Lessons Learned

For mature thought there is no mechanical substitute.

Vannevar Bush
"As We May Think"
Atlantic Monthly, July 1945

Brad Cox and I founded Stepstone[1] on June 6, 1983. For five years, we developed commercial software products using object-oriented programming. I would like to share some important lessons I learned in the hope that you will forge ahead to make different and more interesting mistakes.

The order of the following lessons does not indicate anything other than the order in which I thought of them.

DEVELOPMENT LESSONS

Prototyping

Professor Fred Brooks counseled us years ago to "plan to throw one away; you will anyway."[2] He almost got it right.

Actually, plan to throw two away. Each iteration of a product's development should involve the complete development cycle—from requirements analysis and design to system test and customer acceptance.

It is a myth that object-oriented programming provides a magical way to transform research into a final, engineered product. Object-oriented programming is a wonderful tool for research; it allows us to press the limits of the application of software technology. But engineering is a different activity, with a different process and a different objective. It cannot be done in a vacuum. It requires customer evaluation and quality assurance at every stage.

Requirements and design

Requirements exist when they are publicly recorded and formal customer agreement has been obtained. They do not exist informally.

An idea is not a design. Like requirements, a design is a formal record of decisions that have been made during the design process. These decisions must be formally reviewed with the customer to ensure that the developers have correctly understood the requirements and transformed them into a designed solution. Misunderstandings must be corrected at the earliest possible stage. A formal design is required before product development can begin.

Quality

Quality may be free in the long term, but in the near term it seems expensive. This expense cannot be considered optional for a producer of commercial software components.

Software-ICs are the encapsulated, collective knowledge of some system or application domain. A knowledge representation of this type must be rigorously validated and verified by independent, external sources. Validation involves checking the logic and consistency of the knowledge representation; verification involves checking the accuracy of each component and each behavior.

Software-ICs cannot be produced by individual artisans. Their development requires an engineering process with industrial-strength quality assurance at each stage.

Documentation

More than half the effort in constructing commercial-quality software components should go into documenting them. Each component must have a specification sheet. We also found that detailed tutorials and user's guides, showing how to assemble components to form systems or applications, are equally important.

The limitation in using a new component package is the time it takes for a new engineer to become familiar with it. Such learning time is the largest expense borne by the organization that acquires the package. Component suppliers should strive to reduce this time to a minimum.

Never confuse documentation with paper. We must begin to more aggressively use alternative media to communicate the relevant aspects of software components. An example of such an alternative media is interactive CD-ROMs, which can include hypertext, still and animated graphics, and sound along with text. Simple and inexpensive videotapes should also be used much more aggressively. It is too hard to describe the look and feel of interactive graphical applications or systems using text only.

COMPONENTS LESSONS

Components vs. software-ICs

It is easy to be seduced by your own techniques for seduction. As Brad Cox and I began to think about commercializing software components (or Software-ICs as we began to call them), we imagined that components built within one system or application could be reused by someone else in another system or application. We were wrong.

An application or system built using object-oriented programming techniques consists of classes or components. Those internal components are actually quite different from a library of components designed and engineered for reusability. This distinction between internal application classes and commercial reusable components (or, to use Stepstone's term, Software-ICs) is crucial.

Commercial components must be designed for reuse under defined circumstances and they must have an acceptable level of quality. Because a component is being sold does not mean that it is a commercial-grade component. As I am writing this chapter, most components being sold in the market have not been subjected to the most rudimentary levels of testing. Commercial components should be delivered to customers with their associated test cases to verify that they work as advertised. Begin your evaluation process by reading the test cases.

Experience suggests that the number of lines of test code will exceed the number of lines of code in the component libraries. Component libraries will eventually grow to be quite large—thousands of classes for sure. When they do, many management issues will arise. Such issues include:

Naming
What happens when the library contains 3 or 30 different versions of the String class? Five or 50 versions of the Collection class?

Configuration control
The functionality of components will change in ways that cannot always be upwardly compatible. How are multiple versions of the same component managed? What happens when several versions of the same component are required within the same application or system? What happens when several developers want to modify a component at the same time?

Accessing
How do you identify components that might prove useful in a system under development? Can smarter techniques be employed to find appropriate functionality?

Dependencies
Components are typically dependent upon many other components. What constraints should be imposed upon designers regarding these dependencies? How can dependencies be made explicit? Enforceable?

Distribution
Components will be geographically distributed across a variety of hardware and software environments. How can software updates be distributed? How can components be customized efficiently?

Responsibility
Who is responsible if a component fails in a different hardware or software environment from that in which it was built?

Quality
Components inherit capabilities from other components. A complete suite of tests must be developed and run on all behaviors, including inherited behaviors, of all classes.

Some enterprises already have thousands of components; a few have tens of thousands. In those quantities, these issues can easily become the bottleneck to corporate reuse of software components.

Source availability

Although you can now buy source code to a variety of class libraries, I do not believe that you necessarily should. The last thing a competent software manager should want is another few tens of thousands of lines of code to maintain.

Further, successful suppliers of components will steadily improve their products. If their customers have acquired and customized the source code, it can become exceedingly difficult to accommodate updates.

Regardless of recent advice to the contrary,[3] cloned copies of source code cannot be the long-term solution to the software crisis. We need standard components that are sold in a package and used as delivered without modification.

To make this a reality, we must understand the idiosyncratic needs of particular companies and industries, and customize libraries of components to meet those needs. Source code availability is not needed. Accurate, thorough, and usable documentation, quality control, and customization capabilities are needed. We also need specialized components that can be used intact, not generic components that have to be specialized.

PEOPLE LESSONS

Training

To design and engineer commercial-quality component packages requires skills and experiences not ordinarily available in the commercial marketplace. I have found that it takes at least 6 months, and often 12, before new software engineers become fully productive object-oriented software engineers. The more explicit training and employee development you provide, the more rapidly new engineers become fully productive. Therefore, hire in advance of need and invest in extensive training for new employees.

Real programmers don't reuse

The current culture within the software industry can be expressed as, "I am no more interested in reusing a subroutine from Fred than Hemingway was in reusing a paragraph from Shakespeare." This attitude is inappropriate.

Component providers must start building components of exceptional ingenuity and even more exceptional quality. These components may be finely crafted to satisfy a particular requirement, such as needing minimal memory or achieving maximum flexibility. Designers and engineers working for component suppliers will be analogous to designers of integrated circuits. They should have excellent skills and immaculate track records for product quality.

Nevertheless, I have regularly experienced a negative attitude toward reusability. Capable designers and engineers see themselves as gurus who cannot afford the errors or shortcomings of others, and correctly so. But this attitude can lead to a sad mistake. Strokes of brilliance that may be contained within a package of components developed elsewhere will never be found.

Component suppliers must invest in developing a comprehensive knowledge of the possible approaches to implementing a particular component package. Design reviews must contain detailed reviews of alternatives considered but rejected. Previous implementations of similar component packages, whether they come from research labs, careless hackers, or distinguished universities, must all be considered.

Individual differences. Software designers, engineers, and support personnel are not all created equal. Their differences far exceed their similarities. Studies show that productivity differences of 25:1 or even 50:1 are possible among software engineers with comparable training and experience. This fact creates more opportunity, and demands more explicit attention, than any other in this book. (Pity those software managers who stopped reading earlier.)

The contemporary approach to structuring software companies is to create artisan shops where extraordinary individual ability can be maximally amplified. The approach I advocate instead is to create an engineering organization and match the unique talents and skills of individuals to the needs of the engineering organization. This approach takes advantage of each individual's unique abilities; it does not assume that engineers are interchangeable parts.

Among the skills I have found to be unique are prototyping, design, development, tool building, and communicating the result. A common problem in organizations is to have good people in the wrong job. An excellent designer may be a poor tool builder and vice versa.

Prototyping. Some individuals are trailblazers. Their unique skill is being able to discover or invent a myriad of ways to reach an objective—often in record time.

A working program must never be confused with a product. Trailblazers or prototypers do not create products; instead, they create the opportunity for a product. The output of the prototypers demonstrates the technical feasibility of a new product. Their design, approach, and certainly implementation may bear little or no resemblance to the finished product.

Working prototypes are not real products. Internalizing this fact is among the more difficult tasks of the budding software executive. It is even more difficult when one is developing software components rather than full-blown applications. The temptation is to say, "What do you mean, class is not a product-quality class? It has 25 methods that seem to work."

But in a software component library, many classes must work in close harmony. Much of the energy in designing a library of components is in creating this harmony. This design work benefits enormously from repeated technical reviews by others who should consider the implications of each design decision from a variety of viewpoints.

Design. I am often asked how long it takes to train a person to become a competent designer using objects. The answer, described in Chapter 9, is often considered disturbing—from less than a year to never. Some people will never become good designers. Good designers may similarly prove to be lousy implementors.

Design ability must be identified and cultivated. Give designers the resources and constraints required to accomplish the job. These constraints include learning to communicate their designs effectively, first to customers and then to developers. Designers must also understand that budgets (both time and dollars) are real.

One critical characteristic of a good designer is the experience to understand the implications of a design decision down to the lowest level of detail. Designers cannot be blue-sky thinkers or philosophers. They must have comprehensive implementation and systems knowledge; they must understand the full range of problems the developers will encounter when they proceed to implement their designs.

Designers must also have the ability to fully exploit the media provided—be it visual, tactile, or auditory. HyperCard is a good example. Attention was paid specifically to the look and sound of prototype applications built with HyperCard. Graphic artists and musicians were part of the design team, and their contributions are clearly visible in the final product. But the most spectacular success of HyperCard was "design enhancement by elimination." How much can you take away and still provide awesome capability? HyperCard allows only nine classes.

Another critical requirement is that the designer must be able and on occasion willing to implement some critical portion of the system. This portion must be implemented under the same constraints as those the developers must obey, and the results must be of the highest quality. These implementation tests are critical to gaining the respect of developers and should not be considered optional. Bill Gates is the exemplar.

Development. Some people enjoy making computer programs work. Their abilities are different from either prototypers or designers.

As in other branches of engineering, developers work from a detailed design to construct the final product. Their creativity is displayed by ingeniously solving the hundreds of subproblems left unsolved by the designers and the equally large number of problems that were simply not anticipated.

Tool building. When an army begins to engage the enemy, there are more people behind the lines providing logistic support than fighting the battle. So it should be in software development projects. We should not all crowd around the front line. We should recognize that some of us are frankly much better at building innovative tools to support the front-line designers and developers.

I have found that toolsmiths have unique skills and interests. They should be searched out and fully supported within a development organization. My advice is to devote 20% of your head count within a development project to toolsmiths. It always pays a handsome return.

Communication. Software consists of code, but an equally critical component is the collateral information provided to assist the user. Many engineers are poor communicators of this information. Most designers fail to understand that designing the collateral materials may influence the ultimate success of the product as much as properly aligned bits on the floppy disk.

Identify and cultivate individuals who have this skill. They are not just technical writers—that is far too restrictive a definition. As we develop more and more applications using the full range of visual, tactile, and acoustic capabilities of contemporary technology, the traditional skills of the technical writer become only a portion of the full set required.

Successful communication can be measured by how long it takes someone to gain a specified level of understanding, for example, how long it takes an engineer to use a new component pack to help build a certain type of application. Unadorned text is rarely the most effective medium. We must avoid the trap of using the most accessible tools—they are often woefully inadequate or inappropriate. Raw text is the medium of last resort. Good communicators naturally exploit all the tools available to assist their audiences.

Reluctance of developers to use tools

I am forever amazed at how reluctant professional software engineers are to acquire or use a new tool. This cultural heritage originates from the craft shop mentality. It must change. It is far too expensive to build your own tools or, more commonly, to do without them.

How often do we see software development shops with 50 programmers and not a single person whose job it is to acquire, distribute, and train people in the use of new tools? Organizations must be restructured to acquire new tools and use them effectively.

I often recommend that knowledge of available tools be carefully tested during interviews. If professional software engineers do not remain current in their knowledge of available software tools, they are all too likely to either do without or, worse yet, build something of lower quality than something that already exists.

ORGANIZATIONAL LESSONS

Leadership vs. managing

One theory of management states that a competent manager can manage anything—content-free management, I call it. In my experience, this simply does not work for software projects.

I suggest to corporate executives that team leaders of software development teams should be required to read and review every line of code delivered by that team. Second-level managers, those to whom the team leaders report, must be able to read every line of code being produced within their organization. Second-level managers should regularly read what is being produced, but do not have the obligation to read every line.

Understanding how software development should be structured and managed is not sufficient, either. Innovative software development projects require a healthy dose of leadership as well as technical and managerial understanding of the fundamentals.

A leader must lead, not direct. Leaders must be willing to take personal risks, make crisp decisions, communicate effectively, and challenge others to do their best. To lead a software development project, a leader must understand what is happening at an appropriate level of detail.

Building teams

Teams are required to build commercial software products. Initial versions of products may be built by a team as small as two. From that initial version, success brings increasing numbers of "helpers." There must be tens of thousands of people working on the UNIX operating system around the world today. In 1972, there were two. Lots of new help has arrived in 20 years.

Most software products are built with teams of developers, marketers, and documentation experts.

Teams should be resilient to product changes and personnel turnover. When a smoothly working team is constructed, every effort should be made to keep the team together and to cultivate it. There are a few examples of teams that have worked together building software for more than two decades, and I know of one that has been working together for three decades. They have become very efficient.

In practice, this is difficult within any company, but a manager should think twice before reassigning a smoothly working team. If there is a 25:1 productivity difference among individuals, there could easily be a 10:1 difference among teams. When you disband a smoothly working team operating at maximum potential, you may have reduced overall productivity 900%.

Conway's Law

Mel Conway observed years ago that "organizations that design systems are constrained to produce designs that are copies of the communication structures of these organizations."[4] To our peril, it is easy to forget Conway's Law.

We must organize our teams carefully and make sure that the organization has the flexibility to change if the system design changes. For example, if you want an integrated development environment, create a team to develop an integrated development environment–not several teams to build its components.

But on the other hand, a prudent manager can take advantage of this fact to restructure a software product. Just change the organization to the desired structure and wait a few months!

CULTURE LESSONS

Not invented here

"My component is better than your component" still echoes through the halls of companies dedicated to reusability. It is not that the speakers do not believe in reuse or appreciate the virtues of object-oriented programming. Instead, prior technical obstacles have made the "not invented here" syndrome an adaptive behavior. The "NIH" syndrome was adaptive because even those sub-routines that appeared to do almost exactly what we wanted done turned out to be incredibly difficult to understand and modify correctly. Once modified, we have all been heard to say "if I had only known how tough that was going to be, I would have just written it from scratch." Managers have all said "by the time we made the changes we needed to make and fixed their errors, we could have just built it ourselves."

The NIH syndrome need no longer be adaptive with object-oriented technology for two reasons:

1. The technology allows us to more clearly specify the conditions under which we expect a given piece of software to work correctly.
2. As an industry, we are learning how to design and build reusable components with acceptable performance and quality.

However, never assume that well-learned behaviors will fade quickly. Stay alert for the NIH syndrome in your organization, and for the "from scratch excuse."

Rewards for bulk

How often have you heard a manager say something to the effect of "Do you realize she developed 30,000 lines of code last year, by herself? She deserves an award."

Like it or not, we have grown up in a "rewards for bulk" culture. It is the responsibility of the new generation of real software engineers to purge this tradition from our culture. The best way to begin the purge is to make a public list of all the ways in which software engineers in your organization are rewarded for bulk production. Using the list, a tabulation of specific instances of each class of behavior can also be constructed.

Rewards must be given to the people who figure out how to provide functionality comparable to 30,000 lines of code in only 1,500. In the software business, *bulk is bad*.

TECHNOLOGY TRANSFER LESSONS

Don't oversell

It is easy to get so engrossed in a particular product or technology that you focus exclusively upon its benefits. Enthusiastic entrepreneurs can be the worst culprits. They often make the mistake of creating unrealistically high expectations for their products.

The best example I have seen of this came from a competent, professional manager who was disappointed because his measured reusability from applied object-oriented programming was only 60%. This seemed disturbingly low because his predecessor had expected 90% reuse. However, prior to adopting object-oriented programming their measured reuse was 5–10%. Because of inflated expectations, a manager of a substantial organization of software engineers was disappointed because reusability had increased more than 600%!

Distribute directly

Small (and even some large) companies often delegate the sales and servicing of their products. If you are using innovative new technologies, you must be careful. Your distributors cannot understand leading-edge technology as well as the developing organization, nor will they be as motivated to ensure the success of their customers. Countless U.S. software companies have been visited by international companies asking to distribute their products in their respective country, region, or continent. Woe to the company that chooses its distributors in the order of arrival at the home office!

Financial investors often get growth requirements confused with monthly or quarterly financial growth objectives. What is really important is building the customer base and delivery systems that produce growth and stability. A little patience can improve the stability of the company immensely. But all patience is a recipe for certain disaster.

Pick important, not unimportant, projects

When introducing object-oriented programming into an organization, people typically recommend starting with a small pilot project. I no longer make this recommendation.

Instead, pick a project large and important enough to attract the best people and to get and keep the attention of upper management. Objects, like microprocessors, are a proven success, so use them on projects that can materially improve the business.

This does not mean, however, that you should pick the biggest, most important project in the company as the first project for any new technology. The software world seems more likely to make this mistake than any other industry. Remember the discussion about creating a "margin of safety" in Chapter 10.

The best choice for introducing objects is what I call a "metaproject." Initiate a project to build reusable components that will be required for the next three development projects in the company or organization. Budget 18 months for this metaproject. Plan the project so that the designers can complete three iterations of the design—one every 6 months. Ensure that the project is large enough to impact the business if it fails. Also, ensure that the projects that follow it directly impact the bottom line of the company.

Immersion works best

Learning a foreign language cannot be done in the few days of a commercial training course. The best technique is to become immersed in the culture where the language is spoken. Such an immersion process takes months, not weeks or days. A month can help tremendously; six months has a major effect. Most people can be fluent in one year.

My oldest daughter just returned from spending four weeks in Spain on an exchange program. She had studied the language for two years, but made incredible progress after spending a month in a home where Spanish was the only language spoken. Her assessment is that it would take another few months to be completely competent in the spoken language, and possibly as much as a year to gain equal fluency in the written language.

We tend not to think in these time-scales when we plan corporate training programs for new programming methods, tools, and languages. We want to think days, might be willing to assume weeks, but rarely assume it will take months or years.

Like the spoken language, the best way to transfer software language technology is to immerse would-be practitioners in a culture where the technology is in mature use. We should have many more apprentice programs in this industry and fewer quickie training courses in airport hotel conference rooms.

Service really counts

Software is an information product. Information constantly changes. Software changes almost constantly. Such changes can create value for our customers, but may also create large amounts of seemingly unproductive work for our customers. That work is sometimes greatly appreciated but often is despised.

Companies in the business of providing class libraries know these problems only too well. A class library product has the characteristic of a broad and deep interface with the customer's product. Considerable value is created by the depth and breadth of this interface, but a certain inflexibility is also inevitable. The class library provider cannot make major changes to the structure of the classes and the names of the methods on each release. Customers want high innovation, responsiveness to changes in technology, and stability in the class library design. Those are a tough combination of requirements.

Providers of class libraries must view themselves as providers of a service. That service involves a religious adherence to the constraints imposed by previous versions of products, unless a major change is actually required. A major change every decade may be okay; every year, it would never be tolerated.

Technical lessons

Reviewers of this book have repeatedly asked me to say more about a topic that I would really rather not get involved in. But, at their request, I will. The topic is object-oriented languages. The primary questions are which language should we use for a particular project, and does the choice of language matter?

I will answer a set of the most commonly asked questions I hear concerning object-oriented programming languages. I will not suggest any one recommended language. But I do believe that the choice of language matters.

I must make one fact clear from the start. At this point in time, I have no commercial interest in any particular object-oriented language. Until June 6, 1988, I did have a substantial interest in the Objective-C programming language by virtue of having been a founder of the company that developed it. But my consulting practice is worth more to me than Stepstone stock ever could be.

My history with regard to programming languages and object-oriented languages should also be made public so that any historic or technical biases can at least be known. Note that I have had little direct experience with Object-Pascal, Eiffel, ProGraph, Actor, CLOS, Dylan, Self, or Pro-Kappa. But I do have regular professional contact with companies involved with these languages as both suppliers and consumers.

If I sit down to develop code for my own use (which frankly I do not have time to do very often), I am most likely to use Smalltalk on either a Mac or a DOS-based laptop.

Personal Programming Language Experience

I began programming in 1968 using a homegrown FORTRAN compiler written at the University of Alabama, called "Bama Belle." Three years of FORTRAN experience doing mathematical and statistical programming was followed by real-time laboratory control programming using the SDS Sigma 7 computer at the University of Washington, also using FORTRAN. From there, I moved to small minicomputers, programming in Basic and FORTRAN on PDP-11 and Data General computers. Once I got seriously interested in computer science and software engineering, I learned Pascal and Snobol. My dissertation project was done using Snobol on a CDC-6000 mainframe. Then, as I went into industry, I met PDP-11s again with the AOS operating system until I was able to acquire a copy of UNIX in 1978. The first computer-aided software engineering (CASE) tool I was involved in building was using Pascal on UNIX. At the same time, I had been loaned the first-generation IBM personal computer, an IBM 5100. I learned APL on this machine. Then, a company move found me purchasing a VAX-UNIX machine and managing a project that used C language for nearly three years. It was during the last year of this project that Brad Cox developed OOPC and it began to be used. Another company move brought me to Xerox Dolphin workstations, VMS, and Smalltalk-80. I was the first commercial user of Smalltalk-80 from Xerox Special Information Systems. I spent at least nine months learning Smalltalk-80 by reading source code and the rather scanty documentation available at that time. Then came my first entrepreneurial venture (with Brad Cox), the founding of Productivity Products International—where Objective-C was born, grown, and promoted. I had some significant influence on the requirements for and design of the language. In particular, I insisted that we have a language that would be acceptable to engineers and scientists, not just C programmers with a degree in computer science. Since 1989, I have had long-term relationships with two companies using C++ to build products. I have been a consultant to Ascent Logic Corporation since 1988, where Smalltalk is used for all product development. Accent Logic's product, RDD-100, is the largest known commercial Smalltalk application. I have also worked as a consultant with tens of companies using languages that include Assembler, COBOL, C, TAL, Objective-C, Smalltalk, and C++ to develop commercial products.

I have a lot of direct experience and a reasonable amount of knowledge about various object-oriented languages. There are only a handful of people on the planet who have visited as many commercial object-oriented development projects as I have. Yet, there are a fair number of people better equipped to provide a detailed feature-by-feature comparison of language A vs. language B.

Why should anyone use an object-oriented programming language?

Based upon my experience, there are two overpowering reasons to use an object-oriented language:

- to gain the benefits from reusability of previously developed code—productivity
- to reduce the complexity of new systems or applications so that they are easier to build and will be easier to maintain over the years — maintainability

The generic recommendation is to use the highest-level language possible for the given application or system. Increasingly powerful microprocessors make it possible to use languages for applications today that would have been unthinkable years ago. Also, don't choose the language needed for the most time-critical portion of the system for use in all the system. Use a higher-level language for the bulk of the system; then, drop to the lower-level language for the 5 or 10% that requires additional optimization.

When is it not appropriate to use object-oriented programming?

The one class of system where objects are clearly inappropriate as an implementation language is tiny embedded systems that are either so CPU constrained or RAM constrained that the additional overhead of objects is simply unacceptable. If I were writing code to control an embedded microprocessor sitting atop an automobile transmission, I would design with objects but implement using C or Assembler.

Another class of system where the decision is tough in 1993 is mainframe computer applications. While technology advocates are rushing to apply objects in various ways to these types of applications, the experience is modest and the tools are nonexistent or immature. Great caution would be advised here. However, for large enough mainframe systems having appropriate tools built as a joint venture with existing suppliers of object-oriented languages, it would be well worth it. Brooklyn Union Gas did exactly this.

The third and final class of system is the unbuildable system. Customers and inexperienced executives will from time to time convince inexperienced managers of development organizations that they should put their career on the line to build some amazing new system at warp speed. Please don't use objects on these systems, because failure will be prolonged and both you and objects will get a bad reputation.

What properties of object-oriented languages seem most important to commercial development projects?

A commercial development project typically involves two or more teams of programmers building a product that should last for at least 10 years after its first release. Any thoughtful project manager should trade initial productivity for reductions in complexity and gains in extensibility over the long haul.

I would begin by evaluating languages based upon the maintainability and extensibility of the software written in that language. How easy will it be for a 23-year-old programmer coming from a reasonable state university to understand this code and make the required set of changes and add the required set of new features? What are the odds that, once made, those changes will be the correct changes?

We in the software business often get our priorities confused. When selecting a programming language, we should understand that its primary purpose is to communicate with some other human being and its secondary objective is to communicate that same intention to a computer. The second objective is much easier to satisfy than the first.

A second consideration would be which languages allow me to avoid work by virtue of my ability to acquire existing class libraries and integrate them into my company's products. No language technology beats component purchasing for increasing productivity. A related consideration is how well the proposed object-oriented programming language can work with existing applications. Even better than integrating components is integrating completed applications.

A third language criteria would be the quality of commercially available class libraries. A perfect language with a void class library is not perfect. Basic building blocks must be there from the start, and they must work as documented. More than one building block should be able to be assembled to create new applications or systems.

A good language must be a well-supported language. Language compilers outlive successful applications and systems. Projects should not have to invest in supporting such basic capabilities as compilers or especially debuggers. Ike Nassi does a wonderful job of explaining why dynamic object-oriented programming languages are important in the preface to *Dylan: An Object-Oriented Dynamic Language.*[5]

The pity is that Apple chose to design yet another LISP-based object-oriented programming language instead of improving Smalltalk, supporting and improving Objective-C, or redefining C++. As good as Dylan undoubtedly is, it will have a tough time in the market. Development managers have simply had too many bad experiences with LISP. Dylan also is just a language, not a complete development environment.

The competition in the marketplace is now well aligned with object-oriented languages. Apple is using two languages: C++ and Dylan. Sun and Hewlett-Packard are using C++. NeXT is using Objective-C. IBM is using C++ and Smalltalk. How would you bet?

How should I choose between static and dynamic object-oriented programming languages?

It is really quite easy. Choose a dynamic object-oriented language unless you are absolutely confident that you can write the detailed functional specification for the system you are designing and that this specification will not change for three years.

We invented software because it took so long to rewire computers. Dynamic object-oriented languages make it easy to rewire computers. Static object-oriented languages use lots of solder. Resoldering is expensive and error prone.

Most applications and systems are in a high degree of flux. Choose a tool that accommodates rather than hinders this change.

What features of object-oriented languages seem to add more complexity than value?

At the top of the list for all experienced object-oriented developers is multiple inheritance. I will not say that there is no place for this language feature. There are certainly applications or systems whose design could be materially improved by the availability of multiple inheritance. I give a simple recommendation to my consulting clients: "Do not even consider using multiple inheritance until you have used single inheritance to design and test at least one commercial system involving two teams of programmers."

Judiciously used, it is a powerful feature. Overused, it adds only complexity. On average, its value does not exceed its costs for most applications or systems.

Another feature about which I have serious commercial reservations is operator overloading. I understand it can make programs a little more elegant by redefining an operator to perform a different physical operation. But consider all the ways in which a feature such as this could be misused. Think how challenging it might be to discover that unbeknownst to you a familiar operator had been redefined by someone else. Or imagine the challenge of integrating 10 class libraries, each of which had a different set of operators. Or, imagine writing the standards for operator overloading that four teams of developers could agree upon.

I am not convinced that operator overloading adds sufficient value. In Smalltalk, there is no such thing as operators. All operators are messages; some are binary messages (e.g., +, -, etc.) to increase the readability of the programs. It is possible to change the behavior of binary messages, but it is unwise to do so often. It is easy to define a new binary operator for a new class so that it exhibits a known behavior, e.g., "+". For those binary messages that get used often, a primitive is defined and implemented efficiently, e.g., in Assembler.

What features of development environments should a commercial development project insist upon?

In object-oriented development projects, the problem is not to develop and debug new code. More likely than not, the problems derive from an ability to generate new code and change existing code too easily.

For pure object-oriented languages, the key features of development environments are group development tools, which include documentation tools, configuration control tools, build management tools, testing tools, and interpersonal communication tools.

In hybrid languages, the priorities include debuggers, memory management facilities, testing tools, and design tools. In C++, speed of compilation is absolutely critical, with a strong preference for a distributed compilation environment. Also, because a lot of recompilation is required with C++ (due to changes in class designs) one should put special emphasis on design tools to reduce the number of subsequent design modifications.

Dynamic binding and strong typing are both desirable features, but incompatible; how do I choose?

Strong typing has been shown to help in finding about 10% of the errors introduced in a new application. Dynamic binding facilitates the widespread reuse of code. The productivity benefits of reuse are not limited. Competent reports indicate 500% increases in productivity in some cases. EDS has one experience indicating a 1,400% increase in productivity. Experiences in building the NeXT computer software suggest than dynamic binding has made it possible to build products and add capability with a fraction of the effort required in a staticly bound language. Hewlett-Packard's VEE product is a visual programming environment for engineers. They say it could not have been built without dynamic binding.

Dynamic binding is much more important commercially than strong typing ever can be. Of course, there are those who say we should have both dynamic binding and strong typing. Eiffel is a case in point. Maybe?

Application vs. system programming languages

The portable C compiler included with the UNIX operating system from AT&T made it possible for the world to have one common programming language on all machines. Until then, we had application programming languages (FORTRAN, COBOL, PL/1, APL) and system programming languages (PLM, JOVIAL, BLISS, Assembler).

C is a good system implementation language and an acceptable application programming language. C++ is a system programming language. Smalltalk is an application programming language. Objective-C can be used as either, but like many multipurpose tools it isn't quite as good at either as the best of breed.

That sounds too easy. It is. The problem is that systems are looking more like applications and applications more like systems. To me, the distinction can be made based upon entropy. The more uncertainty involved in what you are building, the more it resembles applications. The more certain you are that components within the system are stable and that the desired behavior will be stable, the more rational it is to use a system programming language.

THE FINAL LESSON

Brad and I should really have had better sense than to start a company on the anniversary of D-Day.

NOTES

1. Actually, it was Productivity Products, Inc. (PPI) until the name was changed subsequent to a couple of rounds of venture capital negotiations.
2. Fred Brooks, *The Mythical Man-Month, Essays on Software Engineering*, ©1975, Addison–Wesley Publishing Company, Reading, Mass.
3. Recent Computer article lauding the virtues of source availability.
4. Melvin E.Conway, How do committees invent? *Datamation*, April 1968.
5. Published by Apple Computer, and available by calling (617)374-5300.

14

Software Component Foundries

In order that the producer and consumer may speak a common language in discussing quality, it is necessary that quality be described in precise terms. This situation has led to establishing definite specifications that define quality and test procedures.

Article on Metallurgy
Encyclopedia Britannica
15th edition, p. 1077

About 3500 B.C., it was discovered that you did not have to forge every object out of raw metal. Instead, you could pour molten metal into a mold and make many similar objects rather easily and efficiently. Complicated objects were made as an ensemble of individually cast objects. Complicated jobs involved only assembly of the pieces rather than working it all from raw metal.

After about 30 years of hand-forging software, we are also beginning to see the value of a new process. Our new process for developing software will require that we develop foundries for producing software objects, just like the metal and semiconductor industries have done before us.

THE CONCEPT OF A SOFTWARE COMPONENT FOUNDRY

Since the time of Lady Lovelace, we have been searching for the proper way to communicate our understanding of the world, or our directives to machines. Real progress in the software industry occurs when we invent a new language that allows us to accurately express models or directives that have never before been expressed.

Software components are executable, machine intelligence. To the extent that we can write a computer program to accurately model an object or describe some concept, we understand that object or concept.

Objects provide the latest improvement in computer languages. Object languages allow us to construct complicated ensembles of models that can be developed independently of specific applications or systems. These independently designed and constructed ensembles of objects will be built in "software component foundries."

A software component foundry is a software company that specializes in the construction of components, not finished applications or systems. Initially, we will see foundries developing generic components that can be used for many different applications or systems. Over time, we will see increasingly specialized software component foundries emerging.

THE RATIONALE FOR COMPONENT FOUNDRIES

Let's take a specific example to see how software component foundries could work. As a developer of a new telecommunications system in 2002, I would like to be able to go to the Object Mall (which might be a physical place, a CD-ROM, or a service bureau). There, I would like to find several varieties of each object or ensemble of objects that I need in my new system. I would then like to compare these components based upon performance, reliability, size, documentation, and price.

Once I had selected an appropriate set of components, I would like to be able to assemble these components into an initial working version of my system at high speed, say in a week. Once working, there would be many opportunities for improving what had been assembled. But I would not be working from scratch, and I would have a working version of my desired system quickly.

For this shopping scenario to become a reality, we must create a business entity, the software component foundry. That entity will be in the business of stocking the warehouse with appropriate components. But "stocking the warehouse" is a slow, expensive, and iterative process. What it means is that we must figure out what components are required, then design, build, and certify ensembles of components.

The reality is that we don't build a single component and sell it. We build ensembles of components that are sold and used together. A typical ensemble of components contains 50 classes or individual components. The development cost for such an ensemble is 15 to 30 person-years of effort. Those costs include the marketing activity to determine what should be built, the development costs of actually building the components, the documentation, and the quality assurance activities associated with both the code and the documentation. The initial selling price will vary depending upon the size of the available market and the uniqueness of the components. Ensembles of classes addressing the large PC market might sell for less than $1,000, whereas ensembles addressing a more specialized market might sell for $50,000 or more.

The rationale on the part of the purchaser is simple. Would you pay $50,000 for a software product that exists today and will require some customization, or would you choose to begin a development project that will surely cost you $500,000 and take 18 months to produce components of lower quality? No experienced development manager spends much time thinking about that question if he or she is sure that the purchased product provides the needed capability and is of reasonable quality.

But our warehouses are not fully stocked. So all we need to do is re-express all the software we have previously written in other languages using object-oriented languages. And we must do this while writing all the new software that our businesses demand. Hmmm . . . sounds like we are going to be very occupied over the next few years.

THE CURRENT DEMAND

Isn't it a terrible waste of precious human resources to develop the same capabilities independently all over the globe? How many spreadsheet applications, window packages, text processors, communication packages, or editors do you suppose have been built from scratch in the last decade? How many times have hashed lists been implemented in the last year? Is there really enough innovation in each to justify the time and expense of building them all from scratch?

At ITT in 1982, I discovered that there were 12 independent projects building text processing software for 8086 microprocessors using the C language. Other companies of comparable size will undoubtedly have similar examples, even today. What is most interesting is that ITT is not even the place where text processing software should have been built in the first place. Wang or InterLeaf or Xerox should have been doing that kind of work while ITT solved the many communications software problems that remained.

A software component typically involves 10–15 methods, equivalent to 200–300 uncommented lines of source code. Experience suggests that it takes about two person-months of effort to build a commercial software component once the design is well understood. By contrast, it takes only one person-day of effort to understand it well enough to reuse it. This 20:1 discrepancy is the fundamental stimulus for the software components industry.

For example, suppose that 50% of the components required for your next system could be purchased at a price equal to your development cost. From previous experience, you have faith in the quality of these components. As a developer, your technical risk is reduced dramatically. In addition, you reach the market sooner; you can develop the product in four fewer person-years than if you had to build it all. Your energies are thus directed toward the true value-added aspects of the system, not toward a lot of scaffolding or substrate that your customers never pay for anyway.

Purchased components should be of higher quality than you could have afforded to make them, and their documentation should be first rate. Your risk of total failure is lower and your sales will begin months earlier. What a deal! Besides, you are comparing a fixed expenditure for a known product against an historically inaccurate estimate for a to-be-developed product. It's a "no-brainer"—even if you had to pay what it would cost you to develop the components. In fact, most components being sold today are sold for a tiny fraction of the development costs.

The table on the next page summarizes the benefit due to reuse. It compares the effort (measured in person-years) to construct a system consisting of 100 classes given five different percentages of code reuse.

To select a modest level of reuse, say 30%, 2.3 person-years of effort could be saved by purchasing and reusing existing components. At a typical burden rate of $120,000 per person-year, reusing those components would have saved $281,000 - the purchase price of the components + the benefit accrued by virtue of delivering the product earlier + the benefit from not having to maintain those components indefinitely.

Amount of reuse (%)	Development (person-months)	Effort to reuse (person-days)	Development effort (person-years)	Savings (%)
0	100	0	8.3	0
10	90	10	7.5	9
30	70	30	6.0	28
50	50	50	4.4	47
80	20	80	2.0	76

This analysis assumes that you are acquiring high-quality components that provide the needed capabilities. If quality is lower or the capabilities are not adequate, the savings will be less because rework will be required. This rework is especially expensive because it implies that the development group will have to take over the maintenance and enhancement responsibility for those components perpetually. Cloning is better and more desirable than starting from scratch; it is not nearly as attractive as "pure reuse," however.

DESIGNING A FOUNDRY

This chapter is written not only with the direct experience of having founded and been CEO of one of the first companies to build and sell an object-oriented class library as a standalone product (ICpak 201 in 1987), but also as someone who was intimately involved in the planning for an international software component foundry in 1986. The international joint venture partners changed their mind the day of the press conference,[1] *after* the facility had been leased. Months of analysis and planning had preceded that event.

How then should a software components foundry be organized? Software components should be constructed at the software component foundry, then sold through distributors and local sales organizations to developers, who will reuse these components in a variety of products.

ORGANIZING THE FOUNDRY

Foundries[2] will employ about 100 people each. They will focus on the production of software components for well-defined markets such as IBM communications protocols, robotics, process control, banking, integrated circuits, computer-aided design (CAD), or specialized end-user applications (see Figure 14.1). The foundry will be a software products company requiring marketing, sales, engineering, quali-

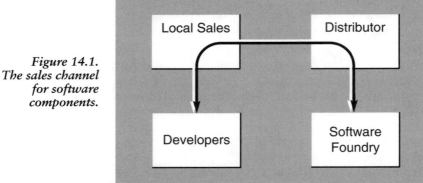

Figure 14.1.
The sales channel
for software
components.

ty assurance, shipping, and research activities. Less than 20% of the staff will be devoted to engineering (including documentation), 10% to quality assurance, 45% to marketing and sales, 20% to customer support, shipping, and administration, and 5% to research.

Software is developed best when the engineering organization employs a strong team orientation. Development teams provide the fundamental productive unit of the foundry. Each team should be led by an individual with three object-oriented projects under his or her belt and some supervisory experience. This leader can provide both technical leadership and team management.

The team members will have two to five years of diverse experience, including several programming languages and some specialty exposure, be it IBM's System Network Architecture (SNA), graphics, or artificial intelligence. Each team also needs support staff, including administrative support, a professional technical writer, and an individual responsible for quality assurance.

Teams should remain together to develop many components. Most companies make a terrible mistake by assembling and disassembling teams on every project or even every time there is a reorganization. Design and development teams should be thought of as the fundamental unit of production within the foundry. Restructuring a team is like replacing all the machinery in a factory. The new machines may be better, but there will be a major cost to make the change. If the change occurs too frequently, productivity approaches zero.

A new foundry must begin with at least two teams, designated and trained as such from the beginning. Planning, budgeting, and production must be in terms of teams and software components. They should take into account:

- time to learn a new language and development tools
- time to learn new software components

- time to work out individual roles and responsibilities within the team
- time to work with content specialists to learn what must be built

A particularly important team to create from the start is the quality team. To be successful, a foundry must produce software of immaculate quality. Every step of the development process must be viewed with an eye toward quality.

Some helpful hints

I have four simple hints for anyone considering building software components:

1. *Uniqueness:* Don't build the same class library that everyone else is currently building—we have enough user interface libraries now!
2. *Solve a common problem:* Don't solve a trivial or esoteric problem; instead, find a common need and service it.
3. *High performance:* Time and space always matter in the software business; build small and fast components that do some real work and could save some significant energy for anyone considering building the same functionality.
4. *Build deep, not broad:* Too many small companies get distracted by trying to port their products to every platform in sight; choose a platform that provides an adequate market for your product, then dominate that market. Once your product has more than 50% of the market, consider another.

PLANNING FOR A FOUNDRY

The foundry is a software products business, and, like any such business, must be carefully planned and managed. The first step is to construct a business plan. To help in understanding all the issues involved, I developed a miniature plan to guide the discussion.

A financial model of the foundry

In the spreadsheet (see Figure 14.2), I developed a simple model of a software component foundry business. From this hypothetical example, some important recommendations will emerge for anyone considering the founding of a foundry.

Plan on two years of development. As we have learned elsewhere in this book, it will take at least three refactorings of the design to "get it right." Do not ship a component library too early. It will create too much grief for both the supplier and consumer.

Figure 14.2. Hypothetical pro-forma.

	YEAR –2	YEAR –1	YEAR 1	YEAR 2	YEAR 3	YEAR 4	YEAR 5
Development staff	5	10	12	12	8	6	4
Marketing	2	4	6	6	5	4	4
Management/admin.	3	3	4	6	7	5	4
Sales	0	2	7	9	20	20	12
Total staff	10	19	29	33	40	35	24
Cost/PY	$120,000	$127,200	$134,832	$142,922	$151,497	$160,587	$170,322
Total expenses	$1,200,000	$2,416,800	$3,910,128	$4,716,423	$6,059,889	$5,620,547	$4,085,335
Cumulative costs ($M)	$1.2	$3.6	$7.5	$12.2	$18.3	$23.9	$28.0
Copies sold	0	0	360	720	1,440	1,440	720
Price per copy			$9,500	$9,500	$9,500	$7,600	$5,700
Annual revenue			$3,420,000	$6,840,000	$13,680,000	$10,944,000	$4,104,000
Monthly revenue			$285,000	$570,000	$1,140,000	$912,000	$342,000
Cumulative revenue			$3,420,000	$10,260,000	$23,940,000	$34,884,000	$38,988,000
Annual P/L	-1,200,000	-2,416,800	-490,128	2,123,577	7,620,111	5,323,453	18,665
Cumulative P/L	-1,200,000	-3,616,800	-4,106,928	-1,983,351	5,636,759	10,960,212	10,978,877
Revenue per employee ($)			117,931	207,273	342,000	312,686	171,000
Sales/marketing			12	13	16	14	10
Salespeople			7	8	10	8	6
Revenue per salesperson ($)			491,379	863,636	1,425,000	1,302,857	712,500
% invested in R&D	50%	53%	41%	36%	20%	17%	17%
Company value ($)			6,840,000	13,680,000	27,360,000	21,888,000	8,208,000
Investor equity ($)			5,130,000	10,260,000	20,520,000	16,416,000	6,156,000
Investment ($)				-4,106,928	-4,106,928	-4,104,928	-4,106,928
Return on investment (%)				250	500	400	150

Set a goal of being cash flow break-even in the first year you start selling the product. But, as the plan above shows, don't plan on making that goal. It is tough to do and only the very successful companies achieve this goal.

The number of copies of product sold the first year multiplied by the selling price should equal the expenses for that year. One of the most commonly seen mistakes in software companies is that they undercharge for their products. It is a recipe for going out of business. Especially in the foundry business, one should be reluctant to immediately start selling a product for low-end mail order prices. At Stepstone, we found it much easier to sell a $35,000 library of components than a $2,500 compiler that included a set of components. If you have the right product with an appropriate level of quality, your product will be cheap at most any price.

Plan to recoup all investments during the second year of selling the product. It seems that when people run businesses with other people's money there is a tendency to do something other than recoup investments and turn profits. Successful software companies have a tradition of profitability that begins early in the life of the company.

Keep development costs under control. Successful software companies spend less than 20% of total expenses on R&D. As technical people, we often make the mistake of assuming that all revenue problems of the company are related to missing features or lack of ports to new platforms. Most likely, the real problem is inadequate marketing and inefficient sales.

There are expenses associated with each sale. Do not forget that someone has to find the prospect, convince them to buy the product, take the order, ship the product, and answer the phone when there is a problem.

Software is durable, but it does not last forever. Plan for 5 years of sales for your product. New products or major changes to the existing one must begin 2 or 3 years before the business needs the revenue. Do not get caught up with the "bulldozer effect" —too busy pushing the current product to build the next.

Building professional-quality software components is expensive. The business model shown above would produce 50–60 commercial-strength classes. As a part of an application development project, it would cost a user of these components about 50 person-months of effort, or $500,000, to develop this capability. For a selling price of $9,500, it becomes an easy decision process.

Foundries can be highly profitable businesses. Venture capitalists want to believe that they can get a 500% return on their money in 5 years. It is possible with foundries, as we can see from the final row in the table. But, notice that the venture capitalist has to be careful. It is becoming harder and harder to float a public offering for a software company doing less than $20 million in annual sales. To cash out with the highest return, the venture capitalist has to encourage development of follow-up products, so that annual revenues can continue to grow in years 4 and 5.

Revenue per salesperson is finite and variable. For a product like software components, a competent and well-trained salesperson should be able to generate $1 million in annual sales. If the number is considerably higher than that metric, be skeptical of the plan. If the number is much lower, scrutinize the sales force and the product.

Revenue per employee is an important metric of a software company. It should be greater than or equal to the fully burdened annual cost of two engineers. If it is much less, pass on the investment. If it is much higher, be skeptical of the plan.

Revenues do not linearly increase forever. Any entrepreneur who hasn't thought about declining revenues hasn't thought through the business adequately. The corollary is that sales are never monotonic. There has to be a cash cushion available to account for certain variances in revenue—3 months is a minimum; 6 months is secure.

Is there an adequate market and how can I find it? It is easy to plug sales figures into a powerful spreadsheet, but it is a bit more challenging to deliver on those projected sales figures. If you are first into a market, assume that the best you could ever do would be to secure 30% of the available market. The second entrant in the market gets 30% of the remainder, etc. Once you become convinced that the market is adequately large, the next issue is how to locate appropriate targets within that proven market.

Have adequate cash. For the plan above, the business should have at least $5 million available; $6 million is an even better number. If you don't have adequate cash to develop the product, then develop a product whose ambition level is well suited to the cash you have available. The prototype plan shown above could be scaled to a two-person company in the first year of operation. In that case, one person would be doing all development and the other doing marketing, management, and administrative functions. A different product would be built, but it could be built for about $1 million in investment.

Product prices will erode in time. Just like the semiconductor industry, we must assume that the value of a new set of software components will erode in time. For planning purposes, I have assumed competition and thus price erosion in year 4 of the venture.

Pricing should be modeled after the semiconductor industry. New components will have a much higher price than older ones. The price of a new software component will be a function of its engineering cost and the degree of innovation it represents. Manufacturing rights can be sold on a limited basis to provide for alternative sources. Customers will pay a royalty for each component they use in their own products, just as they now do with semiconductors.

Many of today's software product managers may find this scenario disturbing. The very idea that another software company should get a royalty based upon every copy of their product sold seems preposterous. But, the alternative will be to build everything from scratch and see how competitive you can be.

A royalty-free price would naturally be possible, but it needs to be high enough to discourage that approach. For example, a specialized component that sells for $35,000 and a $5 royalty per copy might sell for $300,000 if no royalties were collected.

There are other approaches that can also be considered. These approaches include leasing, pay per use, and royalties as a percentage of sales that is adjusted based upon percentage of purchased code. In my opinion, the most practical alternatives are purchase with fixed royalties, or an annual lease arrangement that guarantees continuing revenue to the component developers.

Component developers and suppliers must be compensated based upon the quality of their work. Ultimately, competition will determine prices. For general-purpose components, the developer market might be large enough that charging royalties might not be necessary. As software components become more specialized, however, the market for each component shrinks; thus, the price must increase. Remember, foundries will be investing heavily in new product development. Without earnings from prior sales to stimulate this research, the flow of new software components will be pinched.

Nevertheless, a foundry can be a remarkably profitable business. It can derive revenue from direct sales, services, and royalties; the software foundry can be much more stable than the typical software products business today. After all, it is unlikely that all the products sold by all of your customers will suffer simultaneous and precipitous sales drops. "Components are often more profitable, more broadly based, and their market more secure than the end products of which they are a part." Harold Geneen, ex-CEO of ITT Corporation, described his experience after acquiring a number of pump, valve and electronic component companies. "[These component companies] are earners in good times and bad."[3]

Preparing yourself for the future

Any significant new technological innovation creates opportunities and causes change within the existing industrial infrastructure. But, industries do not change quickly. The fundamental restructuring of the software industry sketched here will require at least a decade.

But, just imagine what it will be like to begin a major new development project with the realization that 80% of the required software components can be purchased! With your help, that opportunity will actually arise for some systems before the end of this century.

Skeptics might point out that it took 5,400 years from the invention of metal casting until the industrial revolution began. Being able to make individual objects more efficiently did not create the revolution. Being able to build more complicated objects from interchangeable parts and to consistently manufacture products of uniformly high quality did create the revolution.

So shall it be in the software industry, I predict. Once we learn how to produce quality objects using an industrial process, we will create a revolution in the information industry. Software component foundries are a necessary but partial step in that direction.

Don't forget to invest in the development of a repeatable, industrial-strength manufacturing process.

NOTES

1. Because of a misunderstanding regarding the liquidity of an associated equity investment in a privately held U.S. corporation.
2. When I use the word "foundry," I do not mean to imply that foundry workers should be treated like unskilled laborers. Instead, my vision is the exact opposite. Foundries should generate handsome profits and provide high-quality working environments. Nothing would be more fun than to see a foundry parking lot filled with debt-free BMWs and Lexuses!
3. Harold Geneen, *Managing*, Doubleday & Company, New York, 1984, p. 205.

15

Software Development–2002

The easiest way to predict the future is to create it.

Alan Kay

M uch earlier in this book, I described a humbling experience—attempting to predict the future. Object technology is now mature enough to allow some predictions.

When the previous predictions concerning the development of workstations and software development environments were made, they were the property of ITT Corporation. If they had not turned out to be somewhat accurate, you would have never known that they existed.

As I ponder the upcoming decade, I do it from the perspective of a three-person company and in a public forum. Should I even take the chance?

I will take the chance, but with an important constraint. I do not have the resources to make the quantitative estimates we made back in 1980. Essentially, I will try to identify some important trends the software industry must recognize and prepare for. I will also harness my optimism based upon our lousy results at predicting progress in the software industry during the 1980s. But, unlike the 1980 prediction, I will address software products as well as software production environments.

PROGRAMMING IN 2002

Predicting the future is difficult, yet planning for it is mandatory. Our planning should also assume that some of the predictions will be incorrect.

A lesson from the 1980 ITT prediction was that the leading-edge development environment of 1980 (UNIX) had been improved (workstations), commercialized [Sun, Hewlett-Packard (HP), IBM, Digital Equipment Corporation (DEC), NeXT], and adopted (check workstation sales figures) in 10 years. It has not been standardized. Competitors have spent lots of money to develop comparable capability and only one seems likely to succeed (Microsoft). Others like IBM, Apple, and DEC are still spending a lot of money to develop proprietary development environments. They alone believe in their success.

What development environment in 1992 is comparable in power and early adoption to UNIX in 1980? Smalltalk is the clear answer. If we assume the same rate of progress, we can look forward to a few million copies of Smalltalk by 2002. But, we should not expect standard development environments to emerge. Instead, we will see intense competition. By the same logic, the Object Management Group (OMG) has its work cut out for itself; it will not be an easy road.[1]

On the other hand, prior experience may prove incorrect on the issue of standards. Productivity from objects requires some degree of standardization. The OMG is very much out in front, developing standards for objects. To the degree that the OMG can be successful in preemptive "standards strikes," we will all benefit. To the extent that premature and inappropriate standards are promoted, we will suffer.

Development tools that were just barely operational in 1980 have become commonplace in 1990. Developers in the 1990s can assume configuration control and build management tools. They also routinely employ integrated text/graphics documentation and presentation tools. Those were just beginning to be used in a handful of highly capitalized research organizations in 1980.

We should expect to see groupware tools as commonplace in development organizations of 2002. We should find real-time, full-motion video-conferencing facilities in every sizable development facility in five years.

Tightly integrated development tools that are considered expensive and "research-oriented" will be the norm in a decade. A batch compile will have gone the way of the punched card. High-resolution color screens will be the norm. Processing power will be abundant. RAM will continue to get cheaper and cheaper.

In 10 years, single processors will be as interesting and useful as single memory chips. Local and wide area networks of massively parallel computers will be the norm. Bandwidths will grow steadily, making it possible for groupware applications to work over large physical distances. Multimedia will be in routine use well before 2002.

Use of mainframes will begin to atrophy in a decade's time. Small network-based compute servers (consisting of massively parallel computers) will replace the mainframe. But these compute servers will resemble today's supercomputers more than today's mainframes. Mainframes exist in 1992 because of software constraints, not hardware capabilities. These same software constraints will keep these machines running as a server on a network for decades to come. Even today, in many sizable companies new applications are rarely mainframe-based. So, the era of the mainframe is waning.

There is a fascinating prediction that the mainframe computer industry will cease to exist on the first day of the next century.[2] When I first read that prediction, I was enchanted that anyone would make such a precise prediction. The prediction was actually a refinement of a similar prediction made by Bill Gates. But, the more I thought about it and tested such a bold assertion, the more I began to agree with it. So much software is going to break on that day and so much of that software will be easier to rebuild than to repair that many mainframe programs will have to be rewritten to run on contemporary computers. Those computers are not likely to be running MVS.

Robert Cringely says "there is mainframe software in this country that cost at least $50 billion to develop for which no source code exists today." No one can know for sure whether the number is $50 billion, $3 billion, or $100 billion. But, no one doubts that the units are billions and most likely tens of billions. It is a fair guess that a trained object-oriented software engineer could duplicate a block of this code for 20% of the original development cost (in person-years of effort). Working backward from Cringely's number, we must grow the population of object-oriented MIS programmers at least 300% per year for the balance of the decade to produce this amount of new code before the beginning of the next millennium.

Do not, however, be surprised to discover that the operating system that this new code runs on will be a variant of today's OS/2. OS/2 is a contemporary interactive operating system that can be scaled up reasonably well. MVS can't make the cut. VM/CMS was a patch to make programming tolerable and it seemed outdated in 1980. Its stretch marks and wrinkles can no longer be ignored.

The other operating system's name that uses the same letters (DEC's VMS) will be with us, but its market share will be rapidly diminishing by 2002. Its design and implementation will allow it a few more years of life. But, a new operating system will be needed at DEC as well by this time.

The odds of a new object-oriented operating system gaining enough support and maturity to be selected as the basis for another quarter of a century of application development seems low for some years to come.

Object-oriented extensions to UNIX will be successful in the technical community, but will represent a long shot to succeed in "glass houses."[3] UNIX suppliers have not historically made much progress in glass houses. Companies like Sun, HP, and NeXT have to learn new techniques of selling and, especially, supporting their hardware and software to be successful in the traditional MIS world.

As the big guys invest their billions to repair, extend, and replace their monoliths, technologists will be snapping at their heels. The Pink operating system developed by Apple and funded by IBM exists in 1992. It could be a force in the industry in 10 years. I have never seen it. I cannot judge its fate. The victory that they must win is to be sufficiently capable and mature for the rapid migration of mainframe applications that will happen this decade. The sooner they deliver, the greater their odds.

Microsoft's "NT++" will still be a major player in the market in 2002. They might even be capable of developing a real object-oriented, distributed operating environment and have it well planted in the landscape in 10 years. But, such a product must be well underway as this is being written.

Pure object-oriented languages will be the norm as we move into the new millennium. Hybrid's will still be used for system programming or other high-performance/low-entropy applications. Mega-mippers don't need bitfields and pointers! Pure objects make it possible to build software for massively parallel computers. Whatever benefits might accrue as a result of language-level optimization will be insignificant relative to the benefits coming from massive parallelism.

Pure languages will also make widespread adoption of reusable components more likely. Nonlinear increases in both compute and programming power have never happened before. It will be an exciting decade.

Programming should be a social activity. In 10 years, this fact will be even better understood. Team programming will become the accepted practice. Higher-level languages will also make it much easier to read and understand "code" that is being developed.

THE SOLUTION TO THE SOFTWARE CRISIS

Many attempts have been made to solve the software crisis. The first may have taken place one week after April Fool's Day in 1958. Six people, including Grace Hopper, convened in the office of Professor Saul Gorn at the University of Pennsylvania to develop the specifications for a common business language for automatic digital computers.[4] From this meeting, COBOL was conceived. COBOL solved some important and practical problems of the day—most notably the proliferation of incompatible, machine-dependent programming languages for business applications.

But business managers did not become COBOL programmers. Today it is estimated that we have more than 1,000,000 COBOL programmers in the United States alone. Yet the application backlog in most large companies is measured in person-centuries of effort and is still growing.

Other attempts to solve this crisis have included structured programming, software engineering, computer-aided software engineering (CASE), relational databases, artificial intelligence, fourth-generation languages, and visual programming. All have made some contribution. None has made an order of magnitude contribution.

In contrast spreadsheets have made an order of magnitude impact. Important work within small and large companies is now being routinely done by millions of "nonprogrammers." A small percentage of these spreadsheet users are involved in building applications using the macrolanguages included as a part of the spreadsheet packages.

While at Schlumberger, I was a member of a group whose objective was to build advanced programming tools to support the mainline business of the company, geophysical data collection and analysis. I observed that the best solution was not to make the handful of software engineers in the company more productive, but rather to turn the physicists, chemists, and petroleum engineers into programmers. A few hundred programmers could never keep up with 10,000 engineers.

The way we solved the problem of not enough telephone operators was to turn all telephone users into operators. Today, telephone users must know area codes, dialing conventions, and calling card numbers. The systems have changed so that it is easier to do the job ourselves rather than wait for an operator to "assist us." We have done exactly the same thing in the office. Office tools like word processors, electronic mail systems, spreadsheets, and presentation tools make it easier for us to accomplish work directly than to have an assistant do it for us.

The MIS bottleneck in some companies has been ameliorated by the widespread availability of powerful spreadsheet packages that allow access to corporate

data so that *ad hoc* analysis can be done on the individual workstation. Many analysts require more powerful and more specialized tools than spreadsheets.

THE SOLUTION TO THE SOFTWARE CRISIS IS TO CREATE MORE PROGRAMMERS

We must enable our "users" to access the data they require and to analyze and
transform it as they see fit. In other words, turn them into application developers
(or programmers).

Object-oriented programming languages have the fundamental property of
being extensible. Every time we design and implement a new class, what we are
really doing is extending the programming language. If we choose languages and
development tools that are accessible to a broad population of users, then we have
the very real opportunity to "cure the crisis."

Extending object-oriented programming languages and providing powerful
programming tools will be necessary but not sufficient to effect important changes.
We will also have to design higher-level multimedia environments that will allow
"users" to assemble custom solutions from a set of powerful, preexisting building
blocks. This assembly process will not involve low-level programming languages
such as Smalltalk. Instead, it will be third-generation interface and application
builders, based upon the experiences of using early primitive products, like NeXT's
Interface Builder.

Another early instance of a class of appropriate solutions is HP's recent Test
and Measurement product, Visual Engineering Environment (VEE). VEE allows an
engineer to design experiments using real instruments or simulated measurements
and to display the results using powerful graphic tools. What VEE provides is a
graphic language for assembling high-quality components into meaningful applications without having to write code. This assembly process relies upon a dynamically bound object-oriented programming language and a large number of efficiently
programmed objects.

These new environments for assembling powerful components will still require
lots of creative programmers to build new and better components and make them
available to the market. Programmers will become software component providers;
users will construct the final applications and systems based upon the available
repertoire of components.

SUMMARIZING THE FUTURE

If we attempt to train everyone to become system programmers, we will fail. If we
continue to invent new incompatible languages instead of extending existing lan-

guages by building system- and application-specific classes, we only aggravate the crisis.

To solve the software crisis, we must meet the users on their turf with solutions to their problems. These solutions must allow users to solve their problems in a manner that is easier than describing the solution to someone else who could then do it.

Objects are the enabling technology to make us all application developers without having to be programmers.

NOTES

1. The OMG is a nonprofit consortium promoting object technology and industrial standards. It was formed in 1990 and is located in Framingham, Massachusetts.
2. Robert X. Cringely, *Accidental Empires: How the Boys of Silicon Valley Make Their Millions, Battle Foreign Competition, and Still Can't Get a Date*, Addison-Wesley, Reading, MA, 1992.
3. Glass house is a euphemism for IBM mainframe installations, which were commonly placed in the centers of buildings and provided with glass walls so that important people could see the major investment the company had made in business automation.
4. Robert Slater, *Portraits in Silicon*, MIT Press, Cambridge, MA, 1987, p. 226.

Index

ABB Process Automation, Inc., 85, 86

Accessing, 73, 218

AccuRay, 85, 86

ACS, 20

Actor, 41, 50, 74, 151, 277

Ada, 46, 149

Advanced Programming Environment (APE), 144

Aegis, 41

AI (*see* Artificial intelligence)

Åke Larson AB, 180n

Aldus Corporation, 94

Alternative media, 217

American Airlines, 95-96

AOS, 228

APL, 228, 232

Apple Computer, 83-84, 151, 233n

Apple Scientific Computing, 73

Applied Intelligent Systems (AIS), 89-90

Apprentice, 161

Architect, 84, 100-103, 160, 163, 171-174

Architectural partitioning, 150n

ARPA (*see* DARPA)

Artecon, Inc., 84

ArteDraft, 84

ArteGKS, 84

Articulate Systems, 154n

Artificial Intelligence (AI), 17, 22n, 253

Ascent Logic Corporation, 87, 228

AT&T:
  Bell Laboratories, 151
  UNIX, 14, passim

Automatic Teller Machine (ATM), 109, 186

AXE telephone switching system, 80

Behavior:
  functional, 110
  inherited, 192
  of objects, 43, 64, 687
  polymorphic, 192

Behavioral specification, 113

Bell Labs (*see* AT&T)

Bildschrimtext, 20, 21

Binary messages, 231

Binding, dynamic, 29-30, 42, 46, 50, 87, 91, 139, 232

BLISS, 233

Borland C++, 152

Browser, 64

C, 228, passim (*see also* C++, Objective C, Complete C)

C++, 65, passim

CAD (*see* Computer-aided design)

CAM, 11

CareView 9000, 90

CASE, 122, 136, 138, passim

CASE tools, 204

CD-Rom, 217

Champions, 209, 213n

Change process, 208-209

Checkpoints, 209

CHILL compiler, 81

CIM (*see* Computer-integrated manufacturing)

Clascal, 83

Classes, 31-39, 59-60, 64, 83, 87-94, 108-118, 121, 191, passim

Cloned, 219

Cloning, 239

CLOS, 227

COBOL, 17, 80, 151, 204, 205, 228, 232, 253

Code reading, 191-194

Coding, 20, 119, 178
    phase, 20

Comments, 43, 58, 64, 75, 89, 195

Communications, 204-205
    packages, 237
    protocol, 237

Complete C (*see* C)

Component:
    design, 117, 211, 236
    integration, 210
    library, 51, 140, 150, 153, 162-165, 190, 217-218, 243
    packages, 153
    reusable, 148, 150
    suppliers, 217-218

Computer-aided design (CAD), 11, 128-130, 133-134, 239

Computer-aided software engineering (CASE) (*see* CASE)

Computer-integrated manufacturing (CIM), 11, 82

Compute servers, 250

Concurrency, 81, 119, 126, 134
    control, 126, 130, 131, 140

Configuration control, 251

Consistency checking, 127

Constraints, 17, 108, 117, 137, 154, 218, 221, 227

Construction management, 172-173

Contact tools (*see* Tools)

Corporate culture, 207

CRC cards, 114-115

Customer Information Control System (CICS), 14

Customer Information System (CIS), 88

DARPA, 145

Data:
    access, 201
    fusion, 201
    modeling, 204

Data General, 228

Database, 84, 95, 126-136, 151-153, 202, 203

Database Management System (DBMS), 126,-128, 131-138, 179

DataDesk, 204

Debugging, 152, 188

Dependency graph, 116-117

Design:
    phase, 171
    process, 102-104, 121, 216
    validation, 120

Digital Equipment Corporation (DEC), 250, 252

Documentation tools, 204, 232
Dylan, 151, 152, 227

Econometric modeling, 202
EDS, 232
Eiffel, 74, 152, 227
EMACS, 149
Enator Functional Systems, 86
Encapsulation, 30, 33, 34, 50, 80,
    86, 146, 181
Ensemble, 110-112, 117, 118, 237
Entity-relationship attribute (ERA),
    132
Ergonomics, 105, 187
Ericsson, L.M., 80
Environment, 150-152
    development, 40, 64-65, 121,
        154, 230, 232, 250
    object-oriented, 152, 163
    programming, 20, 47n, 141n,
        144, 145, 232
Error message, 96, 203
Executive champion, 209
Extensibility, 37, 230

Factory, 188n
    methods, 32, 42-43
Fairchild, 165
Falcon Framework, 92
Finite Message Machine (FMM),
    81
Flavors, 91
FORTRAN, 17, passim
Foundry, 236-246

General Electric (GE), 88
General Motors (GM), 11
Generic:
    code, 34
    components (*see also*
        Components), 211, 219, 236
    user interface, 211
Geographic Information Systems,
    87
GKS graphics standard, 84
Godfather in system implementa-
    tion, 209
Gunakara Sun Systems, 71

Hewlett-Packard Corporation (HP),
    51, 86, 90, 93, 97n, 250, 254
HP (*see* Hewlett-Packard
    Corporation)
Hybrid vs. pure object systems, 39
    languages (*see* Languages)
    object-oriented languages (*see*
        Languages)
HyperCard, 50, 65, 69, 71, 121
Hypertext, 141, 217

IBM 3083, 108, 203, 205
IBM 5100, 228
Icon, 93
ICpak 101, 153
ICpak 201, 153, 190, 194, 195
IDE, 74
Incremental compilers, 204
Information Technology Institute of
    Singapore, 90
Inheritance:

[Inheritance]
  of behavior (*see* Behavior)
  classes and metaclasses, 35-37
  defined, 34, 47n
  lattices, 37
  multiple, 231
  property of, 118
  trees, 43, 118, 121, 192
Instance, 31, 42
  methods, 42
  variables, 42, 64, 116, 119
IntelliCorp., 40
Intelligent C, 89
Interaction diagrams, 114, 123n
Interface Builder, 91
Interleaf, 238
Interlisp, 149
Interoperability, 105
Interpreter, 86, 147, 151, 204
IS-A relationship, 134
ISDN, 20
IS-PART-OF relationship, 134
Iterative development process, 177
ITT, 11, passim

JOVIAL, 232

KEE, 40
Knowledge-based-systems, 133
Knowledge Systems Corporation
  (KSC), 50, 51, 58, 97n, 114,
  164

LAN (*see* Local Area Network)
Languages:
  extended, 151
  higher-level, 36
  hybrid, 151
  object-oriented, 41, 131, 152,
    passim
  procedural , 29, 46, 15, 204
    programming (*see also*
      Modeling), 27, 40, 42,
      43, 82
  pure, 150
Laptop, 55, 58
Large-system development, 105
Lawrence Livermore National
Laboratory, 84-85
Leitz, 78
Lisp, 40, 90, 165, 230
    Common, 90
Local Area Network (LAN), 129
LOOPS, 46
Lotus 1-2-3, 12, 210

Mac, 227
MacApp, 73
Mainframe, 153, passim
Maintainability, 85, 105, 230
Margin of safety, 148, 171, 226
Massachusetts Computer
Associates, 154n
Massachusetts Institute of
Technology (MIT), 135, 190, 209
Memory management, 94, 151,
  152
Mentor graphics, 92
Message, 28-31, 33, 41-43, 81, 96,
  101, 114, 116, 131, 139, 151,
  189, 203, 231
Metaclass, (*see also* Classes), 32, 37

Metaproject, 226
Method, 28-31, 39, 42-43, 64, 110,
    118, 121, 130, 134, 146, 151,
    173, 191, 220, 227
  and data definition, 115
  of design/development, 106,
    107, 148, 152
  elaboration, 117
  inherited, 116, 193
  private, 116
Microsoft, 12, 213n, 250
Microsoft NT++, 252
Microsoft Word, 74
MIS, 88, 204
MIT (*see* Massachusetts Institute
    of Technology)
Modeling (*see also* Programming),
    43, 44, 46, 54, 85, 127, 133,
    140, 180n, 201, 204, 205
  data model, 127
Modifiability, 105
Modularity, 85, 86
Multimedia, 135, 251, 254
Multiple inheritance, 38, 118, 231
MVS, 18, 203, 252

Names, 131
Naming, 131, 218
Neon, 41
Network, 108, 129, 150, 153, 205,
    240, 251
NeXT, 91, 97n, passim
NeXTstep Application Kit, 91
NLS, 145n, 154n
NT++, 252

Object, 26, 28-40, 43-47, 53-54,
    passim
Object Expo '92, 93
Objective-C, 41, passim
Objective Systems, 123n
Object Management Group
    (OMG), 250
Object-oriented:
  applications, 25, 126, 131-132
  databases (OODBs), 126, 132
  design, 106
  languages, 29-31, 33, 39, 41,
    45, 50, passim
  programming, 28, 58, 131,
    139, 141n, 153, 252
  software engineering, 41, 46,
    165, passim
  technology, 40-41, 46, 96, 139,
    250, 254
Object-Pascal, 41, 46, 50, 65, 73-
    75, 83, 151, 228
ObjectWorks, 95
Ontologic Inc., 129, 196n
OODBs (*see* Objects)
OOPC, 228
OOPSLA, 51, 89, 97n, 114, 141n
Operating systems, 18, 184, 203,
    251, 252
Operator, 231
  overloading, 231
Optimization, 151, 165
Oracle, 14, 15

PageMaker, 94
ParcPlace Systems, 95, 153
Pascal, 17, 83, 151, 159, 160, 228
Pay per use, 245
Persistence, 128
  object bases, 136

objects, 126, 130-131, 133
Pink operating system, 252
Plex, 80
PLM, 232
Polymorphism (*see* Objects)
Portability, 14
Port of Singapore, 82, 90
PPI, 41, 233n
Prime Computer, 87
Procedural language (*see*
    Languages)
Process control, 85, 115, 239
Product champion (*see* Champions)
Productivity, 14, 17, 85, passim
    coordinator, 208
Productivity Products International,
    228
Programmer's Assistant, 149
Programming environment (*see*
    Environment)
Program segments, 80
ProGraph, 72, 50, 65, 71, 227
Project teams (*see* Teams)
Pro-Kappa, 227
Prototypers, 220
Protypes, 119, 220, 153, 161
Prototyping, 40, 144, 153, 162,
    216, 220
Pseudocode, 118
Purchased components, 208, 210,
    238
Pure object-oriented system, 39
Pure object systems, 40, 152, 184-
    196, 218

Quality Assurance (QA), 16, 109,
    120, 165, 189-192, 195
    methods and techniques, 191-
    195

Quality College, 186

RAT (*see* Recorder of ad hoc tests)
RDBMSs (*see* Relational database
    management systems)
RDD-100, 87, 115
Receiver (*see* Message)
Recorder of ad hoc tests (RAT),
    191-192
Redundancy, 34, 38, 92, 111, 131,
    135
Refactoring, 120-121
Relational database management
    systems (RDBMSs), 129, 136,
Requirements, 16, 30, 40, 103,
    107-108, 110, 216, passim
    analysis, 107, 108, 186, 210
    phase, 174
Reusability, 19, 33, 55, 149, 178,
    191, 225, 229
Reusable, 34, 148
    components, 149-150, 217
Reuse, 21, 38, 50, 104, 118, 121,
    219-220, 225, 232, 237-239
Robotics, 239
Royalties, 244
Rule-based programming, 58
Run time, 130

Saturn, 11
Scenarios, 108-112, 120, 123n
Schlumberger, 83, 253
Scientific Data Systems (SDS)
Sigma-7, 228
Security, 127, 130, 135, 172

Self, 227
Semantics, 133, 151
Sender (*see* Message)
Simplicity, 14, 34
Single inheritance, 231
SLOC, 11
Smalltalk, 58, 64, 71, 75, 82, 88,
    149, 184, 228, 230, 250
Smalltalk-80 (ST-80), 30, 37, 46,
    47n, 50, 82, 83, 95, 149, 150,
    152, 153, 163, 228
Smalltalk-V, 41, 46, 50
SNA, 240
Snobol, 228
Software:
    assets, 148
    components, 21, 38
    costs, 11
    development, 18
    engineering, 14, 213n, passim
    industry, 11
    products, 14
    projects, 16
    quality (*see* Quality Assurance)
    revolution, 18
    team, 170
Software-ICs, 47n, 189, 217-218
Software development environ-
    ment, 147
SPSS, 204
Standard Electric Lorenz, 21
Standard query language (SQL),
    130
State diagram, 114
Static:
    binding of procedures and data,
        43
    object-oriented languages, 231
Statistical Analysis Institute, 16
Statistical Analysis System (SAS),
    16, 204
SASGRAF, 204
Statpack, 16

Stepstone Corporation, 41, 42,
    153, 190, 217
Strong typing, 232
Structured:
    analysis, 19
    design, 19
    programming, 19, 23n, 229
Subclass, (*see* Classes)
Subroutine, 27, passim
Superclasses (*see* Classes)
Support staff, 161
Suzuki, 158, 166n
System:
    administration, 40
    design, 112
    development:
        champions in, 209
        Godfather in, 209
        object-oriented, 40, 106
    verification and validation,
        120, 121
System 9, 87
System 1240, 11, 81

Tasks, concurrent, 119
Teams, 117, 149, 170-171, 176,
    178, 223, 229, 240
Technical writers, 161, 165
Technology general contractor, 208
Test, 82, 121, passim
    class, 192
    method, 192
    process, 193-194
    scripts, 188
TestDroid, 191, 193
Tester (*see* Test)
Testing tools (*see* Tools)
Texas Instruments, 165
Tools, 189, 222, 147, passim

building of, 221-222
for contact (i.e., mutual) use, 149, 150
maintenance of, 184
for optimization, 204
software, 184, 222
for solitary use, 149
for testing, 147, 204
toolsmithing of, 221-222
Traceability, 108, 147
Traditional databases, (*see* Database)
Training, 14, 19, passim
Transaction management, 14
Trellis, 74
Troubled projects, 19
TRW Defense Systems Group, 177
TSO, (*see* MVS)

UCC, 22n
Ultrix, 86
Uniforum, 22n
University of Alabama, 228
University of Pennsylvania, 253
University of Washington, 228
UNIX (*see* AT&T)
Unsuccessful software projects, 18
Usage scenarios, 108-110
User annoyance rating (UAR), 190
User interface, 54, 65, 75, 203, 211, 240

Validation, 119, 120
Vamp, 94, 97n
VAX, 83, 203, 204

VAX-UNIX, 228
VEE, 93-94, 232, 254
Verification, 1220, 107
VisiCalc, 17
VISTA, 85
VLSI, 128
VMS, 18, 41, 203, 228, 252
Voice Navigator, 140n
Voice recognition, 140n, 149

Wang Laboratories, 209
Waterfall model, 104, 177
Whirlwind, 190
Wild Heerbrug, 86
Workstation, 133, 149, 250, 251

Xerox, 40, 97n, 228, 238
PARC, 39, 149, 150
Special Information Systems, 82

Permissions

Chapter One, opening figure and figures 1.1-1.3 are reprinted with permission of Landström, Björn, *The Royal Warship Vasa*, Stenström Interpublishing AB, Stockholm, Sweden, 1988.

Chapter Two, opening figure is reprinted with permission of Hall, Asa E., and Langworth, Richard M., *The Studebaker Century—A National Heritage, 2nd Edition*, Dragonwyck Publishing, Inc., Contoocook, New Hampshire, 1983.

Chapter Three, figure 3.5 is reprinted with permission of Taylor, David A., *Object-Oriented Technology: A Manager's Guide*, Addison-Wesley Publishing, Reading, Massachusetts, Copyright ©1990, Servio Corporation.

Chapter Five, opening figure is reprinted with permission of Chouinard, Yvon, *Climbing Ice*, Sierra Club Books, San Francisco, California, 1978.

Chapter Six, opening figure is reprinted with permission of the Nebraska State Historical Society, Lincoln, Nebraska.

Chapter Seven, opening figure is a photograph by Catherine Guarnieri.

Chapter Seven, figure 7.1 is reprinted with permission of ONTOS, Inc.

Chapter Eight, opening figure is reprinted with permission of Henry Holt & Company, New York, New York, 1988.

Chapter Nine, opening figure is reprinted by permission of the Norman Rockwell Family Trust, Copyright ©1946, the Norman Rockwell Family Trust, Poughkeepsie, New York.

Chapter Ten, opening figure is reprinted with permission of Adams, James L., *Flying Buttresses, Entrophy, and O-Rings*, Roger-Violet, Paris, France, 1991.

Chapter Eleven, opening figure is reprinted with permission of Bang and Olufsen ®, Mount Prospect, Illinois.

Chapter Twelve, opening figure is reprinted by permission of the Norman Rockwell Family Trust, Copyright ©1967, the Norman Rockwell Family Trust, Poughkeepsie, NY. Although it is assumed that the Norman Rockwell Family Trust holds the copyright on this figure, it is possible that *Rampart's Magazine*, San Francisco, California, held the copyright as it was originally printed on its May, 1967 cover. The magazine has since been dissolved. Publisher has made best effort to obtain permission from this source to no avail.